# The Two Faces of Democracy

# The Two Faces of Democracy

*Decentering Agonism and Deliberation*

**MARY F. SCUDDER**

AND

**STEPHEN K. WHITE**

**OXFORD**
UNIVERSITY PRESS

Oxford University Press is a department of the University of Oxford. It furthers
the University's objective of excellence in research, scholarship, and education
by publishing worldwide. Oxford is a registered trade mark of Oxford University
Press in the UK and certain other countries.

Published in the United States of America by Oxford University Press
198 Madison Avenue, New York, NY 10016, United States of America.

© Oxford University Press 2023

All rights reserved. No part of this publication may be reproduced, stored in
a retrieval system, or transmitted, in any form or by any means, without the
prior permission in writing of Oxford University Press, or as expressly permitted
by law, by license, or under terms agreed with the appropriate reproduction
rights organization. Inquiries concerning reproduction outside the scope of the
above should be sent to the Rights Department, Oxford University Press, at the
address above.

You must not circulate this work in any other form
and you must impose this same condition on any acquirer.

Library of Congress Control Number: 2022058614

ISBN 978-0-19-762389-3 (pbk.)
ISBN 978-0-19-762388-6 (hbk.)

DOI: 10.1093/oso/9780197623886.001.0001

Paperback printed by Marquis Book Printing, Canada
Hardback printed by Bridgeport National Bindery, Inc., United States of America

*Molly dedicates this book to Jack*

*Stephen dedicates this book to his grandson,
Jones Kieffer Dunay*

## CONTENTS

Acknowledgments ix

1. Introduction: The Challenge of Imagining Democracy Today 1
2. The Deliberative Turn and U-Turn in Democratic Theory 19
3. The Deliberative Face 45
4. The Agonistic Face 71
5. Re-envisioning the Core of Democracy 107
6. An Exemplary Scene of the Moral Equality of Voice 144
7. Conclusion: The Communicative Model of Democracy 171

Bibliography 181
Index 191

# ACKNOWLEDGMENTS

Stephen and I began work on this book in the Summer of 2020. At the time, we each were working on papers independently, exchanging them with each other for comments. My paper sought to defend the normative core of deliberative democracy while acknowledging the limitations of deliberativists' responses to compelling critiques. Stephen was investigating how the clearly valuable democratic insights carried by some variants of agonism have been subtly undermined by certain framings of that tradition. Taking a step back, we realized that both of our papers pointed to the need for a fuller understanding of what we call the "two faces of democracy." By joining together we intended to articulate how to best comprehend those two faces and explain why we feel the persistent, intuitive force of each. We hope this book achieves these goals.

In those early days of the project, I was emailing Stephen from the road. After months of isolation due to the COVID-19 pandemic, Kyle, Lola (eighteen months old), and I set out on a contactless road trip from Indiana to California. Once we arrived in Sonoma, we formed a pod and childcare co-op with my sister, her family, and my parents. Without their help, especially that of my mom and dad, John and Judy Scudder, I would not have had the time or energy to begin working on this project. I am so grateful for the love and assistance they provided my family and me. I also want to acknowledge the care shown to us by Bonnie and Tim Haynes whose willingness to drive thirteen hours for a visit never ceases to amaze me.

My colleagues and friends at Purdue have improved my ideas as much as my day-to-day life. A special thanks to Tara Grillos for the sustained friendship and speedy advice she has provided me these past years. I am indebted to my mentors Rosie Clawson and Nadia Brown, two Academic Moms who have worked tirelessly to make our department and our discipline more diverse and inclusive. I am lucky to have them as role models and mentors. I am also thankful to have Valeria Sinclair-Chapman as a colleague and friend. In many ways, she embodies the two faces of democracy, always seeming to know when to resist and when to cooperate to achieve shared goals. I am grateful to my comrade-in-writing, Ann Clark, for talking me through the highs and lows of the academic writing process. Jimena Cosso and Macarena Guerrero, as well as their respective partners, my colleagues, Giancarlo Visconti and Reed Kurtz, have been great cheerleaders as I tried to write with a new baby in a pandemic. I am grateful to have them and their families in my life.

I presented some of the material in the book at the University of Virginia's Political Theory Colloquium in November 2020. I thank the participants and my discussant, Ferdinand Flagstad, for their comments and suggestions. I also want to thank Michael MacKenzie and Patricia Boling for feedback they provided on earlier drafts of portions of this manuscript. I appreciate the permission to reprint material previously published in Mary F. Scudder, "Deliberative Democracy, More Than Deliberation," *Political Studies*, Online First, pp. 1–18, https://doi.org/10.1177/00323217211032624.

I cannot imagine a better coauthor than Stephen. He was nothing but supportive and understanding when chapters got held up on my desk, including for the length of my parental leave in 2021. From the energizing Zoom meetings to the constructive conversations via track changes, writing this book with him has been a joy.

Finally, I would like to thank Kyle Haynes for his partnership. I am not exaggerating when I say that I could not have survived having two children on the tenure track if it were not for him (and his coffee). He never doubted me for a second, and it made a world of difference. Finding the time for me to work on this book was often a team effort. Lola, too, was a great help in this regard. Her curiosity and enthusiasm are contagious and her love for her baby brother convenient. For my part, I dedicate the book to my son Jack Scudder-Haynes who was born during its writing. Jack seems intent on making me a morning person and deserves credit for his persistence.

—Mary F. (Molly) Scudder

I presented some of the material in the book at the Political Theory Colloquium, University of Virginia, September 2020 and at the Institute for Advanced Studies in Culture, September 2021. I thank the participants for their many insights.

I appreciate the permission of the following publishers to reprint material previously published: Sage Publications for reprinting portions of Chapter 4 from Stephen K. White, "Agonism, Democracy, and the Moral Equality of Voice," *Political Theory* 50, no. 1 (Feb. 2022): 59–85; and the Institute for Advanced Studies in Culture for reprinting portions of "A Democratic Mythic?," *The Hedgehog Review* 24, no. 1 (Spring 2022).

Thanks to the following individuals who read and offered helpful critical insights on some portion of the manuscript: Lawrie Balfour, Kevin Duong, Rita Felski, Jill Frank, Bonnie Honig, George Klosko, Brittany Leach, Lori Marso, Isaac Reed, Shalini Satkunanandan, William Scheuerman, Jay Tolson, Rachel Wahl, and Robert Wylie. I would especially like to thank those who provided more sustained commentary on the project as a whole: Murad Idris, Tae-Yeoun Keum, and Jaeyoon Park. Also, my appreciation goes to my coauthor, Molly, who has been the ideal partner in this intellectual adventure.

We would both like to thank the two anonymous reviewers for Oxford University Press and our highly skilled editors at the press, Angela Chnapko and Alexcee Bechthold, who made the whole process a pleasure.

Finally, I thank Pat for all her copyediting expertise, but even more for being as wonderful a life companion as one could imagine.

—Stephen K. White

# 1

# Introduction

## The Challenge of Imagining Democracy Today

When we think about classic moments we associate with democracy, one or the other of two sorts of pictures usually comes to mind. One is of public scenes where people are speaking, listening, debating, arguing, voting. Vivid, classical instances include the agora in ancient Athens, where democracy was born; scenes of town hall meetings in colonial New England and televised "town hall" meetings today; or the Constitutional Convention in Philadelphia in 1787. The other sort of classic moment involves scenes of protest and resistance against injustices perpetrated by tyrants or elites. Here we think of the Tennis Court Oath at the beginning of the French Revolution, where members of the Third Estate vowed not to be cowed by the king's efforts to shut down their meetings; the resistance that came to be known as the Boston Tea Party or the Minutemen at Lexington and Concord before the American Revolution; or the street demonstrations against authoritarian rule in Egypt's Tahrir Square in 2011 or during the "umbrella protest" in Hong Kong in 2014.

We might call these two portrayals of democratic life the two faces of democracy. Although they present to us somewhat different qualities, each captures essential intuitions about that political form, and both are assumed to represent core ideals. The first face portrays ideas of popular discussion, deliberation, and other activities central to the life of a legitimate democratic order. The second speaks to us about the necessity of oppositional protest against efforts to hold back or undermine democratic political arrangements, including protests that claim a legitimacy even when they turn violent, as in the case of colonists' actions leading up to the Declaration of Independence.

In referring to the two faces of democracy, we don't mean two faces in the sense of the visages of two different people. Rather we mean the different "faces" a single person may display at different times; as when we say that a person's face now shows anger but later curiosity. In the case of a single actor, we would normally be interested to know how the interaction between her character and her circumstances might have given rise to a face that expressed anger and then why it shifted to curiosity. Similarly, in the case of a democratic society, we are interested in providing an account of why a given set of circumstances should elicit activities that express one face more than another.

We certainly affirm that the two faces are tied together through their relation to comprehensive democratic intuitions and values, but we are concerned that the character of that connection and its underlying moral infrastructure are poorly understood. This lack of clarity has become more evident and unsettling recently, both in the world of real politics and in the efforts of scholars to conceptualize democracy.

One reason for a sense of distress is that in contemporary politics the face associated with classic instances of vehement democratic resistance has been repeatedly coopted by movements on the political right to advance ideas of white nationalism and other disturbing political orientations in ways that corrode democratic processes and the rule of law. In the last decade, right-wing, populist groups appropriated the images and names of the Boston Tea Party and the Minutemen. This process continued in the broader movement associated with the rise of Donald Trump.[1] The American revolutionary flag picturing a snake coiled to strike against the boot of tyranny has also become a popular vanity license plate for this

---

1. For an analysis of this phenomenon, see Stephen K. White, *A Democratic Bearing: Admirable Citizens, Uneven Injustice, and Critical Theory* (Cambridge: Cambridge University Press, 2017), Ch. 2.

movement in a number of states. For many in these movements, and the armed, self-styled "militias" that have metastasized in recent decades, President Obama and the federal government became the agents of tyranny, against whom righteous resistance was directed. And that flag was flown proudly by the Trump supporters as they stormed the U.S. Capitol in an attempt to prevent the transition of power mandated by the 2020 presidential election. In short, the classic call to political resistance against supposed *threats* to democracy has become increasingly associated with unprecedented *violations* of deep democratic norms. Thus, one sort of pictorial representation of democracy has become joined, on the right, with activities that are decidedly undemocratic, if not proto-fascistic.

Unsurprisingly, there have been vigorous, recent efforts across the political spectrum to push back against violations of basic democratic norms. These have occurred in the streets, the popular media, and academic publications. As one would expect, this upwelling has been most prevalent in the broadly defined political left in the United States. Concerns there accumulated into a flood of active and sometimes violent resistance in the wake of the police killing of George Floyd in May of 2020. As an illustration of such push back in the media, consider a 2019 article in the *New Republic*, under the title "Give War a Chance." Alex Pareene speaks there of the growing number of voices within the Democratic Party who have become convinced of the need to meet the right's "muscular and coherent 'antagonistic' approach to politics" with a comparable one on the left that unapologetically divides the world into political friends and enemies and urges us toward battle, as opposed to a more traditional orientation toward respectful engagement and mutual compromise.[2] In relation to the two faces of democracy, the affective force behind Pareene's essay draws us to determinately plant in the foreground the image of vehement and courageous resistance to those who threaten the basic norms of democracy, while backgrounding the picture of reason, deliberation, and compromise

---

2. Alex Pareene, "Give War a Chance: In Search of the Democratic Party's Fighting Spirit," *The New Republic*, June 20, 2019, https://newrepublic.com/article/154113/democratic-party-fighting-spirit-give-war-chance.

across lines of political difference. The left and center simply need to "give war a chance."

If this distinctive foregrounding of one face of democracy is relatively recent in practical politics in the U.S., its contemporary intellectual roots extend somewhat further back. Pareene refers to these when he mentions the growing influence of a Belgian political theorist, Chantal Mouffe. Since the early 1990s, Mouffe has become increasingly prominent (along with her now-deceased coauthor, Ernesto Laclau) in several European countries as well as the U.S.[3] This elevation is based on her consistently arguing that conflict and resistance constitute the essential character—the ontology—of all political life, an account that has come to be called "agonistic." The term "agonism" comes from the ancient Greek word, "agon," meaning conflict or contest.[4] Mouffe is hardly alone in embracing this orientation; she is part of a broader movement that has been gaining strength among political thinkers for some time.

This intellectual shift toward agonism emerged at least partially in reaction to the work of two of the most prominent political theorists of the late twentieth century, John Rawls and Jürgen Habermas. Rawls and Habermas came to be perceived as too tied to the assumption that Western political orders were tolerably just, and that the main job for political theory was to conceptually reconstruct the foundations of that democratic legitimacy. This orientation was apparent in Rawls's immensely influential theory of justice and Habermas's account of deliberative democracy.[5] For the critics, these approaches offered idealized versions of liberal democratic orders

---

3. See Chantal Mouffe, *The Democratic Paradox* (London and New York: Verso Books, 2000). Mouffe and Laclau, espousing agonism and populist "hegemony," have been drawn upon by politicians (some of whom were their students) across the European continent; see Benjamin McKean, "Toward an Inclusive Populism? On the Role of Race and Difference in Laclau's Politics," *Political Theory* 44, no. 6 (Dec. 2016): 797–820.

4. The first deployment of the idea of agonism relevant to current usage is in Nietzsche's "Homer's Contest," in *On the Genealogy of Morals* ed. Keith Ansell Pearson (Cambridge: Cambridge University Press, 1994), 187–194.

5. John Rawls, *A Theory of Justice* (Cambridge, MA: Harvard University Press, 1971); and Jürgen Habermas, *Between Facts and Norms Between Facts and Norms: Contributions to a Discourse Theory of Law and Democracy*, trans. William Rehg (Cambridge, MA: MIT Press, 1996).

grounded in reason, deliberation, and consensus about just political arrangements. Such works seemed to imply that any extant injustices in such regimes were secondary matters to be subsequently recognized and critically addressed on the basis of these constructs. In effect, they decidedly foregrounded one face of democracy: the one focused on reason, procedures, and debate.

Criticism of that broad intellectual strategy gathered momentum through the 1990s and has taken a multitude of forms. Perhaps the most significant commonality shared by these attacks on what has come to be called "ideal theory" is the charge that it inevitably tends to render secondary what should be primary. Such theory subtly slides concerns about persisting forms of domination and injustice into the background, thus providing an inflated sense of legitimation to the status quo.

This backgrounding, even if unintentional, runs the risk of giving ideological cover to those harms, making them appear less pressing. One of the first entrants onto this terrain of battle was Judith Shklar's 1990 *The Faces of Injustice* in which she argued for a global reorientation of attention in political theory: we should start political reflection from the patent reality of concrete instances of *in*justice and the struggles against it, and not from hypothetical, complex constructions of justice such as those of Rawls.[6]

Similar sentiments were expressed by many who began to style themselves as "realists" and attack "ideal theory."[7] Despite its popularity in recent years, what this movement substantively affirms has never become quite as coherent as the character of its attacks. After one has deflated the idealists, the actual normative direction in which one should go has remained somewhat amorphous. Perhaps this is one reason that the

---

6. Judith N. Shklar, *The Faces of Injustice* (New Haven and London: Yale University Press, 1990).

7. See, e.g., Raymond Geuss, *Philosophy and Real Politics* (Princeton: Princeton University Press, 2008); and Bernard Williams, *In the Beginning Was the Deed: Realism and Moralism in Political Argument*, ed. with an introduction by Geoffrey Hawthorn (Princeton: Princeton University Press, 2005).

"agonist" version of realism has become so popular: it seems to have a clearer shape and more vivid character than the general calls to be more "realistic."

"Agonism," at least in its most emphatic form, is a specific variant of realism that proffers not only the idea that we should pay more attention to the conflictual elements of political life but also the specific claim that the concept of politics itself is *constituted* by the struggle of "friends" and "enemies." And, proponents argue, the sooner we acknowledge this reality, the better. This call has achieved substantial resonance. As the editors of the American Political Science Association journal, *Perspectives on Politics*, declared in 2019, we "inevitably" face an "agonistic conception of the political."[8] Moreover, as others contend, this should not disturb us because it is now "uncontroversial" that agonism is a "democratic good."[9]

In sum, we are in an era in which one face of democracy has, for many, increasingly receded into the background of public consciousness, while the other has moved into the foreground. Now, on one level, this is part of an expectable ebb and flow of democratic life; at any given time, one face will seem more relevant and appropriately prominent than the other. But, on a second level of reflection, there may be grounds for not being entirely comfortable with the present state of affairs. As we have indicated, the current shift toward the face of conflict and resistance has been accompanied on the political right with a deeply disturbing slide toward actions that undermine basic democratic norms. And many of those involved in this slide seem to have placed themselves, even if only tacitly, on a path of self-justification that affirms potential democratic losses so long as they allow for the subduing of those who are now defined as their enemies.[10]

---

8. Daniel O'Neill and Michael Bernhard, "Perspectival Political Theory," *Perspectives on Politics* 17, no. 4 (Dec. 2019): 953.

9. Lida Maxwell, introductory statement to the critical exchange, "The 'Agonistic Turn': *Political Theory and the Displacement of Politics* in New Contexts," *Contemporary Political Theory* 18, no. 4 (2019): 640.

10. This kind of logic could not have been more vividly displayed than in the multidimensional crescendo of Trump-supporter efforts to overturn the 2020 election results in the U.S. based on a willful denial of facts and confident sense that behavior that would normally be judged

This phenomenon raises a challenge for all those committed to democracy. Clearly, there must be protracted contestation of this antidemocratic onslaught from the right. As citizens and academics, we wholeheartedly affirm this stance of resistance. But we also think it is wise to consider an intimately related question: Could there be some danger in this fight that our warranted contestation might also begin to corrode commitments to democratic norms? For some on the political right, resentment and self-righteousness are so intertwined with perceptions of warfare that they seem to miss the danger of such corrosion. Should combatants on the center and left feel immaculately immune from a comparable toxic amalgam of ideas and affects?

There have certainly been sobering examples in the past of leftist groups, like the Red Army Faction in Germany and the Weather Underground in the U.S. in the 1970s, who espoused the necessity of exterminating their enemies in democratic societies. Fortunately, there are few such movements now on the left. And with the electoral defeat of Trump in 2020, it could be that the immediate danger on the right will recede somewhat in the U.S., if not in other democratic countries such as Hungary. Little is certain at this point. Perhaps this juncture in the career of virulent forms of agonism provides us with a timely opportunity to reflect more carefully on the implicit pull of its corrosive framing of political life, without at the same time inordinately downgrading the enduring significance of the second face of democratic life with its portrayal of contestation and resistance.

But even if this sort of global practical relevance of our project seems apt, these concerns may still appear to be relatively academic and remote from grassroots-level politics. For a given group of protesters in the streets or a community organization resisting some palpable injustice, any mandate of attunement to both faces of democracy may understandably seem to be a remote matter of concern only to intellectuals. Only the agonistic face will be immediately relevant. In relation to questions of immediate

---

corrupt and insurrectionary was to be esteemed as heroic (by friends) and necessary to save the republic from mortal danger (at the hands of domestic enemies).

strategy, this may be entirely correct. But if, in such cases, we expand the time frame or scope of actors involved, then the issues revolving around the other face will likely begin to seep into the relevant problem space. For example, questions about internal group structure and strategy may need to be extensively debated, as well as ones about the character of relations with other groups affirming somewhat different priorities. In these contexts, appeals that have recourse to normative criteria associated with the first face will likely surface. And if that expansion of concerns is actively precluded, it is probably an indicator that the group is trying to freeze out a kind of questioning intrinsic to a healthy democracy.

In short, there are ample practical reasons to inquire into the relation between the two faces. But the task of moving from this simple declaration to a lucid explanation of the connectedness of the two faces within the democratic imagination is no simple matter. Our book undertakes this task by trying to make clearer and more compelling the grounds upon which the two pictures, as well as the intuitions they embody, are interrelated. This requires a better theorization of the core normative commitments of democracy. We might think of this knot of commitments as functioning something like the role of character in understanding why a given individual's face shows anger in certain circumstances but shifts to curiosity as those circumstances change; only here we will be trying to sketch what one might call the character of an admirable democratic political actor.

Toward that end we begin by exploring the two perspectives that offer the best insights into each face. For the face of conflict and contestation, we consider the agonistic turn in democratic theory, looking for the most persuasive formulations that have emerged. For the face of reason and debate, we consider the tradition of deliberative democracy, looking for a version that could offer openings to the insights of agonism. Our ultimate aim is to articulate a distinct account of democracy, from the perspective of which one can assess the character, strengths, and limitations of both perspectives, revising each as necessary in order to illuminate how they might be persuasively imagined as existing in a relationship characterized by both tension and congruence.

Any effort to bring these two perspectives into alignment will likely have to confront the criticism that one or the other is subtly being accorded priority. This strikes us as a useful sort of initial suspicion of any attempt to do justice to both. In our case, many will suspect that the deliberative model is being assigned an initial privilege. And, in a way, it is. But the real test of whether our effort is successful is not where it starts, but whether our partially deliberative starting point can be integrated ultimately into a convincing way of comprehending the two pictures of democracy and the sorts of intuitions and values implied by both. That is what we hope to achieve by the end of the book.

For some, a figure prominent at our starting point will be maximally suspicious: Jürgen Habermas. After all, his account of deliberation, according to critics, is one of the primary poster children for one-sided accounts of democracy. Although there is some truth in this claim, there is just as much in the way of distortion. What we will offer is a partial borrowing from, but also a distinct revision of, what is at the core of his thought. Conceptually, we start from his theory of "communicative action," rather than his specific idea of deliberation, with the intention of showing how the latter needs to be seen as derivative from a broader conception of normativity and interaction. Ultimately, this approach to democracy might be better called "communicative" than "deliberative" because it is oriented around the implicit norms that circulate in the linguistic intersubjectivity through which modern social life is symbolically reproduced. Iris Marion Young tried to signal her distance from the deliberative model by announcing a preference for the term "communicative democracy."[11] She was an early admirer of Habermas's approach to communicative action generally, as it emerged out of the central concerns of the Frankfurt School, but she was also consistently critical of the way the term "deliberative democracy" threatened to reduce our scope of critical vision. We share her sentiments, as well as her terminological preference. And, following that general tack, we aim to further develop a basis

---

11. Iris Marion Young, *Inclusion and Democracy* (Oxford: Oxford University Press, 2000), 40.

for conceptualizing democracy that *decenters both* the deliberative perspective and the agonistic one, with its greater focus on contestation and resistance.

When the term "deliberative democracy" is used today it refers to a broad movement in recent decades to center one's assessment of democracy more precisely on the quality of the processes through which individuals come to discuss, debate, and mutually justify their respective stances before voting or taking other sorts of political action. Perhaps the most famous encapsulation of this slant is the general idea that the discursive means by which a majority becomes a majority in a democracy is just as important as the fact that a majority has voted in one way or the other.[12] The movement to give such concerns a guiding role in our thinking about democracy has, over the last three decades, become a full-scale research tradition in the sense of encompassing a multitude of publications, research groups, and practical experiments designed to enhance deliberation about significant public issues, both in the U.S. and around the world. But, as we indicated above, this movement has also spawned an enormous amount of opposition that generally accuses it of emphasizing too heavily only what we have called the first face of democracy and thereby obfuscating how power operates inconspicuously to keep various issues and groups out of forums of deliberation. In short, deliberative democrats systematically draw our attention away from the connotations, affects, and motivations associated with the second face of democratic life.

As noted earlier, the agonistic turn in democratic theory emerged partially out of this context of critique and partially out of a general feeling that leading liberal democracies today should not be accorded the benefit of the doubt in being identified as moderately just, given persisting racial and ethnic injustices, as well as the rapid growth of economic inequality since the late 1970s. Perspectives on justice and democracy that do not front-load such concerns need to be replaced by ones that make conflict and resistance to elites the starting point and center of attention. Agonism has been fleshed out in a variety of ways, but they all share this general

---

12. Habermas, *Between Facts and Norms*, 304.

motivation to accord an emphatic prominence to the resistant face of democracy. Despite the warranted sense of achievement that is shared by proponents of this new prominence, the question that emerges with this reversal of status between the two faces is whether we now get any better comprehension of *the relationship* between them than we did when the first face was given unquestioned prominence.[13] The goal of this book is to provide a persuasive answer to this question in a way that grants one-sided prominence to neither but sees both as intertwined with a common

---

13. Ours is hardly the first effort to grapple with the question how to comprehend this relationship. Marie Paxton's *Agonistic Democracy: Rethinking Political Institutions in Pluralist Times* (London and New York: Routledge, 2020) tends to take the good of agonism to be largely unproblematic and then works to show that we can negotiate a straightforward settlement with more traditional frameworks in political theory. This allows her to move on relatively effortlessly to her proposals to reform democratic institutions in a way that reflects this settlement. From our perspective she resolves the whole dispute between agonism and deliberation too quickly, without sufficiently probing the depth of the disagreement involved. See especially 1–22, 139–141.

Others take the dispute more seriously and look in more detail, as we do, at how one might better conceive the relationship between agonism and traditional approaches to democracy. Ed Wingenbach's *Institutionalizing Agonistic Democracy: Post-Foundationalism and Political Liberalism* (London: Routledge, 2011) proposes a reconciliation of Mouffean agonism and Rawlsian political liberalism; see especially xv and Ch. 7. He argues that an "agonistic liberalism can emerge from Rawlsian premises" (159). We don't find this marriage to be well-conceived on either end. Mouffe's agonism is never subjected to sufficient critical analysis, and Wingenbach's watering down of Rawls's central ideas of "overlapping consensus" and a "well-ordered society" leaves the force of that perspective in a rather unclear state.

Another somewhat related attempt at negotiation is Steven Gormley, *Deliberative Theory and Deconstruction: A Democratic Venture* (Edinburgh: Edinburgh University Press, 2020). He tries to chart a course between deliberation and Derridean deconstruction that takes the insights of both seriously, develops criticisms of both, and sees an "overlap in their shared hope . . . in the promise of democracy to open up the possibility of doing justice to the other." His admirable effort has some slight parallels with ours, but, given that he is not taking on agonism per se but deconstruction, the project is not exactly the same. See 4–5, 190–192.

Finally, there is Arletta Norval's excellent work, *Aversive Democracy: Inheritance and Originality in the Democratic Tradition* (Cambridge: Cambridge University Press, 2009). Although committed to the agonistic approach, she nevertheless perceptively highlights many of its shortcomings, turning to Wittgenstein and Cavell to remedy them, as well as critiques standard deliberative approaches. There is much to admire in this effort, but we would argue that she does not offer an adequate articulation of the key value of equality of voice. Moreover, we think that her criticisms of deliberative democracy, as well as her affirmation of aspects of Wittgenstein and Cavell, can be encompassed within our portrait of a "communicative model" of democracy.

normative core; our preference for the term "communicative democracy" is intended to highlight this reorientation.

As we pursue this goal, it is important to emphasize that the role we envision for our efforts is not reducible to that of a peace negotiator who strives simply to bring two antagonists to some negotiated end of hostilities. Others have chosen that strategy, seeking to find a way to have these opponents simply "converge in the middle sharing similar values."[14] In contrast, we attempt to articulate an independent, constructive perspective on democracy and its moral core that provides a distinctive viewpoint, from the perspective of which one can then relocate the significance of both the agonistic and deliberative approaches.

Chapter 2 begins with a broad attempt to construe the deliberative approach in such a way that it can be taken as the best representative of the first face of democracy, and thus the fittest contender among competing conceptions of democracy to take on the challenge of agonism. Accordingly, we will offer an account of the emergence of the deliberative perspective around 1990, as it appears in Habermas and others, consider its evolving shape over time, and evaluate some of the ways it has responded to a variety of specific criticisms.

Two criticisms, however, stand out as especially challenging and thus worthy of separate and more sustained treatment. These are global assaults on the whole enterprise of the deliberative perspective, as opposed to the more specific criticisms examined in Chapter 2. The first of these broader critiques surveys the train of particular complaints against this perspective over the last couple decades and concludes that the best way forward is to simply abandon any emphasis on deliberation as the core concept animating the first face. The problem, these critics argue, is that the many efforts to save the deliberative perspective by expanding what can count as "deliberation" end up amounting to nothing more than "concept stretching." In short, accumulating piecemeal modifications of the model have so expanded the notion of deliberation as to render it

---

14. Paxton, *Agonistic Democracy*, 139. Compare the similar strategy pursued in Wingenbach, *Institutionalizing Agonistic Democracy*, xv.

effectively useless.[15] As a consequence, the idea of making deliberation the centerpiece of democratic theory should just be dropped. It makes better sense to simply return to an emphasis on some of the more familiar ideals traditionally associated with democracy, such as inclusion in agenda formation and decision-making.[16]

In Chapter 3, we argue instead that the real problem lies with those advocates of deliberative democracy who overly concentrate attention on *practices* of deliberation and fail to comprehend adequately the *normative core* that should animate this perspective as a whole. That core, properly conceived, orients our understanding of the deliberative model to its commitment to a complex, central value, *the moral equality of voice*. On our interpretation this provides a minimal conceptualization of both autonomy and equality. In regard to the latter, it offers a way of conceptualizing how individual autonomy necessarily opens into democratic autonomy. Chapter 3 focuses primarily on this last value, showing how understanding it within our frame helps deliberative democrats decenter the specific practice of deliberation. Deliberation can now be seen as one variant of communication among a variety of others, each of which may play a role in enhancing democratic autonomy and equality. Accordingly, a range of modes of communication, including, for example, rhetorical expression, storytelling, and expressive protest, can be assessed not as watered-down variants of deliberation but in terms of their contribution to promoting or undermining the values of autonomy and equality in a given political order.

When understood in this sense, we suggest that the deliberative approach does not have to devolve into an increasingly amorphous conglomeration of insights lacking coherence. Rather, it deserves to be ranked as the best way to conceptualize the first face of democracy. At the same

---

15. David Owen and Graham Smith, "Deliberation, Democracy, and the Systemic Turn," *Journal of Political Philosophy* 23, no. 2 (2015): 213–234.

16. Mark E. Warren, "A Problem-Based Approach to Democratic Theory," *American Political Science Review* 111, no. 1 (2017): 39–53.

time, however, one can also see why it makes sense to begin referring to our conceptualization not as a deliberative but as a "communicative" model.

Still, our arguments up to this point are not sufficient to answer the second global challenge we identified above, namely, the one arising from agonism. The main charge here is not so much that the idea of deliberative democracy is conceptually useless; rather, that it ends up being ideologically biased. Our goal in Chapter 4 is not to demonstrate that this critique is wrong but to construe it in a fashion that allows agonism to take a crucial place in the democratic imagination, without it also exerting a corrosive force on other democratic values. The concern here is to carefully explore how any given take on agonism, which interprets the political world as essentially characterized by conflict, might be capable of negotiating its way from that stance to the affirmation of some normative infrastructure that can democratically constrain such conflict.

This concern about the potential danger of agonism is not merely imagined. Mouffe is the outstanding case in point. The reason is that she has grounded herself in the work of the twentieth-century German jurist and political thinker, Carl Schmitt, who quite clearly believed his agonism accorded well with Nazism. Our point in calling attention to this is not to score easy points against Mouffe but to argue that we must be extremely careful in how we construe the claims of agonism. Although Mouffe thinks she can free her version from the less attractive features of Schmitt's thought, we have our doubts, and the difficulties we elaborate highlight a serious challenge to any variant of agonism. What resources does agonism and its ontology of conflict have to ensure an adversarial orientation toward our enemies stays within democratic bounds? Fortunately, Mouffe is not the only game in town; there are other, better conceptualizations of this perspective that make insightful efforts to more persuasively imagine how we might construe the claims of agonism. Although such work takes us some of the way toward the sort of capacious perspective that is needed, we nevertheless conclude that it does not offer a fully convincing path to understanding the tensional congruence that should characterize the relation between the two faces of democracy. The central problem revolves around equality and autonomy. An appeal to these values is clearly central to these agonists' concerns about domination and injustice, but, as we show, they have not presented adequate conceptualizations of them.

Thus, just as Chapters 2 and 3 show the faults of deliberative theory, Chapter 4 does the same for agonism. Having developed these critiques, our overall goal then is to articulate an account of the moral core of democracy that is capacious enough to incorporate the valid insights of both perspectives and yet avoid their shortcomings. If this can be done persuasively, it will allow one to see how the two faces of democracy are interrelated. Progress toward that goal requires two steps. First, in Chapter 5, we clarify and defend what it might mean today to speak generally of a moral core or 'foundational' account of politics in what one of us has called elsewhere a "weak-ontological" sense.[17] Such a core needs to be elucidated in the form of what we call an "originary exemplary scene."[18] A significant part of the task of unpacking this notion involves explaining how its persuasiveness depends not just on its appeal to our reason but also to our imagination; in short, the proto-narrative it relates has to engage us with affective force. One of the key tasks of that chapter, as well as the following one, is to make clear what this implies. A prominent concern that emerges when an appeal to the imagination is allowed such an enhanced role in political thinking is that it would seem to entangle the moral core of politics in a relationship with myth. For many, any involvement of myth with democratic thinking carries significant danger. Hence, our turn onto this terrain will need to proceed carefully.

After elucidating, in Chapter 5, the general criteria that a broadly acceptable idea of 'foundations' must satisfy today, we turn in Chapter 6 to the second step: an elucidation of the specific moral core of our communicative model of democracy, and how it is portrayed as an originary scene that embodies the central value of moral equality of voice. We unpack the

---

17. Stephen K. White, *Sustaining Affirmation: The Strengths of Weak Ontology in Political Theory* (Princeton: Princeton University Press, 2001).

18. The idea of appealing to such a scene, is sketched in a preliminary (and rather flawed) way in White, *A Democratic Bearing*, 57–68. In Chapters 5 and 6, we will delineate the relation between such an originary scene and more particular scenes from history or literature, such as the two types we appealed to at the beginning of this chapter.

notion of equality and show why, in our framework, it must be conceived not as a stand-alone value but as one embedded within the dynamics of an originary scene and constitutively related to democratic autonomy. Although this idea of orienting a democratic citizen's imagination around such a generative scene might sound unfamiliar, even jarring, in the present context, that initial reaction might be lessened by considering how often in the history of political thought appeals have been made to generative "scenes" of some sort. Consider the role of the venerable notion of the "state of nature" in social contract theory or of the more contemporary idea of the "original position" in Rawls. Although our notion shares with these kinds of scenes a sort of primary status, the exemplary scene we have in mind differs quite significantly from them. It is not tied to a sense of strong ontology with God at the center, as is Locke's scene, nor is it a sketch of what a generic rational actor would choose, as is the case with Rawls's scene (at least in its initial form). Our exemplary scene's role is to orient our reflection and imagination in relation to how communicative interactions open themselves to our most basic democratic intuitions and perceptions. Such a scene helps make vivid to us both how we should react to the social dynamics in which we are embedded and why we modern democrats find the two faces so consistently moving: they embody our basic intuitions about democratic life. Moreover, the originary exemplary scene developed here specifically enhances our ability to see the appropriateness of a shift from one picture to the other, not just as an occasional, one-dimensional reaction to a given set of political events but also as reflecting a judgment that cogently expresses a fuller democratic citizen bearing.

If our efforts in this book are successful, we will have helped make it a little easier to see the place and appropriateness of both faces of a healthy democratic body politic that is continually in the process of rethinking itself. What exactly do we mean by this claim and why is it important? Consider a recurrent tension in American politics between vehement protest in the name of redressing grievances about deep-seated injustices, on the one hand, and vehement objections to that in the name defending normal democratic arrangements of "law and order," on the other hand.

This tension has played out multiple times in recent American history. One way of describing it is as a dispute over which face of democracy should be prioritized. Among some Americans in recent decades, protest and resistance have often been met with insistent demands that politics show more "civility." Accordingly, in times of such turmoil in the streets, a venerable and reliable strategy for some political leaders has been to righteously demand the restoration of law and order. President Richard Nixon was a master at making this sort of appeal to the "silent majority" who saw protest as essentially "un-American." He banked on the propensity of many white Americans to affirm only the first face of democratic politics and vote for him based on that commitment.

In mid-2020, President Trump returned to this playbook in as cynical a way as one could imagine, attempting to rally white Americans to affirm his condemnation of the huge wave of protest emerging out of outrage at police killings of George Floyd and other African Americans. Clearly, Trump found some resonance for his demands for law and order. But there is also evidence that increasing numbers of Americans showed themselves more resistant to such appeals than in the past. Polls in states where some of the killings occurred and where large, sometimes violent, protests followed indicated that Trump's simple calls to law and order were relatively ineffective.[19] We would contend that this is evidence that perhaps there is an incipient learning process going on here, in which growing numbers of people are coming to better understand that democracy has not one, but two, faces, and that especially in societies with deep and persisting injustices, actions expressing the second face are as much a part

---

19. In states like Minnesota and Wisconsin, which suffered some of the most violent and disruptive protests in summer, 2020, Trump got little if any traction from such appeals and failed to win these in the ensuing election. See Alexander Burns and Jonathan Martin, "Trump Onslaught Against Biden Falls Short of a Breakthrough," *New York Times*, September 12, 2020, https://www.nytimes.com/2020/09/12/us/politics/biden-trump-poll-wisconsin-minnesota.html. Of course, many on the political right did affirm Trump's law and order appeal, but in the weeks leading up to the 2020 election, a New York Times/Siena College poll, October 15–20, 2021, showed that, nationally, likely voters found that Joe Biden would "do a better job" in "maintaining law and order" than Donald Trump by a margin of 6 percentage points. See https://scri.siena.edu/2020/10/20/the-new-york-times-siena-college-national-poll-biden-leads-trump-50-41/.

of democratic life as actions expressing the first. Our aim in this book is to bring the modest tools of political theory to bear, helping people see more clearly the stakes of this controversy and thus perhaps to contribute in a small way to this slow, but hopefully ongoing, process of civic education. The appearance of such positive signs should never be construed, however, as simple markers of irreversible progress; significant forces always push against such Whiggish expectations. The communicative model of democracy we articulate here aims to embody such a complex awareness.

# 2

# The Deliberative Turn and U-Turn in Democratic Theory

The deliberative model of democracy has enjoyed relative dominance in the study of democratic theory since it emerged in the 1990s. It has blossomed into a full-blown research paradigm. The deliberative model's prominence is especially visible when we consider how it has been adopted and developed by scholars studying democracy from an empirical perspective.[1] Empirical studies of deliberative democracy aim to identify when and under what conditions political communication rises to the level of "democratic deliberation" and to understand the effects of that deliberation in practice.[2] Does deliberation lead to pro-social behavior or other desirable outcomes?[3] Who wants to deliberate and

---

1. Diana C. Mutz, "Is Deliberative Democracy a Falsifiable Theory?," *Annual Review of Political Science* 11, no. 1 (2008): 521–538; André Bächtiger and Dominik Hangartner, "When Deliberative Theory Meets Empirical Political Science: Theoretical and Methodological Challenges in Political Deliberation," *Political Studies* 58, no. 4 (2010): 609–629; André Bächtiger and John Parkinson, *Mapping and Measuring Deliberation: Towards a New Deliberative Quality* (Oxford: Oxford University Press, 2019).

2. Marco R. Steenbergen et al., "Measuring Political Deliberation: A Discourse Quality Index," *Comparative European Politics* 1, no. 1 (2003): 21–48.

3. Rui Wang, James S. Fishkin, and Robert C. Luskin, "Does Deliberation Increase Public-Spiritedness?," *Social Science Quarterly* 101, no. 6 (2020): 2163–2182, https://doi.org/10.1111/ssqu.12863.

why?[4] What are the barriers to achieving deliberation? And can deliberation help us make headway on intractable social or political issues both domestically and internationally?

Despite the prominence of this broad empirical research paradigm, intense debate over the normative value of deliberation and the deliberative model has continued. This chapter presents the deliberative approach to democratic politics as it originated in the work of Habermas and others. Of particular interest to us is the extent to which deliberative democratic theory has succeeded in doing justice to both faces of democracy. It might seem, given its emphasis on reasoned argumentation and consensus, that the deliberative model all but ignores the face of democracy dealing with resistance and contestation. And given how debates between deliberative and agonistic democrats evolved in the years after democratic theory's deliberative turn, it is easy to overlook the extent to which the deliberative model itself grew out of a sensitivity to difference and disagreement in democracy.

Going back to the earliest articulations of the model, however, we identify a general attempt to account for both faces of democracy. Through this discussion, we come to see this model as the best representation of the first face of democracy, and thus the fittest contender among competing conceptions of democracy to take on the challenge of agonism. Ultimately, however, while we argue that the deliberative model is crucial to our understanding of democracy amid deep difference, it is nevertheless still missing important normative components that would allow it to do full justice to both faces of democracy.

This chapter begins by tracing the emergence and development of the core claims of the deliberative idea of politics in the last three decades of the twentieth century (Section I). We analyze the earliest articulations of this idea, paying special attention to the common themes that unite them. Specifically, we consider the unique way that deliberative democracy conceives of (A) legitimacy, (B) procedure, and (C) disagreement.

---

4. Michael A. Neblo et al., "Who Wants to Deliberate—And Why?," *American Political Science Review* 104, no. 3 (2010): 566–583.

For deliberative democrats, legitimacy, especially in contexts of difference and disagreement, emanates from specific communication-based, decision-making procedures. Next, we consider the model's evolving shape over time as it has tried to respond to a variety of criticisms from within and without. In Section II, we consider challenges to both the feasibility and desirability of the deliberative ideal in large complex plural societies, and we survey some ways that deliberativists have responded to these challenges. As we show, a key strategy for responding to these criticisms has been to expand the deliberative ideal so that it is not so focused on rational discourse, narrowly understood. In Section III we turn our attention to what has come to be called the systems approach to deliberative democracy. This approach emerged as a way to bring a more expansive view of deliberation in line with the deliberative ideal. We consider the extent to which this systemic turn was successful at offering a reliable path to democratic legitimacy in large complex societies.

## I. DELIBERATIVE FIRST STATEMENTS

The first statements of deliberative democratic theory appeared in the 1990s in the work of Jurgen Habermas, Iris Marion Young, Simone Chambers, Joshua Cohen, and others.[5] In this early work, one can see the outline of a constellation connecting (A) the concept of legitimacy with (B) ideal procedure in (C) contexts of disagreement brought about due to deep pluralism. As we show, deliberative democratic theory is, at its core, an account of how to achieve legitimate political decisions in contexts of difference and disagreement. Specifically, deliberative theorists offer a

---

5. Some might wonder about our omission of John Rawls from this discussion of the first statements of deliberative democracy. Rawls's ideas on democracy have certainly influenced deliberative democratic theory, especially via Joshua Cohen's work on the subject. Still, we agree with Simone Chambers, who argues that although Rawls, like many other political theorists, endorses deliberative democracy, he is not, himself, a "theorist of deliberative democracy." Simone Chambers, "Deliberative Democratic Theory," *Annual Review of Political Science* 6, no. 1 (2003): 308.

proceduralist account of legitimacy, connecting the adoption of inclusive communicative procedures to legitimate outcomes. A key claim of deliberative democracy is that, despite the moral and political disagreement that persists among people in large complex societies, we can still arrive at mutually acceptable decision-making procedures. When agreement cannot be reached, these procedures aim not just at compromise but also at compromise based on criteria of fairness, part of which is the existence of deliberative participation.[6]

In what follows, we consider the central concepts of legitimacy, procedure, and disagreement as they are presented in these early articulations of deliberative democracy. Ultimately, these key concepts are inextricably linked in the model. As such, it can be awkward to present them independently of one another. Still, for the sake of analysis, we will take each of these concepts in turn. Doing so helps clarify the distinctiveness of the deliberative approach as it emerged in the 1990s.

## A. Legitimacy

At the core of deliberative democratic theory is the claim "that outcomes are legitimate to the extent they receive reflective assent through participation in authentic deliberation by all those subject to the decision in question."[7] Joshua Cohen makes clear the centrality of legitimacy to deliberative democratic theory in his essay "Deliberation and Democratic Legitimacy." There, he draws on Habermas's *Legitimation Crisis* to argue

---

6. Jürgen Habermas, *Between Facts and Norms: Contributions to a Discourse Theory of Law and Democracy* (Cambridge, MA: MIT Press, 1996), 167.

7. John S. Dryzek, *Foundations and Frontiers of Deliberative Governance* (Oxford: Oxford University Press, 2010), 23. See also Habermas, *Between Facts and Norms*; Iris Marion Young, "Justice and Communicative Democracy," in *Radical Philosophy: Tradition, Counter-Tradition, Politics*, ed. Roger S. Gottlieb (Philadelphia: Temple University Press, 1993), 123–142; Simone Chambers, *Reasonable Democracy: Jürgen Habermas and the Politics of Discourse* (Ithaca, NY: Cornell University Press, 1996); Joshua Cohen, "Deliberation and Democratic Legitimacy," in *The Good Polity: Normative Analysis of the State*, ed. Alan Hamlin and Philip Petit (Oxford: Basil Blackwell,1989), 17–34.

that citizens "regard their basic institutions as legitimate in so far as they establish the framework for free public deliberation."[8] Deliberative processes are essential for any decision-making process to be considered legitimate or legitimating. Cohen proceeds to outline the ideal deliberative procedures.[9] We discuss this in greater detail in the next section. For now, it's important to recognize the central claim that political "outcomes are democratically legitimate if and only if they could be the object of a free and reasoned agreement among equals."[10]

The link between democratic procedure and legitimacy is nothing new and goes back at least as far as the Enlightenment.[11] Deliberative democrats, however, revised the generic democratic link between legitimacy and procedure by defending a specifically deliberative procedure.[12] Early defenders of deliberative democracy presented the deliberative model as an improvement over aggregative or interest-based models of democracy that rely solely on voting procedures to achieve democratic self-rule. As Seyla Benhabib explains, democratically legitimate decisions are those that are in the best interest of all, and while voting is one way to determine what people believe to be in their best interest, decisions reached after a simple aggregation of votes do not always or necessarily

---

8. Cohen, "Deliberation and Democratic Legitimacy," 21. As Cohen makes clear, his early articulation of what can now be identified as the deliberative model of democracy, was inspired in large part by earlier work of Jürgen Habermas including his *Legitimation Crisis* (1975) and *Theory of Communicative Action* (1984).

9. Cohen, "Deliberation and Democratic Legitimacy," 22.

10. Ibid.

11. Jean-Jacques Rousseau, *The Social Contract and Other Later Political Writings*, ed. Victor Gourevitch (Cambridge: Cambridge University Press, 1997).

12. It's worth noting that the connection deliberativists draw between communication and good decision-making is also not particularly new. Consider, for example, the etymology of the word "parliament," originating from the word "to speak." Importantly, however, deliberative democrats emphasize communication among everyday people and not just elites. In other words, deliberative democrats care about the people's deliberation and not just the deliberation of those for whom they vote.

take into account the collective interest.[13] Benhabib maintains that *what* is in the best interest of all can "only be determined through processes of collective deliberation conducted rationally and fairly among free and equal individuals."[14] Merely aggregating people's private interests through fair voting procedures will not necessarily result in decisions that all can accept as in their best interest and therefore legitimate.[15]

The deliberative model's comparative advantage vis-à-vis an aggregative model of democracy rests precisely in its legitimating force. More deliberative decision-making procedures are supposed to generate more legitimacy.[16] Additionally, the *kind* of legitimacy that a deliberative democracy can offer is supposed to be a stronger sort than that which is available in a purely aggregative model. Admittedly, it can be odd to talk about the relative "strength" of legitimacy emanating from various procedures. Is legitimacy not a categorical quality, one that is either present or absent in a political system? We would argue, however, that the deliberative model not only offers an account of *how* to achieve democratic legitimacy (e.g., the particular procedures that will or will not result in legitimate outcomes), it actually offers its own account of how we ought to think about legitimacy in the first place.

For deliberative democrats, democratic legitimacy goes beyond simple questions of fair participation. As Cohen notes, if fair opportunity to participate was the only goal, we would have no reason to prefer the deliberative model over "the pluralist conception of democratic politics as a

---

13. Seyla Benhabib, "Toward a Deliberative Model of Democratic Legitimacy," in *Democracy and Difference: Contesting the Boundaries of the Political*, ed. Seyla Benhabib (Princeton: Princeton University Press, 1996), 69.

14. Ibid.

15. Jürgen Habermas, "Three Normative Models of Democracy," *Constellations* 1, no. 1 (1994): 1–10.

16. Again, this link between deliberation and legitimate decision-making was not original to the deliberative turn in the 1990s. But while others drew the connection between deliberation and legitimacy, often by way of a critique of democracy which was seen as non-deliberative, it was Habermas who gave deliberation "a more thoroughly democratic foundation." Amy Gutmann and Dennis Thompson, *Why Deliberative Democracy?* (Princeton: Princeton University Press, 2004), 9.

system of bargaining with fair representation for all groups."[17] When it comes to ensuring democratic legitimacy, deliberative democrats maintain that the *kind* of participation matters as much as whether that participation is fair. More specifically, decisions must be made on the basis of open communication among those affected. Fair voting procedures should be seen as a necessary but insufficient condition for legitimacy. As Dryzek notes, "Deliberative democrats generally believe that legitimacy is achieved by deliberative participation on the part of those subject to a collective decision."[18]

In her articulation of deliberative politics, Simone Chambers contends that the key is maintaining a distinction between "talking and fighting, persuasion and coercion, and by extension, reason and power."[19] Thus, a key tenet of deliberative democracy is holding out for the very possibility of legitimacy. Deliberative democrats deny the realist position of "might makes right." Legitimate decisions are those reached through persuasion rather than coercion. By keeping alive this possibility of persuasion, deliberative democracy elevates itself above "mere majority rule" and the simple aggregation of given individual preferences. Deliberatively derived decisions are those that have held up to the scrutiny of public interrogation and not just the private interrogation of individuals.

Ultimately, deliberative democracy's legitimacy claims rest on the expectation that people can and should try to persuade each other and remain open to persuasion by others. This kind of process, wherein participants provide reasons for their positions and adapt their positions based on the reasons provided by others, is seen as offering a path to a more robust kind of legitimacy. Compared to decisions resulting from even the fairest aggregation procedures, deliberatively derived decisions have a claim to greater legitimacy and not just a greater claim of legitimacy. Deliberative legitimacy is of a different, more substantive sort than

---

17. Cohen, "Deliberation and Democratic Legitimacy," 20.
18. Dryzek, *Foundations and Frontiers of Deliberative Governance*, 21.
19. Chambers, *Reasonable Democracy*, 9.

aggregative legitimacy or the fair opportunity to participate in a vote. That is to say, it is seen as being of a higher quality and not just a greater quantity than that the legitimacy on offer in a purely aggregative model. It is to the question of these specifically deliberative procedures that we turn now.

## B. Procedure

As evidenced by the discussion above, early articulations of deliberative democracy established that the model's legitimating force comes from particular decision-making procedures. Here again, the comparison to aggregative or interest-based theories of democracy is instructive. Like deliberative democracy, aggregative theories of democracy rely on procedural guarantees of legitimacy. But as Young explains, "the role of discussion separates this conception of democracy from the interest-based theory."[20]

Famously, deliberative democracy has been described as "talk-centric" compared to the more "vote-centric" aggregative model.[21] And throughout the first statements of deliberative democratic theory, this emphasis on communication is clear. Still, it's worth noting that we would expect to observe both voting and talking in deliberative and aggregative models of democracy alike. In our view, the deliberative model's key procedural innovation is its call to "be more sensitive to what precedes and underlies" a vote.[22] The debate and communication preceding a political decision determine the democratic nature or legitimacy of the decision itself.[23] In other words, the process by which people come to hold the opinions they express in a vote impacts the legitimacy of the resulting decision.

---

20. Young, "Justice and Communicative Democracy," 129.
21. Chambers, "Deliberative Democratic Theory."
22. Robert E. Goodin, *Reflective Democracy* (Oxford: Oxford University Press, 2003), 2.
23. Habermas, *Between Facts and Norms*, 304.

Deliberative democratic theory has, from its inception, emphasized the importance of looking beyond institutional moments of decision or will-formation. That is to say, deliberative democrats also care deeply about the entire informal process of opinion-formation that takes place before the formal deliberation over a particular policy or decision. We see this attention to processes of opinion-formation most obviously in Habermas's "two-track" model of deliberative democracy. The first track involves the "informal channels of political communication" along which collective opinions are formed.[24] The second track involves deliberation that occurs in empowered spaces or decision-making bodies like Parliament and Congress. According to Habermas, deliberative democracy develops "in the interplay" between these two tracks.[25] Specifically, the administrative power of the state manifested through legislation must be bound by the communicative power or influence generated by citizens' deliberations in the public spheres.[26] Crucially, the two tracks are given equal billing in Habermas's work.

This focus on the various informal communicative processes of public opinion formation helps distinguish deliberative democracy from theories of direct democracy. For example, deliberative democrats would say that it's okay if we cannot point to a time or a place when all or even most citizens gathered to formally discuss particular proposals in advance of a specific decision. They look instead for evidence of broad "resonance of collective decisions with public opinion."[27] Moreover, for someone like Cohen, this resonance need not result from actual processes of deliberation but could be merely hypothetical. Cohen explains that "outcomes

---

24. Ibid., 275.

25. Ibid., 275.

26. Ibid., 133. The informal processes of opinion formation that generate "communicative power" in the first track must be "permeable to the free-floating values, issues, contributions, and arguments of a surrounding political communication." And the formal deliberation made in the second track must remain permeable to the contributions of the first track. Jürgen Habermas, "Popular Sovereignty as Procedure," in *Deliberative Democracy: Essays on Reason and Politics*, ed. William Rehg and James Bohman (Cambridge, MA: MIT Press, 1997), 57.

27. Dryzek, *Foundations and Frontiers of Deliberative Governance*, 40.

are legitimate if and only if they *could* be the object of a free and reasoned argument among equals."[28]

Contra Cohen, Simone Chambers follows Habermas in insisting that the deliberation be real, not hypothetical: "The discursive model of moral deliberation precludes the possibility of hypothetically working out, let alone deducing, what participants would agree to."[29] There is no way, independent of discursive procedure itself, to determine what norms people would agree to. This preference for real, existing communication has led some deliberative democrats to focus on the deliberation preceding formal moments of decision in empowered spaces, from Congress to citizens' assemblies.[30] But the forms of deliberation that deliberative democrats consider to be part of processes of opinion- and will-formation extend far beyond these domains. Just as important as the formal deliberation among elites, for example, is the "real-existing" deliberation always already occurring among citizens in their everyday lives.[31] It is not up to deliberative democrats to determine whether this or that decision could be, in theory, supported by the people subject to it. Instead, the relevant question is whether there is resonance between collective opinions emerging from informal public spheres and the actual decisions made in more formal, empowered spaces.

Still, it's not enough, democratically speaking, for formal decisions to simply map roughly onto public opinion. Deliberative democrats also care about the degree to which that public opinion developed in a deliberative way. As Habermas famously explains, quoting John Dewey, "the means by which a majority comes to be a majority is the most important thing."[32]

28. Cohen, "Deliberation and Democratic Legitimacy," 22. Emphasis added.

29. Chambers, *Reasonable Democracy*, 104. Jürgen Habermas, "Reconciliation Through the Public Use of Reason: Remarks on John Rawls's Political Liberalism," *Habermas and Rawls: Disputing the Political* 92, no. 3 (1995): 117.

30. John Rawls, "The Idea of Public Reason Revisited," *The University of Chicago Law Review* 3 (1997): 765–807.

31. Ana Tanasoca, *Deliberation Naturalized: Improving Real Existing Deliberative Democracy* (Oxford: Oxford University Press, 2020).

32. Habermas, *Between Facts and Norms*, 302.

According to Habermas's two-track model of deliberative democracy, legitimacy actually takes root (or not) in the diffuse and informal discourse preceding formal decisions, which takes place in the public sphere.[33] Thus, another challenge for deliberative democrats is to identify and assess the communicative processes by which collective opinions formed.

Filling in details regarding the ideal procedure, Cohen draws on Habermas's work to explain that legitimating procedures are those that ensure free, reasoned, equal, and consensual deliberation.[34] By *free*, Cohen means that citizens must be bound only by the results of the deliberation. In other words, they are free to make one decision over another. Deliberative procedures are *reasoned* insofar as people provide reasons for their preferences, and those reasons—and not something else—are what "settle the fate of their proposal."[35] Parties in deliberation must be *equal*, both formally and substantively. By this, Cohen means that everyone must have an equal opportunity to participate and that the ideas of a person should be judged independently of the relative power they have. Finally, the deliberation must be *aimed at consensus*, even if consensus is not ultimately achieved. When consensus is not realized, decisions should be made according to a vote.[36] As Cohen explains, however, even when deliberation ends in a vote, "the results of voting among those who are committed to finding reasons that are persuasive to all are likely to differ from the results of an aggregation that proceeds in the absence of this commitment."[37]

Importantly, these procedural specifics are not reflected in all early articulations of a deliberative kind of democracy. In her deliberative first

---

33. Habermas, "Three Normative Models of Democracy," 8.

34. Cohen, "Deliberation and Democratic Legitimacy," 22. Jürgen Habermas, *Legitimation Crisis* (Boston: Beacon Press, 1975); Jürgen Habermas, *The Theory of Communicative Action*, vol. 1 (Boston: Beacon Press, 1984).

35. Cohen, "Deliberation and Democratic Legitimacy," 22.

36. Habermas goes into greater detail about the conditions under which the results of bargaining procedures should be accepted as fair. Habermas, *Between Facts and Norms*.

37. Cohen, "Deliberation and Democratic Legitimacy," 23.

statement, for example, Young challenges various procedural assumptions made by deliberative democrats, including the value of reaching or even aiming for consensus. Young agrees with other deliberative democrats that legitimacy relies on procedures being free from coercion so that no influence is "exercised over people's agreement except the force of the better argument."[38] And yet she reveals how an overly narrow understanding of persuasive reasoning as well as the pursuit of consensus can result in precisely the non-neutral and coercive decision-making procedures that are anathema to deliberative democrats. Ultimately, Young urges deliberative democrats to remain vigilant to threats to democratic legitimacy that can originate *from* specific deliberative procedures rather than focus only on threats that stem from the absence of deliberative procedures.

Rejecting the notion that deliberative procedures ought to be oriented toward consensus, Young still seeks to keep alive the possibility of persuasion, the possibility of people changing their minds through communication with others. For her, this focus on persuasion means that decisions are not reached "merely through the identification and aggregation of preexisting preferences" but through some collective form of communication.[39] The goal of communication, therefore, is not mutual agreement but the transformation of a person's partial perspective to a more inclusive perspective brought about through communication with others.[40] Young continually looks for ways to enhance communication and to expose constraints on it. As such, she takes a relatively broad view of the communicative procedures that can contribute to the legitimacy of collective decisions.

Given Young's deep concern with issues of exclusion and domination in deliberation, she is often taken to be a critic of the whole enterprise rather than a supporter. But we see Young also as a key contributor to deliberative

---

38. Young, "Justice and Communicative Democracy," 125–126.

39. Ibid., 129.

40. Iris Marion Young, "Communication and the Other: Beyond Deliberative Democracy," in *Democracy and Difference: Contesting the Boundaries of the Political*, ed. Seyla Benhabib (Princeton: Princeton University Press, 1996), 127.

democratic theory. Crucially, Young endorses the "broad outlines" of deliberative or discursive democracy as presented by Habermas, Cohen, and Dryzek.[41] To the extent that she departs from these and other deliberative democrats, it is to avoid imposing what she identifies as non-neutral standards of fairness and impartiality on diverse and complex polities.

For Young, the concept of "deliberation" or "discourse" is too narrow "to include all the forms of communication that can legitimately persuade others in situations of democratic decision making."[42] Offering a more expansive understanding of democratic communication, Young's "communicative" model of democracy departs from other early deliberative models in its endorsement of rhetoric, greeting, storytelling, or what she argues are more inclusive modes of communication.[43] As will become clear in later chapters, we see Young's work in this vein as contributing to precisely the kind of revised thinking about democratic theory that we argue is warranted.

In her articulation of the deliberative ideal, Simone Chambers also interrogates the relationship of legitimacy and deliberative procedure. In *Reasonable Democracy*, she seeks to defend the assumption that talking is better than fighting, where better means more legitimate. Legitimate decisions are those that are made freely. At the front of Chambers's mind, however, is the objection that persuasion and dialogue might, themselves, undermine the free nature of collective decisions. As such, she investigates how persuasion and dialogue might be themselves a kind of force and coercion.[44] Ultimately, Chambers finds that the procedural specifics matter a great deal. Drawing from Habermas's discourse ethics and theory of communicative action, she shows that deliberative procedures aimed at persuasion cannot, in and of themselves, guarantee legitimate outcomes. This is especially true if the deliberative procedures are not adequately

---

41. Young, "Justice and Communicative Democracy," 127.

42. Ibid., 127.

43. Iris Marion Young, *Inclusion and Democracy* (Oxford: Oxford University Press, 2000).

44. Chambers, *Reasonable Democracy*, 5.

open and receptive to disagreement and dissent. It is to the question of the status of disagreement in deliberative democracy that we turn now.

## C. Disagreement

As we've shown, early proponents of deliberative democracy attended especially to the theme of legitimacy. They sought to identify a decision-making procedure that would keep open the possibility of legitimacy even in the face of persistent disagreement. Communicative procedures were the key to reaching legitimate collective decisions in contexts of pluralism. If one looks only at the later debates between deliberativists and their agonist critics, however, it's easy to miss the extent to which the deliberative turn itself grew out of a desire to design decision-making procedures sensitive to difference and disagreement in large pluralistic societies. While some might dispute the success of deliberativists' attempts to accommodate difference and disagreement in their preferred model of democracy, it is clear that such attempts were made. From the earliest articulations of deliberative democracy, we see that there is a general attunement to both faces of democracy—the cooperative and the conflictual, the one focused on reason and the other focused on resistance. The deliberative model is, after all, a "discursive approach *to the dilemmas, conflicts, and tensions of modern society.*"[45]

But while, as Chambers notes, Habermas's deliberative theory "does not devalue contestation" and "indeed points to the critical and productive force of contestation, it does not 'valorize' contestation either."[46] She elaborates that while "contestation, naysaying, and struggle" are integral parts of the "dialectical forum," they are not "ends in themselves."[47] Deliberative democratic theory, in short, represents a middle ground between "the view

---

45. Ibid., 158. Emphasis added.
46. Ibid., 162.
47. Ibid.

that all problems are amenable to rational solutions ... and an approach that accentuates the intractability of the dilemmas, conflicts, and tensions of collective life."[48]

Crucially, the communicative procedures at the center of the deliberative model not only permit "disagreement, conflict, dispute, argumentation, opposition, in short, naysaying," they also directly depend on it.[49] These elements of discourse "furnish the very conditions that make universalized norms possible."[50] Moreover, the deliberative ideal can be achieved even in the absence of agreement. In other words, the deliberative ideal does not require that we achieve common ground but that we search for it, and just as importantly that we remain committed to resolving disputes *through* communication precisely when common ground cannot be found.[51]

According to Habermas's notion of "fair compromise," even when a "generalizable interest" is not apparent and decisions must be made through bargaining procedures aimed at compromise instead of discursive ones aimed at persuasion, we must not abandon a commitment to communication. As he explains, it is only through communicative procedures that we can determine that there is no generalizable interest and that fair bargaining procedures need to commence. Similarly, there is no way, independent of moral discourse, to determine "the procedural conditions under which actual compromises enjoy the presumption of fairness."[52]

The deliberative imperative is not that we try to reach agreement at all costs, but that we remain committed to communication even in the presence of disagreement. We see this in many of the earliest articulations of deliberative democracy that were quite sensitive to issues of difference and disagreement. Young, for example, pointed to the ways that difference

---

48. Ibid., 158.
49. Ibid., 158–159.
50. Ibid.
51. Ibid., 162.
52. Habermas, *Between Facts and Norms*, 167.

and disagreement could serve as a resource in democratic communication. Indeed, it is *through* deliberation that diverse and varied viewpoints are brought to bear on collective decisions.

Still, while Chambers and others have acknowledged the crucial role that contestation plays in deliberation, this is not the same as being adequately attuned to the second face of democracy. For example, the deliberative model fails to acknowledge any legitimate or democratic reasons for giving up on trying to persuade others using reason. According to the accounts discussed above, to give up on reasoned persuasion is to give in to the lure of force and coercion. But with a view to the second face of democracy, sometimes it might be necessary to give up on trying to persuade, not for the sake of coercing others but to stand up to those who seek to coerce! Additionally, groups or individuals may look outside of strategies of reasoned persuasion in the event that they have been "othered" by an opposing group, whether consciously or unconsciously, such that their voices or interests have been deemed irrelevant or worthy of exclusion from democratic processes. In such cases, people might resort to creative strategies beyond reasoned persuasion, including protest or direct action, to help dismantle that othering attitude. This shift toward the confrontational democratic mood need not amount to a full embrace of an ontology that affirms the existence of only friends or enemies.

In our view, while the deliberative model has remained sensitive to difference and disagreement and to the coercive potential of certain kinds of discourses, it still struggles to fully incorporate the insights animating the second face of democracy. And so, despite the sensitivity to identity and difference that many early articulations of the first face of democracy show, critics have continued, with good reason, to raise concerns over the exclusionary tendencies of deliberative democracy in both theory and practice. In the following section, we consider this model's evolving shape as it responded to these concerns raised by so-called difference democrats.

## II. DELIBERATIVE U-TURN

In reviewing the earliest articulations of the deliberative face of democracy beginning in the early 1990s, we have revealed a conceptual constellation connecting the idea of legitimacy with ideal procedure and the presence of disagreement amid pluralism. We have tried to highlight the extent to which early defenders saw deliberative democracy as offering an account of how we might unite both faces of democracy, the conflictual and the cooperative. According to this account, the deliberative ideal does not deny conflict in politics but tries to offer a way to live cooperatively with others in the face of conflict.

But as the deliberative model grew more dominant in democratic theory, supplanting pluralist conceptions that relied solely on aggregation, it was met with healthy doses of skepticism as well as calls for revision from critics and defenders alike. Much of the reaction against the deliberative model stems from concerns that it fails to deliver on the promise of democracy amid difference and disagreement. For example, "difference democrats," a group that we see as straddling the agonistic and deliberative traditions, have challenged both the feasibility and desirability of pursuing deliberative democracy in contexts of difference and disagreement.[53] In what follows, we discuss various high-profile challenges from this perspective that have brought about what might be called the "deliberative U-turn" in democratic theory. We also discuss various attempts to respond to these challenges. Then, in Section III we present a deliberative innovation that claims to be able to overcome many of the difference democrats' concerns with one theoretical advance: a systems approach.

The deliberative model's prioritizing of ideal procedure, narrowly focused on the practice of deliberation, left it open to familiar but important challenges. Two main shortcomings of the model were identified in the decades after democratic theory's deliberative turn. From the perspective

---

53. For an early discussion of "difference and democracy" see Seyla Benhabib, ed., *Democracy and Difference: Contesting the Boundaries of the Political* (Princeton: Princeton University Press, 1996).

of these two challenges, the deliberative ideal was seen as being at best unrealistic and at worst undemocratic.[54]

The first criticism relates to the feasibility of deliberative democracy. Is the deliberative ideal realistic and can it be implemented in large, complex, plural democracies? This challenge is primarily an empirical one. On the one hand there is the problem of scale. Citizens and even their elected officials rarely, if ever, engage in anything resembling the free, reasoned, equal deliberation aimed at consensus that Cohen outlines. Even in those organized moments of deliberative participation like citizens' assemblies and mini-publics, these deliberative forums could only ever include a very small subset of those impacted by the laws. Is it possible for the deliberation among a tiny subset of citizens to confer meaningful legitimacy on resulting decisions that affect a much larger population?[55] In addition to the problem of scale, there is the question of human nature and unavoidable power dynamics. Even when people do engage in either formal or informal political dialogue are they actually open to being persuaded, to revising their preferences as deliberative democrats insist they should be?[56] Given these practical concerns of feasibility, how much real-world guidance can the deliberative model provide?

The second set of challenges relates to whether the deliberative ideal is ideal at all. Again, deliberative democracy elevates as more legitimate those decisions that are achieved through free, equal, and reasoned discourse aimed at consensus. Some critics worry, however, that pursuing, let alone achieving, this supposedly ideal type of discourse could result in more exclusionary decision-making procedures. Recalling the early questions raised by Young and discussed in the previous section, the concern here is that deliberation, even in its "ideal" form, is not sufficiently inclusive or is otherwise ill-equipped to reckon with social inequality.[57]

---

54. Lynn Sanders, "Against Deliberation," *Political Theory* 25, no. 3 (1997): 347–376; Young, "Communication and the Other"; Young, *Inclusion and Democracy*.

55. Cristina Lafont, "Democracy Without Shortcuts," *Constellations* 26, no. 3 (2019): 355–360.

56. Mary F. Scudder, "The Ideal of Uptake in Democratic Deliberation," *Political Studies* 68, no. 2 (2020): 504–522.

57. Sanders, "Against Deliberation."

Implementing the deliberative model in practice, with its preference for deliberative reason giving and its focus on consensus could take us further away from our democratic aims. Rather than trying to put the stamp of legitimacy on collective decisions, we are better off acknowledging the, at times, zero-sum nature of politics.

Crucially, deliberative democrats are well aware of these concerns regarding the feasibility and desirability of the deliberative model. They have responded to this "U-turn" away from deliberative democracy with a variety of strategies addressing these criticisms. Empirical research studying actual moments of formal deliberation among everyday people shows that participants in deliberative forums are often open to changing their minds and that, in fact, deliberation can bring about depolarization.[58] Other work has shown that people, especially those who are turned off by adversarial partisan politics as usual, are eager and willing to engage in communicative-based modes of political participation.[59] Thus, even if the deliberative ideal has yet to be achieved in practice, the empirical record seems to support our continued pursuit of the ideal.

To respond to the charge that the deliberative ideal itself is undemocratic and exclusionary in its narrowness, theorists have expanded the definition of what qualifies as "deliberation." In other words, they've changed the standards used to define deliberation, loosening the straitjacket of "rational discourse." Young's work on the importance of greeting, rhetoric, and storytelling, for example, has helped enlarge how deliberativists think of democratic communication. Today, the range of the kinds of communication deliberativists admit under the rubric of deliberation is much broader. Along these lines, they now point to everyday talk among people

---

58. James Fishkin et al., "Is Deliberation an Antidote to Extreme Partisan Polarization? Reflections on 'America in One Room,'" *American Political Science Review* 115, no. 4 (2021): 1464–1481, https://doi.org/10.1017/S0003055421000642.

59. Michael A. Neblo, Kevin M. Esterling, and David Lazer, *Politics with the People: Building a Directly Representative Democracy* (Cambridge: Cambridge University Press, 2018).

as well as their casual interactions on social media as instances of deliberative democracy in action.[60]

Others, including one of us (Molly), have worked to make deliberative democracy both more applicable to the real world and more inclusive by identifying the cognitive-affective disposition required of people if they are to achieve a deliberative practice in contexts of deep difference and inequality.[61] The thinking here is that our deliberative aspirations, no matter how realistic, will remain out of reach unless or until we consider the competencies and dispositions of ordinary people. Specifically, democratic theory and practice must account for the challenge of engaging in meaningful deliberation and careful listening across difference and disagreement.

Deliberative democracy is hard work, yes. But it's important to remember that this hard work does not include the impossible task of stripping away affect and emotion in an attempt to isolate pure reason.[62] People participating in practices of public reasoning are and always will be embedded in complex, intersecting, and even contradictory backgrounds. Rather than pursuing the deliberative ideal of cooperation across difference by somehow doing away with these realities, we are better off incorporating them into our theories and recognizing the challenges that they pose.[63] According to this view, the deliberative ideal remains more or less intact, but greater attention is paid to how people interact with that ideal under often messy real-world conditions.

Deliberative democrat Ian O'Flynn writes that "it is probably no exaggeration to say that almost everything that has been written about deliberative democracy since the late twentieth century has been in response

---

60. Jane Mansbridge, "Everyday Talk in the Deliberative System," in *Deliberative Politics: Essays on Democracy and Disagreement* (Oxford: Oxford University Press, 1999), 211–240; Tanasoca, *Deliberation Naturalized*.

61. Mary F. Scudder, *Beyond Empathy and Inclusion: The Challenge of Listening in Democratic Deliberation* (New York: Oxford University Press, 2020).

62. Sharon R. Krause, *Civil Passions: Moral Sentiment and Democratic Deliberation* (Princeton: Princeton University Press, 2008).

63. Scudder, *Beyond Empathy and Inclusion*.

to" criticisms about either the feasibility or desirability of the deliberative ideal.[64] This responsiveness to critique is evident in our discussion of the deliberative U-turn. Throughout, we have offered examples of the various steps deliberativists have taken to turn democratic theory back in a deliberative direction. In the next section, we consider another such attempt to get deliberative democratic theory back on track: the systems approach.

## III. SYSTEMIC ANSWERS TO DELIBERATIVE PROBLEMS

Since the deliberative model's inception, its defenders have explicitly tried to accommodate both aspects of democracy, what we have referred to as the reasonable and the conflictual aspects. While people disagree on the extent to which the deliberative model has been successful, we have tried to show that the goal at least has always been to do justice to both faces of democracy.

Arguably the most promising avenue for bringing the deliberative model to a point where it can do justice to both faces of democracy comes from the systems approach. Indeed, this approach emerged as a way to bring efforts to broaden our understanding of deliberation in line with the normative commitments of the deliberative model that we outlined in Section I.[65] The systems approach is seen as a way to overcome concerns regarding both the feasibility and desirability of deliberative democracy. The deliberative systems approach has roots going back to Habermas's two-track model of deliberative democracy, whereby the diffuse and informal deliberation in multiple public spheres is transmitted to formal political institutions where decisions are made. Here, the unit of deliberative analysis, so to speak, is the political system as a whole.

---

64. Ian O'Flynn, *Deliberative Democracy* (Cambridge: Polity Press, 2021), 7.

65. Jane J. Mansbridge et al., "A Systemic Approach to Deliberative Democracy," in *Deliberative Systems: Deliberative Democracy at the Large Scale. Theories of Institutional Design*, ed. John Parkinson and Jane Mansbridge (Cambridge: Cambridge University Press, 2012), 1–26.

Taking a systems approach, the goal is not necessarily to maximize the amount of deliberation occurring at each and every site or institution but to enhance the deliberativeness of the larger system. And crucially, the deliberativeness of a political system can be greater than the sum of its parts. Such an approach to deliberative democracy offers a more nuanced and holistic view of democratic decision-making and the role of deliberation within it. Taking a *systemic* approach to deliberative democracy means understanding deliberation less as a discrete practice of formal debate and argumentation and more as a communicative activity that occurs across multiple, interlinked, but functionally differentiated, sites. A systemic approach to deliberation helps explain how to achieve deliberative democracy on a large scale, thus addressing concerns of infeasibility. But it also impacts how we understand the democratic value of other kinds of political practices, including protest, elections, and referendums. By broadening the kinds of political acts permitted in a "deliberative democracy," a systems approach helps alleviate concerns over the exclusionary tendencies of an overly narrow view of deliberation.

According to its defenders, only through a systems approach can we identify and appreciate the democratic significance of interactions between, say, diffuse public spheres, mini publics, the media, and legislative bodies.[66] Different parts of a political system will vary in their deliberativeness. Rather than focusing on any one communicative act or institution, we evaluate the overall deliberativeness of a political system. As Jane Mansbridge and her coauthors explain in their essay articulating a systems approach to deliberation:

> A systemic approach allows us to analyse the division of labour among parts of a system, each with its different deliberative strengths and weaknesses, and to conclude that a single part, which in itself may have low or even negative deliberative quality with respect to

---

66. Mansbridge et al., "A Systemic Approach to Deliberative Democracy."

one of several deliberative ideals, may nevertheless make an important contribution to an overall deliberative system.[67]

According to this view, even non-deliberative acts like protest or partisan opposition can contribute to the overall deliberativeness of the system so long as they enhance the system's epistemic, ethical, or democratic quality in some way.[68] According to Mansbridge et al., these are the core functions of a deliberative system. The epistemic function relates to producing "preferences, opinions, and decisions that are appropriately informed by facts and logic and are the outcome of substantive and meaningful consideration of relevant reasons."[69] If the reliance on expert testimony helps incorporate relevant considerations into a decision-making process, thereby enhancing its epistemic quality, we should see it as contributing to deliberative democracy. A deliberative system's ethical function relates to the promotion of "mutual respect," and the democratic function refers to ensuring inclusion and "equal opportunities to participate" in processes of opinion- and will-formation.[70] If a particular protest helps broaden public debate to be more inclusive of marginalized groups, it should be seen as enhancing the democratic function of a political system and therefore enhancing its deliberative quality.

Among other things, the systems approach to deliberative democracy provides normative justification for expanding the kinds of communication we admit under the deliberative ideal. As such, it has helped the deliberative model respond to criticisms regarding its infeasible and exclusionary preference for rational discourse, narrowly defined. Recognizing the need for modes of communication that do not align with a simple view of deliberation is one way to attune the deliberative model to the

---

67. Ibid., 2.
68. Ibid.
69. Ibid., 11.
70. Ibid., 11–12.

second face of democracy. But while this approach has several benefits, it is not without its costs.

Jeff Jackson, for example, has challenged the notion that deliberative democracy can be improved by non-deliberative actions and practices. Specifically, he takes issue with a central implication of the systems approach—the idea that, especially in real-world contexts of social inequality, we may have to turn to practices that do not resemble deliberation, including protest, in order to enhance the democratic nature of decisions.[71] According to Jackson, "the need to stray from deliberation under the conditions we currently confront" reveals limits to both the normative and practical value of democratic deliberation.[72] In these circumstances, we jettison "precisely what deliberative democrats hold to be valuable about the reason-giving process they describe."[73]

In a similar vein, David Owen and Graham Smith contend that Mansbridge et al.'s "systems manifesto" set the deliberative model normatively adrift when it suggested that non-deliberative practices can contribute to the overall deliberativeness of a political system.[74] Take for example, the idea that "highly partisan rhetoric, even while violating some deliberative ideals, may nonetheless help to fulfill other deliberative ideals such as inclusion."[75] The problem, according to Owen and Smith, is that the various efforts to save the deliberative perspective by expanding what can count as "deliberation" end up amounting to nothing more than "concept stretching." If early accounts of deliberative democracy were seen as being too restrictive, then the systems approach has now been charged

---

71. Young, *Inclusion and Democracy*; Archon Fung, "Deliberation Before the Revolution Toward an Ethics of Deliberative Democracy in an Unjust World," *Political Theory* 33, no. 3 (2005): 397–419, https://doi.org/10.1177/0090591704271990.

72. Jeff Jackson, "Dividing Deliberative and Participatory Democracy Through John Dewey," *Democratic Theory* 2, no. 1 (2015): 79, https://doi.org/http://dx.doi.org/10.3167/dt.2015.020105.

73. Ibid., 78.

74. David Owen and Graham Smith, "Deliberation, Democracy, and the Systemic Turn," *Journal of Political Philosophy* 23, no. 2 (2015): 213–234, https://doi.org/10.1111/jopp.12054.

75. Mansbridge et al., "A Systemic Approach to Deliberative Democracy," 3.

with being too permissive. The tendency to accept a more expansive account of what counts as deliberation is said to threaten the model's normative moorings. In short, the accumulation of piecemeal modifications of the deliberative model has so expanded the notion of deliberation as to render it effectively useless.[76]

Given mounting concerns over the coherence of the deliberative model, it would seem that it has not been so easy for deliberativists to attune themselves to both faces of democracy. In trying to make room for democratically legitimate practices of confrontation illuminated by the second face, the deliberative model seems to have lost sight of the first face. In Chapter 3, we take up the suggestion, made by deliberativists themselves, that we ought to back away from the idea of deliberation as the centerpiece of democratic theory.[77]

## IV. CONCLUSION

In this chapter, we reviewed the origin of the deliberative model of democracy and surveyed various criticisms leveled against it by difference democrats and others who distrust its ideal-theory approach to political theory. In tracing the contours of the deliberative turn and subsequent U-turn, we have found ourselves before the now dominant systems approach to deliberative democratic theory.

By opening up deliberative democratic theory to a broader set of communicative political practices, the systems approach helped better orient the model to the second face of democracy. Critics raise concerns, however, that in so doing the systemic turn caused that model to lose touch with the normative commitments of the first face. It is to these concerns

---

76. David Owen and Graham Smith, "Survey Article: Deliberation, Democracy, and the Systemic Turn," *Journal of Political Philosophy* 23, no. 2 (2015): 213–234.

77. Mark E. Warren, "A Problem-Based Approach to Democratic Theory," *American Political Science Review* 111, no. 1 (2017): 39–53.

that we turn in Chapter 3. As we will show in later chapters, however, so too has the agonistic approach struggled to attend adequately to both the reasonable and conflictual aspects of democracy. Important questions thus remain in regards to how we ought to conceive of a democratic theory that cogently encompasses the two faces.

# 3

# The Deliberative Face

In Chapter 2, we presented criticisms leveled against particular aspects of the deliberative model and considered strategies that developed in an effort to respond to them. In this chapter and the one that follows, we consider two global challenges to the deliberative perspective as such. The second of these global challenges, which we address in Chapter 4, arose from outside the deliberative framework and is articulated most clearly by agonists. For these critics, deliberative theory is ideologically biased and democratically dangerous. But first, in this chapter, we turn to a challenge that has been raised recently by deliberativists themselves.

Surveying the charges brought against the deliberative model over the last couple decades, these immanent critics conclude that the best way forward is to simply abandon the emphasis on deliberation as the core feature of democracy. The problem, these critics argue, is that the concept of "deliberation" has been stretched beyond recognition. In short, efforts to save the deliberative model from charges of exclusion have so expanded the notion of deliberation as to render it effectively useless.[1] As such, the emphasis on deliberation as the centerpiece of democratic theory no longer makes sense. We are better off simply

---

1. David Owen and Graham Smith, "Deliberation, Democracy, and the Systemic Turn," *Journal of Political Philosophy* 23, no. 2 (2015): 213–234, https://doi.org/10.1111/jopp.12054.

focusing on more familiar ideals traditionally associated with democracy, such as inclusion in agenda-formation and decision-making.[2]

This chapter begins by outlining these concerns of concept stretching and the general normative unmooring of the deliberative model in Section I. Then, in Section II, we argue that the problem lies primarily with those advocates of deliberative democracy who focus too much on *practices* of deliberation, thereby failing to comprehend the *normative core* that animates this perspective as a whole. Finally, in Section III, we show that if we orient our understanding of the deliberative model to its core sense of the autonomy of political communities, in which the moral equality of each person's voice is recognized, we can effectively decenter specific practices of deliberation, allowing them to become merely one mode of communication among others. In doing this, we are able to critically assess a variety of modes of communication not as watered-down variants of deliberation but in terms of their contribution to promoting or undermining those core values under the conditions of a given political order. When understood in this decentered sense, we argue that the deliberative approach can avoid devolving into an increasingly amorphous conglomeration of useless insights and thus deserves to be ranked as the best conceptualization of the first face of democracy.

## I. THE DELIBERATIVE SYSTEM AND ITS PROBLEMS

If by 2010 deliberative democracy had "entered a kind of adolescence," it would appear that it is now squarely in adulthood.[3] Gone are the awkward and tiresome years of trying to be all things to all people. As it matured, deliberative democracy has come to terms with what it can and cannot do. For example, the recent emphasis on systems-level analysis has relaxed the expectation that all elements of a deliberative system be, themselves,

---

2. Mark E. Warren, "A Problem-Based Approach to Democratic Theory," *American Political Science Review* 111, no. 1 (2017): 39–53, https://doi.org/10.1017/S0003055416000605.

3. Michael A. Neblo et al., "Who Wants to Deliberate—And Why?," *American Political Science Review* 104, no. 3 (2010): 566.

deliberative.[4] According to this view, deliberativeness is a quality of a political system as a whole rather than simply the sum of its deliberative parts. Furthermore, the systems approach recognizes the possibility of non-deliberative actions, including protest or partisanship, contributing to the overall deliberativeness of a political system.

Consider, as an analogy, the idea of a healthy diet. For example, how should we understand the health implications of sugar in a person's diet? Experts would agree that sugar is not healthy, per se. If we take a systemic or holistic view of health, however, we would want to consider this food not on its own but within the context of a person's diet as a whole. While, all else equal, more sugar might reduce the overall health of a diet, we should also consider whether the deprivation of pleasure and strict prohibitions of specific foods could lead to an imbalanced and unsustainable regimen. Taking a broader view, we begin to see how the presence of sugar, in moderation, could be consistent with and even supportive of a healthy diet. Similarly, while protest is not deliberation, taking a systems approach to deliberative democracy reveals how it could be generally supportive of deliberative goods.

According to David Owen and Graham Smith, however, the problem with this kind of systems approach is that we could come to judge a political system as deliberative even if it has "*little, or even nothing, in the way of actual democratic deliberation between citizens taking place.*"[5] Just

---

4. Mansbridge first introduced the concept of a "deliberative system" in "Everyday Talk in the Deliberative System," in *Deliberative Politics: Essays on Democracy and Disagreement*, ed. Stephen Macedo (Oxford: Oxford University Press, 1999), 211–240. Others have discussed the need to evaluate deliberative democracy on a larger scale. See also Robert Goodin, "Sequencing Deliberative Moments," *Acta Politica* 40, no. 2 (2005): 182–196; Michael Neblo, "Thinking through Democracy: Between the Theory and Practice of Deliberative Politics," *Acta Politica* 40, no. 2 (2005): 169–181; John Parkinson, *Deliberating in the Real World: Problems of Legitimacy in Deliberative Democracy* (Oxford: Oxford University Press, 2006). These insights were distilled by Mansbridge et al. into what Owen and Smith have called the "systems manifesto"; Mansbridge et al. "A Systemic Approach to Deliberative Democracy," in *Deliberative Systems: Deliberative Democracy at the Large Scale—Theories of Institutional Design*, ed. John Parkinson and Jane Mansbridge (Cambridge: Cambridge University Press, 2012), 1–26; David Owen and Graham Smith, "Deliberation, Democracy, and the Systemic Turn," *Journal of Political Philosophy* 23, no. 2 (2015): 213–234.

5. Owen and Smith, "Deliberation, Democracy, and the Systemic Turn," 218.

as concerning in their view has been the tendency to stretch the concept of deliberation itself to the point where now "almost every communicative act may qualify as 'deliberative.'"[6]

In responding to criticisms regarding an overly narrow view of deliberation—one that does not account for more agonistic postures of democratic action—theorists of deliberative democracy have given in to two self-defeating tendencies: "concept-stretching" on the one hand and "criteria weakening" on the other hand. The systems approach stretches the concept of deliberation by including non-deliberative acts within its scope while weakening the criteria for evaluation by failing to require any actual deliberation within the system itself.[7] Critics of systems approaches to deliberation make an important point: "If deliberation is everything, maybe it's nothing."[8]

Returning to the health analogy, we would be concerned if, as a result of taking a holistic view of health, we deemed a diet "healthy" that included little or nothing in the way of actual "health food" like fruits or vegetables. If we wish to defend the dietary value of sugar, perhaps we are better off simply admitting that health is not the only dietary consideration. Such an approach would be more coherent than one that, in an effort to include sugar, stretched the concept of "health" beyond recognition.

Several high-profile deliberativists now ask if it's time we let democratic theory off the deliberative hook, so to speak. Reinterpreting the systemic question, Mark Warren and others have called for investigating "the role of deliberation *within* democratic systems" instead of asking "whether democratic systems are deliberative in nature."[9] Breaking with the deliberative model, Warren differentiates a system's deliberativeness from its *democratic-ness*. According to his problem-based approach, it matters

---

6. Ibid., 227; Warren, "A Problem-Based Approach to Democratic Theory," 41.

7. Owen and Smith, "Deliberation, Democracy, and the Systemic Turn," 232.

8. Robert Goodin, "If Deliberation Is Everything, Maybe It's Nothing," in *The Oxford Handbook of Deliberative Democracy*, ed. Andre Bächtiger et al. (Oxford: Oxford University Press, 2018), 883.

9. Owen and Smith, "Deliberation, Democracy, and the Systemic Turn," 232.

more *that* a political system solves certain problems than *how* it solves them, whether through deliberation or some other political practice.

For their part, David Owen and Graham Smith articulate two possible paths for democratic theory to regain solid normative footing: either bring democratic theory back in line with the deliberative ideal, or give up on the deliberative ideal altogether.[10] In other words, democratic theory can either double down on claims regarding the centrality of deliberation or it can simply step away from "the deliberative system as the organizing idea."[11] The first approach, Owen and Smith explain, would require "a more restricted account of the type of everyday talk that can be considered deliberation."[12] The second approach would simply cut democracy loose from essential deliberative commitments.

Importantly, for Owen and Smith, the first option does not mean "falling back on the highly delimited account of deliberation within some ideal theoretical accounts."[13] For example, they acknowledge the need to consider how "non-deliberative acts and practices enable or disable democratic deliberation."[14] But even with this allowance, the focus remains on how non-deliberative acts impact the discrete practice of deliberation. It's not enough to show that protest or partisan opposition have a broad *deliberative effect*. Taking this first approach would mean considering more specifically the effect that these practices have on *deliberation* itself.

Convinced by the critiques discussed in the previous chapter, we think it would be a mistake to return to a more restricted account of deliberation. But what about this second solution to the problem of normative drift? Is it time to cut democratic theory loose from its deliberative anchor? The idea here is to acknowledge that democratic deliberation is "one amongst many practices through which democratic institutions and systems realize

---

10. Ibid., 228.
11. Ibid., 233.
12. Ibid., 228.
13. Ibid.
14. Ibid., 218.

a range of democratic goods. It is not the only democratic practice and will not always be appropriate."[15] As an example of this approach, Owen and Smith cite an early version of Warren's 2017 paper proposing a problem-based approach to democratic theory.

Like Mansbridge et al.'s systems approach, Warren's problem-based approach allows us to recognize the democratic contribution of even those practices that "violate the very core of deliberative persuasion."[16] Importantly, however, Warren's problem-based approach avoids charges of concept stretching and conceptual confusion insofar as it acknowledges the democratic value of, say, resistance without having to claim that it somehow contributes to the deliberativeness of a system. According to this view, a system's democratic nature is not simply a function of its deliberativeness.

In sum, Owen and Smith present two options for addressing the problem of normative drift in deliberative democracy since the systemic turn. The first involves tethering deliberative theory more firmly to the practice of deliberation. The second would mean freeing democratic theory from its deliberative anchor.

We argue that neither of these proposed remedies is satisfactory. Owen and Smith's problematization of deliberative systems assumes a view of the world where political practices can be placed into neat categories of "deliberation" and "not deliberation." This thinking encourages what John Parkinson first referred to as an "injection" approach to deliberative democracy.[17] According to this view, a political system's deliberative quality is the result of *injecting* or *adding* "strictly defined deliberation at critical points of the system."[18] Such an injection approach "assumes that the more deliberation there is in the system's component parts, the higher the

---

15. Ibid., 231.

16. Mansbridge et al., "A Systemic Approach to Deliberative Democracy," 18.

17. John Parkinson, "Models, Metaphors, and Their Consequences: The Curious Case of Deliberative Systems," in *ECPR Joint Sessions*, Pisa, April 24–28, 2016.

18. André Bächtiger and John Parkinson, *Mapping and Measuring Deliberation: Towards a New Deliberative Quality* (Oxford: Oxford University Press, 2019), 104.

deliberativeness of the entire system."[19] If the deliberativeness of a political system is based on how much deliberation occurs within it, then the only way to recognize the deliberative value of practices like protest is to somehow lump them in as a kind of deliberation.

As Bächtiger and Parkinson point out, however, this injection or *additive* approach to assessing and improving a deliberative system is not the only one available. Articulating an alternative, they propose thinking of deliberativeness as a "quality that emerges from the proper working of the parts of a democratic system, no part of which need be fully deliberative (or fully democratic) on its own."[20] Here deliberativeness is a *summative* quality, "a quality that is produced by the scale and complexity of a given system, and not simply an ingredient which goes into a system."[21] In their view, such a summative approach can alleviate Owen and Smith's discomfort with judging the deliberativeness of a system according to something other than the deliberation present in its component parts.[22]

But Bächtiger and Parkinson go on to argue that the deliberativeness of a democratic system is just one quality among several. Specifically, they compare the deliberativeness of a democratic system to the timbre of an instrument.[23] To say that a democratic system or decision-making process has a deliberative timbre means that it puts "special emphasis on a quality that other forms do not."[24] A clarinet's timbre will set it apart from other instruments, but this is not the clarinet's only distinctive feature nor is it always the most relevant feature when it comes to understanding its function and sound or how it compares to other instruments in an ensemble. Applying this timbre metaphor to democratic theory, Bächtiger

---

19. Bächtiger and Parkinson, *Mapping and Measuring Deliberation*, 104.
20. Ibid.
21. Ibid., 8.
22. Ibid.
23. Ibid., 6.
24. Ibid., 7.

and Parkinson argue that the deliberativeness of a democratic system "is just one feature of such processes, albeit a highly salient one."[25]

Rather than narrowing their focus to deliberation, strictly defined, those who take Owen and Smith's second path opt instead to simply drop deliberation as the centerpiece of democratic theory. In their view, we are better off focusing on classic democratic ideals such as inclusion in agenda formation and decision-making.[26]

Here, we consider the implications of such calls to step away from deliberation as an animating feature of democratic theory. In pursuing a *democratic* system instead of a necessarily *deliberative* one, is deliberative democratic theory simply coming to terms with the inherent limitations of deliberation? In doing so, is it better able to account for the second face of democracy? Or is it selling out, making compromises that go against its core commitments and the intuitive pull of the first face of democracy?

Appealing to the normative core of deliberative democracy, we argue that the deliberative model has not, in fact, been set normatively adrift. As such, recent calls to move beyond model-based approaches to democratic theory likely represent an overcorrection to systems thinking that cause us to miss the real normative value of the deliberative model. In our view, the biggest problem for the deliberative face of democracy relates primarily to the tendency of its supporters (and detractors) to focus too much on the discrete *practice* of deliberation, in whatever form. Such a focus causes us to lose sight of its normative contribution.

Reinterpreting the orientation of the deliberative face, we show how we can avoid charges of concept stretching and normative unmooring while remaining committed to an expansive understanding of a specifically deliberative, or what we will ultimately call a communicative, model of democracy. We can move away from an additive or injection model of deliberative democracy—one that centers deliberative theory on one particular practice—without giving up on the key normative insights of

---

25. Ibid., 6.

26. Warren, "A Problem-Based Approach to Democratic Theory"; Bächtiger and Parkinson, *Mapping and Measuring Deliberation*, 9.

deliberative democracy. While acknowledging that the practice of deliberation alone cannot guarantee a political system functions democratically, we maintain that the *deliberativeness* of a democratic system is more than simply one quality among many. Indeed, it relates to how we understand democracy itself.

The deliberative model provides much more than an account of the democratic value of deliberation. Instead, its key contribution is its answer to the question of how to achieve democracy in large pluralistic societies. In other words, the deliberative model is not anchored, normatively speaking, by the practice of deliberation but by the assertion that democratic decisions are those that are arrived at through inclusive, even if diffuse, communication among those who will be affected by them. According to this interpretation of the deliberative model, we are not betraying its key normative commitments by acknowledging either the limitations of deliberation or the value of non-deliberative practices. Furthermore, in light of the normative and critical content the model provides, we show that it would be a mistake to simply give it up.

## II. RECLAIMING THE NORMATIVE CORE OF THE DELIBERATIVE FACE

Our aim here is to better articulate the normative value of a specifically deliberative model of democracy, demonstrating what we lose by pursuing merely a *democratic* system instead of a necessarily *deliberative* one. According to critics, the problem with traditional model-based approaches to democratic theory is that they encourage us "to center our thinking on an ideal typical feature of democracy, such as deliberation or elections, and then to overextend the claims for that feature."[27] This approach has led to unproductive and unnecessary turf wars as theorists defend their preferred democratic practice against competitors.

---

27. Warren, "A Problem-Based Approach to Democratic Theory," 39.

Take, for example, the supposed difficulty deliberative models have with explaining "why deliberation in the context of skewed empowerments (a context, say, in which the wealthy can buy more voice) can undermine democracy."[28] According to Warren, the force of this critique "depends on treating deliberation as if it functions as to empower."[29] He argues that this is wrong, that "we should not expect deliberation to address problems of empowered inclusion," which are better addressed with practices of voting.[30] Deliberativists can lessen the force of these critiques, as well as move on to more productive discussions, by simply admitting the limitations of deliberation in addressing this particular problem.

To move beyond this theoretical impasse, we ought to drop the automatic emphasis on deliberation and return to those core ideals traditionally associated with democracy. Specifically, Warren invites us to adopt a problem-based approach to democratic theory. Such an approach asks two key questions. First, "What problems does a political system need to solve if it is to function democratically?"[31] Second, "What are the strengths and weaknesses of generic political practices as ways and means of addressing these problems."[32]

To the question of democratic problems, Warren answers that so long as "a political system *empowers inclusion, forms collective agendas and wills,* and *organizes collective decision capacity* it will count as 'democratic.'"[33] These functions, he contends, are "probably exhaustive."[34] To answer the second question, our task is to evaluate supposedly democratic practices to find their comparative strengths and weaknesses when it comes to addressing these three specific problems of democracy. The

---

28. Ibid., 48.
29. Ibid.
30. Ibid.
31. Ibid., 39.
32. Ibid.
33. Ibid.
34. Ibid., 43.

non-exhaustive list of generic democratic practices includes recognizing, resisting, deliberating, representing, voting, joining, and exiting.[35] By building a democratic theory around the *problems* that any democracy ought to address—once again, the problems of empowering inclusion, forming collective agendas and wills, and organizing collective decision capacity—we can make use of a variety of practices in the pursuit of democracy.

Following Warren, Bächtiger and Parkinson advocate focusing "on a small number of crucial *democratic* criteria which have a particular relationship—a timbral sympathy, perhaps—with deliberation. These criteria are inclusivity and representation."[36] These innovations sound the death knell for the once lively debates between deliberative democrats and their critics. No longer do we have to choose one model or practice over another. Instead, we can pursue democracy using the best of each.

Again, the problem with model-based approaches to building democratic theory is their tendency to foreground one particular problem, one norm, or—in the case of the deliberative model—one practice to the exclusion of others. Such an approach is unnecessarily limiting. One practice simply cannot accomplish all of our democratic goals, and it is important to recognize the limitations of the practice of deliberation. With these points, we are in total agreement. We disagree, however, in regards to how we ought to interpret these limitations of the practice of deliberation. Specifically, we maintain that the limitations of the deliberative model are not as great as recent work suggests. First, we show that the deliberative model was not, in fact, designed primarily around the specific practice of deliberation. Thus, the real limitations of *practices* of deliberation should not be interpreted as limitations of the deliberative model as such. Second, and relatedly, the contributions of the deliberative model are greater than Warren's problem-based approach and recent interpretations of his approach seem to acknowledge. As such, we think it would be misguided to step away from the deliberative emphasis in democratic theory.

---

35. Ibid., 46.
36. Bächtiger and Parkinson, *Mapping and Measuring Deliberation*, 9.

In regards to the question of model-based approaches to building democratic theory, it's important to differentiate between normative models and empirical ones. While empirical approaches to democratic modeling have been developed around one ideal practice or norm, this is not true of normative models.[37] Deliberative democracy began as a distinctly normative project aimed at identifying the meaning of democracy itself. In order to understand how this democratic theory was constructed, we need to start with Jürgen Habermas's foundational "Three Normative Models of Democracy" essay. There, Habermas introduces his preferred proceduralist or deliberative model of democracy as a middle ground between the liberal model of democracy rooted in individual rights and the republican model of democracy rooted in a community's shared ethical identity. Rather than focusing on particular practices, Habermas articulates the normative core of the deliberative model in contrast to these two models that he finds respectively too weak and too strong in terms of the kind of autonomy they can deliver in large pluralistic societies.[38]

The ideal of democracy, generally speaking, offers a particular conception of legitimacy as being rooted in autonomy. Again, a key tenet of democracy, at least since the Enlightenment, is that the laws governing our lives are legitimate to the extent that we have freely chosen them. Crucially, different normative models of democracy provide different answers to the question of what it means for people to have a meaningful say in the laws to which they are held.[39] Jean-Jacques Rousseau's republican model of democracy, for example, relies on the maintenance of a thick ethical and cultural background consensus among citizens. Public spiritedness

---

37. For example, Bächtiger traces the dominance of model-based thinking to Coppedge et al.'s discussion of six key models of democracy: electoral, liberal, majoritarian, participatory, deliberative, and egalitarian, see Coppedge et al. "Conceptualizing and Measuring Democracy: A New Approach," *Perspectives on Politics* 9, no. 2 (2011): 253. Selen A. Ercan and Andre Bächtiger, "Deliberative Democracy: Taking Stock and Looking Ahead," *Democratic Theory* 6, no. 1 (2019): 98.

38. Jürgen Habermas, "Three Normative Models of Democracy," *Constellations* 1, no. 1 (1994): 7.

39. Amy Gutmann and Dennis Thompson, *Why Deliberative Democracy?* (Princeton: Princeton University Press, 2004), 14, https://doi.org/10.1057/palgrave.cpt.9300287.

and a strong sense of community among citizens are key. According to Rousseau these conditions ensure citizens will recognize their own will in the objective general will and thus remain "as free as before."[40] But this strategy of achieving autonomy through ethical sameness is neither available nor desirable in pluralistic societies.

Like Rousseau before him, Habermas turns to democracy to address the problem of political unfreedom—we are born free and yet everywhere are in chains. The deliberative model is Habermas's attempt to solve the problem of political unfreedom, but this time in large, complex, and plural societies very different from the communitarian ones Rousseau had in mind.

Moving away from Rousseau's pre-political ethical consensus, Habermas's model relies instead on fair and inclusive communicative procedures. This move is crucial for achieving democracy in a pluralistic society marked by deep difference and disagreement.[41] Indeed, inclusive, attentive, and responsive communication is Habermas's answer to the question of how citizens can see themselves as both the authors and addressees of the law despite unresolved disagreement.[42] For Habermas, we answer the problem of democracy amid disagreement by doing justice to our intersubjectivity and acknowledging the speech-act-immanent obligation we have to justify regnant norms to one another.[43]

In large pluralistic societies, we cannot expect citizens to necessarily agree on all decisions. They will not always see their will reflected in the law. Deliberativists contend, however, that a contested outcome can still have the presumption of democratic legitimacy so long as all citizens

---

40. Jean-Jacques Rousseau, *The Social Contract and Other Later Political Writings*, ed. Victor Gourevitch (Cambridge: Cambridge University Press, 1997), 50.

41. Mary F. Scudder, *Beyond Empathy and Inclusion: The Challenge of Listening in Democratic Deliberation* (Oxford: Oxford University Press, 2020), 24.

42. Melissa S. Williams, "The Uneasy Alliance of Group Representation and Deliberative Democracy," in *Citizenship in Diverse Societies*, ed. Will Kymlicka and Wayne Norman (Oxford: Oxford University Press, 2000), 126–127.

43. Stephen K. White, *The Recent Work of Jürgen Habermas: Reason, Justice, and Modernity* (Cambridge: Cambridge University Press, 1988), 51.

helped shape it. Though citizens with diverse and potentially conflicting perspectives may not be able to derive an *objective* general will, they can still coordinate political action *intersubjectively* through communication.

In other words, deliberativists reinterpret democratic self-rule as being rooted in a set of procedures that, if followed, guarantee citizens meaningfully participated in the lawmaking authority.[44] For Habermas, decisions will have the presumption of democratic legitimacy to the extent that they reflect the collective will and so long as the collective will was formed through inclusive, even if informal and diffuse, communication. This complete process is Habermas's solution to the problem of freedom and authority in large pluralistic societies.[45]

With this discussion of the origin of the deliberative model, we mean to show that its main contribution is its clear articulation of what democracy means in large pluralistic societies. And crucially, Warren's problem-based approach celebrated by Owen and Smith draws on these key normative insights of the deliberative model. Consider, for example, the "problems" that Warren says a political system must solve to be considered democratic. A problem-based approach to democratic theory is supposed to help us sidestep protracted arguments between defenders of various models and their critics. But these problems do not simply fall into our laps like Newton's apple. Rather, they are constituted and articulated from within a larger theoretical framework. Indeed, Warren acknowledges that he derives the problems of empowered inclusion, collective agenda and will formation, and collective decision-making from key normative insights of the deliberative model.[46]

The three problems Warren identifies as essential to democracy are constituted as problems only after one has embraced the framework offered by Habermas's version of the deliberative model. Consider, for

---

44. Denise Vitale, "Between Deliberative and Participatory Democracy: A Contribution on Habermas," *Philosophy & Social Criticism* 32, no. 6 (2006): 745.

45. Jürgen Habermas, *Between Facts and Norms: Contributions to a Discourse Theory of Law and Democracy* (Cambridge, MA: MIT Press, 1996), 299.

46. Warren, "A Problem-Based Approach to Democratic Theory," 44–45.

example, Habermas's concerns over the ethical constriction of discourse in Rousseau's republican model. With this discussion, Habermas raises the issue of *empowered inclusion*, or the need for people to be heard even if they do not already buy into the ethical commitments of a given society. Similarly, Habermas discusses the importance of democracy as a means of *collective decision-making* by way of his critique of the Lockean model, which is too thin in terms of its attention to collectivity. Further, according to Habermas, neither Locke nor Rousseau pay enough attention to *collective agenda and will formation*, or what Warren describes as the need for individual preferences "to be related communicatively to collective judgments, so that individual self-government extends through collective self-government."[47] For Locke, again, agenda and will formation need not be a collective enterprise, and for Rousseau they need not be communicative.

Warren ultimately shares the priorities of Habermas's deliberative model, namely, the importance of citizens forming a collective opinion and will through *inclusive* and *communicative* procedures and the need for that collective will to be *reflected* in resulting decisions. Instead of departing from these deliberative commitments, Warren picks up where Habermas leaves off, urging us to consider which specific practices are best suited for empowering inclusion, forming collective agendas, and organizing collective decision-making.

And yet, Warren's call to move past model-based approaches suggests that he sees these problems as freestanding, in the sense that they could be derived without reference to any particular model of democracy. Specifically, Warren maintains that his list of problems is "straightforward" and "common-sense," building on widely held intuitions about democracy.[48] But these essential tasks of democracy are intuitive thanks to important normative work being done by the deliberative model itself.

We argue that by deriving the problems of his problem-based approach from deliberative sources, Warren actually demonstrates the staying

---

47. Ibid., 44.
48. Ibid., 43.

power of the deliberative model.[49] Based on Warren's own account, then, we should not interpret the limitations of the *practice* of deliberation as limitations of the deliberative model as such. In doing so, we lose sight of important normative and critical insights.

Let's return to Warren's concern, discussed above, regarding the limitations of deliberation under conditions of unequal power. At the normative core of the deliberative model is the promise of autonomy and equality, brought together in a commitment to the moral equality of voice.[50] Although a full unpacking of the meaning and significance of the moral equality of voice will be fully taken up in succeeding chapters, a prima facie sense of its role in the deliberative model is all we need for the moment. Appealing to these deliberative ideals, we can very easily explain why social conditions of inequality, under which people could buy unequal voice, are inherently undemocratic. In such a case, either the decision would be found to not reflect the collective will or else the collective will would be corrupted by noncommunicative forces such as money or power. While we can certainly argue that economic inequality is unjust in and of itself, we can strengthen that critique by showing how inequality undermines democratic autonomy by distorting political discourse.

Crucially, while the practice of deliberation cannot, on its own, improve conditions of inequality, deliberative democratic theory *can* explain why deliberation under the unequal conditions Warren describes undermines democracy.[51] In fact, we would argue that the deliberative model is essential to recognizing how inequality and "existing distributions of power in society" undermine the democratic quality of even the most inclusive voting

---

49. Ibid., 44–45.

50. Stephen K. White, *A Democratic Bearing: Admirable Citizens, Uneven Justice, and Critical Theory* (Cambridge: Cambridge University Press, 2017), 65.

51. Joshua Cohen, "Deliberation and Democratic Legitimacy," in *The Good Polity: Normative Analysis of the State*, ed. Alan Hamlin and Philip Petit (Oxford: Basil Blackwell, 1989), 85; Vitale, "Between Deliberative and Participatory Democracy," 757; Simone Chambers, "Rhetoric and the Public Sphere: Has Deliberative Democracy Abandoned Mass Democracy?," *Political Theory* 37, no. 3 (2009): 339.

procedures.⁵² Whatever the preferred practice—whether voting or deliberation—merely injecting it into a political system will not guarantee democratic results.

Calls to move beyond the deliberative model would be analogous to claims that we ought to move beyond health as a guiding principle. If we admit the potential dietary value of sugar or the limitations of vegetables, have we abandoned the goal of a healthy diet? No. We would argue that the ideal of health is still relevant and important even if we come to realize that a person cannot thrive on "health food" alone. A holistic view of health is precisely what tells us that we should care about vitamins, nutrients, and energy while balancing pleasure and practical considerations like affordability and sustainability. Implicit in these claims is a substantive vision of the meaning of health itself, that to be healthy a diet must be balanced and possible to maintain in the long term.

The same can be said about the deliberative model. As we have shown, the deliberative model tells us much more than that we should value the practice of deliberation. Its key contribution is a substantive account of what makes a political system democratic; namely, the extent to which people have had a meaningful say in the laws to which they are held. While deliberative democratic theory has tended to overburden the practice of deliberation— expecting it to do things it simply cannot—this single-minded focus on the practice of deliberation is not essential to the deliberative model.

It's noteworthy that Warren does not see himself as breaking definitively from the systemic turn in deliberative theory that he helped initiate.⁵³ He explains, however, that "the questions [his approach] frames are broader," relating to democratic political systems and not just deliberative ones.⁵⁴ Our point, however, is that in asking these broader questions about

---

52. Gutmann and Thompson, *Why Deliberative Democracy*, 16.

53. Warren has clearly not abandoned deliberative democracy and co-edited the *Oxford Handbook of Deliberative Democracy* published in 2018. And he acknowledges that his problem-based approach is "congruent with the emerging deliberative systems approach in deliberative democratic theory" (41).

54. Warren, "A Problem-Based Approach to Democratic Theory," 41.

democratic political systems more generally, we are not actually moving "beyond models of democracy," or at least not the deliberative model in particular.

The deliberative model of democracy is itself a theory of what democracy *means* as well as the problems a political system must answer to be considered democratic. Warren, with his problem-based approach, and Bächtiger and Parkinson with their "timbral approach," see themselves as moving beyond a deliberation-only model of democracy. We would argue, however, that the deliberative model, at least the one articulated by Habermas, never *was* a deliberation-only model in the first place.

As such, our defense of the deliberative face of democracy does not depend on our showing the unique democratic value of the *practice* of deliberation. Ultimately, critics of deliberative democracy have long focused on the shortcomings of deliberation, and Warren is right to acknowledge that democracy requires more than deliberation. We reject the claim, however, that admitting the limits of the practice of deliberation somehow puts one at odds with the deliberative model of democracy. Still, it's true that deliberative theory has tended to place too much emphasis on the practice of deliberation. We should therefore consider how we might decenter deliberation from the deliberative model while retaining the model's normative insights. We turn to this question in the next section.

## III. DECENTERING PRACTICES OF DELIBERATION

Here, we orient the deliberative face of democracy such that it can acknowledge the strengths of non-deliberative practices, and even the weaknesses of deliberation, while avoiding the charges of conceptual stretching and confusion discussed above. Specifically, we argue that instead of either narrowing our focus on deliberation or discarding the deliberative model, we are better off simply "decentering" the practice of deliberation from the deliberative model's normative core, grounding it instead on the moral equality of voice of all members in a community.[55] This move effectively redistributes the normative weight of the deliberative model so that it is not leaning so heavily on practices of deliberation, even in their ideal form.

Making a similar distinction between the practice of deliberation and the deliberative ideal, Simone Chambers has identified a growing rift between what she calls "theories of *democratic deliberation* (on the ascendancy) . . . and theories of *deliberative democracy* (on the decline)."[56] While theories of *democratic deliberation* "focus on discrete deliberative initiatives within democracies," or what we refer to as the practice of deliberation, theories of *deliberative democracy* "tackle the large questions of how the public, or civil society in general relates to the state."[57]

Returning to the health analogy discussed earlier, much conceptual confusion could be avoided if we distinguished between health foods on the one hand and the ideal of a healthy diet on the other hand. Once we make this kind of distinction, as well as explain our logic behind what goes into the idea of a healthy diet, we can better understand why a healthy diet can admit more than just "health foods," narrowly defined. In this analogy, democracy is the general idea of a healthy diet. The ideal practice of deliberation is health food. And deliberative democracy is the particular school of thought that offers an account of what makes a diet healthy in the first place, offering reasons why a healthy diet is, say, one that is balanced, sustainable, sufficiently caloric, nutrient rich, and tasty. Making this distinction also helps us see why in most cases simply adding lots of carrots to

---

55. Iris Marion Young, "De-Centering Deliberative Democracy," in *Democratizing Deliberation: A Political Theory Anthology*, ed. Derek W. M. Barker, Noelle McAfee, and David W. McIvor (Dayton, OH: Kettering Foundation Press, 2012), 113–128.

56. Chambers, "Rhetoric and the Public Sphere," 324.

57. Ibid. According to Chambers, when it comes to theories of *democratic deliberation*, "what falls out of the picture is the largely inchoate and often unstructured mass public." The ascendency of theories of *democratic deliberation*, with their focus on the practice of deliberation, narrowly construed, means that deliberative theory "pays almost no attention to elections campaigns, referendums, or broad questions of public opinion formation"; Chambers, "Rhetoric and the Public Sphere," 331–333.

an otherwise unhealthy or imbalanced diet would not miraculously transform it into a healthy one.

To decenter deliberation from the deliberative model, we must distinguish between practices of deliberation (even in their ideal form) on the one hand and the deliberative ideal on the other hand. By "practices of deliberation," we mean "practices that generate influence through the offering and receiving of cognitively compelling reasons about matters of common concern."[58] We follow Habermas in defining the "deliberative ideal" as the broader goal of achieving democratic self-authorship amid difference and disagreement through inclusive and communicative procedures marked by fair consideration. Crucially, this deliberative ideal authorizes the use of more than just deliberation and requires our resistance to any communicative procedures that depart too substantially from fair communicative situations.

In decentering deliberation from the normative core of deliberative democracy, we follow Iris Marion Young, who in a 2006 essay articulated her preferred "de-centered approach to democratic deliberation."[59] According to Young, while centered approaches to deliberation "look for, or aim to design, *actual* processes of discussion, exchange, and persuasion leading to an agreed upon conclusion," decentered approaches are interested in conceiving of ways that "political decision-making processes" within large and diverse democratic polities "do or can exemplify norms of deliberative democracy."[60] Taking a decentered approach to deliberation, our main concern is assessing the extent to which decisions are grounded in social and political arrangements that sustain expectations of fair discussion. This criterion applies to both active participants and others not immediately present but who are substantially affected by the norms at issue.

Like Warren, we find the narrow focus on practices of deliberation to be limiting. These approaches fail to consider the broader democratic

---

58. Warren, "A Problem-Based Approach to Democratic Theory," 47.
59. Young, "De-Centering Deliberative Democracy."
60. Ibid., 116–117.

context within which deliberation occurs. But unlike Warren, we do not interpret the inadequacy of deliberative *practices* as evidence of the inadequacy of a specifically deliberative model. Instead, we emphasize the value of decentering deliberation from the model's normative core.

What about the concerns, voiced by Owen and Smith for example, that expanding the reach of deliberative democratic theory to include storytelling, protest, and everyday talk, has inadvertently emptied deliberative democracy of its normative content? By decentering a narrow understanding of deliberation from the deliberative model, do we threaten its normative moorings? We argue that these worries betray a misunderstanding of what the deliberative model's normative moorings are in the first place. As we discussed in Section II, the deliberative model was not constructed around the unique value of the practice of deliberation but around the normative claim that democratic decisions are those arrived at through inclusive, even if diffuse, communication among those who will be affected by them.

In other words, the crucial normative value of the deliberative model is its account of what democracy looks like in large pluralistic societies marked by dissensus. "Providing a simple yea or nay show of hands for a particular policy does not meet the bar of meaningful authorship" or democratic self-rule.[61] Instead, the deliberative model tells us that democracy amounts to having your voice heard and your perspective considered by your fellow citizens and political elites. Once we understand this to be the deliberative ideal, we can see how protest and partisanship might help us achieve it by facilitating the communication of opinions from one site to another.

As such, we argue that decentering the discrete practice of deliberation should not be seen as a violation of the deliberative model's key normative commitments. On the contrary, distinguishing the deliberative ideal from the practice of deliberation strengthens the normative force of the deliberative model by helping deliberativists take up the question of "how citizens form their opinions and come to their policy preferences" beyond the

---

61. Scudder, *Beyond Empathy and Inclusion*, 24.

bounds of discrete deliberative institutions.[62] Again, the crucial normative insight of the deliberative model is the need to consider *how* we form the opinions that go on to shape collective decisions. But while deliberative democracy is unique for centering processes of opinion formation, it does not, or need not, insist those processes be rooted in the *practice* of deliberation. By decentering deliberation, we open a vast amount of space to consider alternative political practices that bear on the relative democratic value of processes of public opinion formation, thereby making headway on issues of practicality and implementation that have long plagued deliberative models of democracy.

As Young explains, "the purpose of a theory of de-centered deliberative democracy" is to "provide norms and criteria through which the normative legitimacy of the process and many of its policy outcomes can be questioned and improved."[63] We need not lower the standard of what counts as deliberation in order to say that non-deliberative practices have deliberative impact. Instead, we must simply broaden the scope of what we consider to be relevant.

Still, Owen and Smith worry that a systems approach could justify forms of conduct incompatible not only with the ideal practice of deliberation but also with the normative commitments of the deliberative ideal, including the moral equality of voice. Here, they refer to outright "*deliberative wrongs*," including racist speech, being interpreted as somehow enhancing the deliberative quality of a political system.[64] Does this concern apply to a decentered approach as well? Returning to the health analogy, we might think about a hard drug like heroin. Heroin, like sugar, is not a health food. But unlike with sugar, most of us are prepared to say that it is fundamentally incompatible with a healthy lifestyle. Here, Owen and Smith correctly urge us to consider whether there are forms of speech

62. Chambers, "Rhetoric and the Public Sphere," 333.
63. Young, "De-Centering Deliberative Democracy," 119.
64. Owen and Smith, "Deliberation, Democracy, and the Systemic Turn," 223.

that violate not only the ideal practice of deliberation but also the ideals at the normative core of the deliberative model more generally.

While it's important not to overstate the deliberative impact of non-deliberative and even anti-deliberative practices, it would be a mistake to leave them out of the study of democratic theory altogether.[65] Sometimes non-deliberative elements will sum to something greater than their parts. Other times, however, they will prove to undermine the functioning of a deliberative democratic system. In these cases, we may still conclude that the system as a whole is meeting certain democratic expectations *despite* these elements. There is no easy way to make these assessments, and it would almost certainly involve making judgments over time. Our point, however, on the one hand, is that in narrowing our focus to include only practices of deliberation, we ignore political practices that are highly relevant to the means by which the majority comes to be the majority. On the other hand, by giving up on the deliberative model altogether, we miss out on critical insights that allow us to make the key assessments regarding what actions are democracy enhancing and which are democracy degrading. Learning from Young, we see that the key takeaway of the systems approach to deliberation is not that most things in our political lives are democracy enhancing but that they are democracy relevant.

With this, we begin to see how, by taking a decentered approach to deliberative democracy, we can respond to Owen and Smith's concern over non-deliberative practices counting as deliberation. To decenter deliberation is not the same as reinterpreting non-deliberative practices such that they become a *kind* of deliberation. Rather, the goal is to bring these practices into our assessment of a system's deliberative, and thus democratic, quality.

For example, protest can improve the deliberativeness of a political system by putting important problems on the agenda or introducing new arguments into the public sphere. Importantly, we can acknowledge that protest contributes to our attainment of the deliberative ideal, helping connect disparate public spheres, without claiming that it constitutes a

---

65. Chambers, "Rhetoric and the Public Sphere," 331.

kind of deliberation. But what's more, to say that protest *can* enhance the deliberative quality of a political system is not to say that it always does.

When deliberation is decentered from the deliberative model, it begins to make sense, as we suggested in the Introduction, to change our terminology and embrace instead the idea of a *communicative* model of democracy. Young, herself, while sharing many of the critical commitments of Habermas's deliberative approach, recognized the value of a more expansive term to refer to this brand of democracy. As she explains, the term "communicative democracy" denotes "a more open context of political communication" and avoids the "connotations of the primacy of argument, dispassionateness, and order in communication," often associated with the term "deliberation."[66]

We find this shift in terminology useful in helping us better understand the first face of democracy. The distinctiveness of the deliberative or communicative face is that popular sovereignty must be interpreted *intersubjectively*. For this, communication among citizens is key. Importantly, however, the goal is not to increase the amount of communication that satisfies ideal standards of deliberation. Instead, the theorist's task is to examine interactions in multiple and diffuse public spheres in order to assess and create opportunities for infusing collective life with democratic meaning. Increasing the deliberativeness of a decision-making process means ensuring citizens have a say in the laws to which they are held.[67] A decentered approach to deliberative democracy reveals that these opportunities will not be limited to practices of deliberation.

And so if, as deliberative theory mandates, we care about *how* opinions are formed and *how* decisions are made, then we have no choice but to take these non-deliberative practices into account. In decentering the practice of deliberation and looking to other practices and interactions between citizens, we are simply acknowledging the complex, informal, and diffuse process of opinion and will formation. The goal in expanding our scope is

---

66. Iris Marion Young, *Inclusion and Democracy* (Oxford: Oxford University Press, 2000), 40.

67. Young, "De-Centering Deliberative Democracy," 116.

to critically assess and improve—not rubberstamp—the means by which a majority came to be a majority.

Crucially, however, such an approach to democracy only generates this sort of critical edge if it is subsumed under the normative sense of a deliberative "model" that we have defended here. And so, while we have argued in favor of decentering the practice of deliberation from the deliberative model, we maintain that we need not decenter or abandon the normative criteria that a specifically deliberative model provides.

In the end, by purposefully adopting a decentered approach to democratic deliberation, we are able to retain key normative insights of the deliberative model while avoiding the charges of "concept stretching" that have been leveled against the systems approach. Following the systems thinking, we must expand our focus to include non-deliberative practices in our analysis. As we have shown here, however, this expansion is done as much for critical purposes as it is for exculpatory ones. Thinking metaphorically again, it is precisely because certain hard drugs may be incompatible with health that we should include them in our assessment of a healthy diet.

## IV. CONCLUSION

As we have shown, there is concern among deliberative democrats that the deliberative model has been set normatively adrift. Even those who have defended the normative value in the deliberative tradition now suggest that it may have outlived its usefulness. We have shown, however, that these concerns are overblown and the proposed solutions, misguided. For the deliberative model to regain solid normative footing it need not tether itself more firmly to discrete practices of deliberation. And it would be a mistake to abandon the deliberative emphasis altogether, even if we now prefer to speak in terms of a more broadly conceived "communicative model."

Calls to move past model-based approaches to democratic theory concede too much normative ground. As we showed above, the deliberative model does crucial normative work in democratic theory, providing the underlying account of what constitutes democracy in large pluralistic societies. As such, we should not be so quick to move past this particular model-based approach. Instead, we argue that a conceptualization of deliberative democracy whereby the practice of deliberation is decentered from its normative core is the best version of the first face.

In the next chapter, we consider another set of criticisms that, although coming from a different tradition and set of assumptions, arrive at the same conclusions: our democratic aspirations require us to back away from deliberative democracy. The agonistic critics discussed in Chapter 4 would celebrate any movement away from the normative presuppositions of that model. Indeed, for someone like Chantal Mouffe, the promise of democracy requires that we not only decenter the *practices* of deliberation but also reject "the very possibility of a non-exclusive public sphere of rational argument where a non-coercive consensus could be attained."[68] The agonistic critics we survey there suggest that we can never do adequate justice to the second face of democracy, the one emphasizing conflict and resistance, if we see it as deriving its significance only from the first, or deliberative, face.

---

68. Chantal Mouffe, *The Democratic Paradox* (New York: Verso, 2000), 33.

# 4

# The Agonistic Face

Chapters 2 and 3 showed that the deliberative tradition, while it has significant problems, is not quite the easy target that many of its critics take it to be. As we indicated in the Introduction, claims about the debilities of a deliberative approach have in recent years encouraged political theorists, journalists, politicians, and ordinary people to embrace the idea that we "inevitably" face an "agonistic conception of the political." Moreover, this state of affairs represents an "uncontroversial" "democratic good."[1] Agonism has become, in effect, "normalized." But, as Foucault reminds us, we should be wary when an orientation settles too comfortably into collective consciousness. In this chapter, we hope to do some unsettling.

What exactly is involved in accepting the legitimacy of greater levels of contestation as a part of democratic thought and politics? For some, this is simply a call to electoral strategies with a greater emphasis on partisan conflict versus consensus. For many others, however, such a call entails a deeper philosophical shift in our understanding of the character of democracy, more specifically, a shift toward one that renounces the emphasis on values like reason and deliberation that figure so prominently in theories of democracy and justice tied to thinkers like Jürgen Habermas or John Rawls. In contrast to the critics discussed in Chapter 3 who fear that democratic theory's emphasis on deliberation has become

---

1. Daniel O'Neill and Michael Bernhard, "Perspectival Political Theory," *Perspectives on Politics* 17, no. 4 (2019): 953.

increasingly self-debilitating, these agonistic critics worry that it systematically undermines democracy itself.

We argue that democratic theory should indeed accept a philosophical revaluing of conflict called for by agonists, but that doing so adequately involves a path of reconceptualization that is more difficult than typically realized. The problem is especially pressing in a popular version of agonism whose implications for democratic life are more questionable than many proponents tend to acknowledge. We call this version "imperializing" because of the default primacy it implicitly accords to subduing one's opponent over any other values. As the normalization of agonism has proceeded, insufficient attention has been paid to this difficulty. Our goal is to elucidate this problem, as well as show what might constitute a more satisfactory way of understanding what the place of agonism should be in political thinking, and, especially, how its relation to the communicative model should be understood.

We will argue that it makes sense to comprehend agonism as falling into two categories, "imperializing" and "tempered." The former anchors itself in the work of the early twentieth-century German jurist and political thinker, Carl Schmitt; the latter tends to emphasize the importance of Nietzsche. In Section I, we elucidate the "imperializing" version and argue that it provides us with an approach that is toxic for democracy. Section II turns to the "tempered" variant and contends that its proponents offer a more promising path. Here we examine the work of William Connolly and Bonnie Honig. Despite their impressive contributions to conceiving a defensible agonism, we suggest that they are not entirely successful because they fail to provide adequate accounts of equality and autonomy, values that are nevertheless at the center of their concerns.[2] This shortcoming is

---

2. There are other thinkers who have substantially contributed to what we call "tempered" agonism. Prominent here would be James Tully. We would argue that our challenges to Connolly and Honig would apply as well to the work of such figures. On the closeness of Tully and Connolly, see Marie Paxton, *Agonistic Democracy: Rethinking Political Institutions in Pluralist Times* (London and New York: Routledge, 2020), 68–74. In other ways, Tully is close to Honig, especially in his reliance on Arendt for his idea of an "ethos of citizenship and democracy," especially the "love of equality" and public "dialogue." Tully, *Public Philosophy in a New Key*, vol. 1: *Democracy and Civic Freedom* (Cambridge: Cambridge University Press, 2008), 136, 145–147,

explored in the present chapter. The task of providing a better account of these values is taken up in Chapters 5 and 6. Our approach there draws partially on a radically revised understanding of the normative core of Habermas's thought. We argue that this core can be modified and fleshed out in such a way that it allows us to see the concerns of at least some communicative democrats as not totally at odds with those of agonists such as Connolly and Honig.

## I. IMPERIALIZING AGONISM

How does one embrace a robust conflictual stance while retaining a strong allegiance to democratic norms and the rule of law? Over the last several decades, many on the political left have looked to the work of Chantal Mouffe for orientation. This includes not only academics but also a number of prominent European politicians who find that her agonism provides a broad strategy for re-energizing the left.[3]

A fundamental intention of Mouffe has been to excoriate Habermas and Rawls for obscuring oppression through their overemphasis on reason, consensus, and ideals of justice.[4] In what follows, we want to interrogate the basis of this charge and the conceptual coherence of the perspective that animates it. Doing so will help illuminate why the articulation of an

---

159. Our claim then would be that, as with Connolly and Honig, he does not provide a clear and convincing enough account of the ideas of autonomy and equality that his position relies on.

3. See John Morgan, "Chantal Mouffe: Only Populism Can Save the Left," *Times Higher Education*, April 4, 2019, https://www.timeshighereducation.com/features/chantal-mouffe-only-populism-can-save-left; Benjamin McKean, "Toward an Inclusive Populism? On the Role of Race and Difference in Laclau's Politics," *Political Theory* 44 no. 6 (2016): 797–820; and Alex Pareene, "Give War a Chance: In Search of the Democratic Party's Fighting Spirit," *The New Republic*, June 20, 2019.

4. Chantal Mouffe, *The Return of the Political* (London and New York: Verso Books, 1993), 3–8, 25–30; and Mouffe, "Introduction: Schmitt's Challenge" and "Carl Schmitt and the Paradox of Liberal Democracy," in *The Challenge of Carl Schmitt*, ed. Chantal Mouffe (London: Verso Books, 1999), 4–5, 43–44.

agonism that accords with, rather than corrodes, democratic values is not an undertaking as easily carried through as many think.

## A. Schmittean Ontology

Mouffe roots her central claims in Carl Schmitt's 1927 essay "The Concept of the Political," which famously defines political life in existential-ontological terms as the struggle between "friends" and "enemies." The decision as to who fits into which category is the originary moment of politics, unconstrained by any ethical-political norms.[5] For Mouffe, this formulation effectively slashes through the liberal democratic "illusion of consensus and unanimity," going directly to the core of what political life is really all about. "Power and antagonism" lie at the "very center" of politics.[6] It is this ontological-existential reality that needs to suffuse and transform our thinking about politics, and that is what an embrace of Schmitt provides. But Mouffe also wants to avoid any dangerous implications carried by a Schmittean stance, given that there is nothing necessarily democratic about his portrait of the struggle of friend and enemy. As she puts it in one of her most quoted lines, the goal is "to transform [Schmittean] *antagonism* into *agonism*," the latter implying a respectful, democratically constrained, struggle between "adversaries."[7]

Pulling off this transformation is a challenge, politically as well as conceptually. Mouffe, who is on the political left, is aware that her bold embrace of Schmitt carries with it a real danger, given the well-known fact that Schmitt was associated with Nazism, and his thought is often accused of being essentially fascist. For present purposes, two interrelated aspects

---

5. Schmitt, *The Concept of the Political*, trans. with an introduction by George Schwab, with a new foreword by Tracy Strong (Chicago and London: University of Chicago Press, 1996). A first version of this essay appeared in 1927; a short book version appeared in 1932. The latter is the one that was translated and to which scholars typically refer to today.

6. Mouffe, *The Democratic Paradox* (New York and London: Verso, 2000), 99.

7. Mouffe, *The Democratic Paradox,* 99, 102–103; *On the Political* (London: Routledge, 2005), 19–20; and *For a Left Populism* (London: Verso, 2018), 90–93.

of this topic need to be considered. First, how tightly is Schmitt himself and his work tied to fascism? If the connections are not serious, then presumably one can borrow liberally from his thought without worrying too much. Second, after embracing Schmitt, is Mouffe's effort to create distance from him as persuasive as she thinks, or does that connection generate serious, unacknowledged problems?

Mouffe is hardly the only thinker on the left who has borrowed from Schmitt over the last few decades.[8] Among this group, there has been a tendency to join apologists on the right and play down his connection with Nazism and argue that those who call attention to it are simply trying to illegitimately smear their attempts to draw valuable insights from his work. Mouffe adopts this strategy, deflecting uncomfortable questions by impugning critics' motives, asserting that "the aversion [that Schmitt's writings] incite probably comes from the truth within them."[9]

Associating one's intellectual opponent with Nazism is indeed a potent weapon of delegitimation, and it has not always been wielded responsibly.[10] On occasion, the political background of German thinkers has been attacked in a tendentious or overblown fashion, and sometimes critics' motives are justifiably questioned. In order to show that such suspicion is not warranted in relation to our claims about Schmitt, it is crucial to proceed with caution on this terrain and carefully untangle competing claims.

---

8. For an overview of the deployment of Schmitt by a variety of thinkers on the left, see Matthew G. Specter, "What's 'Left' in Schmitt? From Aversion to Appropriation in Contemporary Political Theory," in *The Oxford Handbook of Carl Schmitt*, ed. Jens Meierhenrich and Oliver Simons (Oxford: Oxford University Press, 2016), 426–454.

9. Mouffe, "Introduction: Schmitt's Challenge," 2.

10. Perhaps the most outrageous attempt to tar a German intellectual with the charge of Nazi complicity involves Habermas. Some critics have attempted to delegitimate his attachment to democracy with the accusation that he was an active Nazi near the end of World War II. They portray him as an avid leader in the Hitler Youth, citing a letter he wrote to his comrades supposedly encouraging their commitment to the cause. The truth is that he was inducted into that group at fifteen, as the war was drawing to its end, and his "activism" took the form of a letter to others in his unit urging them to attend a first-aid training session he was holding, given his position as a medic. For an account of this controversy, see Stefan Müller-Doohm, *Habermas: A Biography*, trans. Daniel Steuer (Cambridge: Polity Press, 2016). 22–25, 343–346.

With that goal in mind, it is useful to begin with a brief detour, comparing Schmitt's life and work with that of another prominent German philosopher who famously had ties with Nazism, Martin Heidegger. Heidegger accepted the position of rector of Freiburg University in 1933, making it clear in his inaugural speech that he favored the Nazi regime. Moreover, he privately expressed anti-Semitic attitudes at this time. Heidegger resigned several months later, after clashes both with Nazi officials and their opponents in the university over institutional policy. That ended his active, public ties with Nazism. So his personal active association with Nazism was patent and disturbing, even if rather limited. But is there any attachment evident in his philosophy? For many years, it appeared that one might be able to keep his brief association with Nazism largely separate from his major concepts and texts. More recently, however, previously unpublished notebooks have shown that hostility to "world Jewry" was deeply embedded in his central idea of the "history of Being."[11] In light of this revelation, it became clear that any future attempts to draw substantially upon Heidegger's thought must carefully articulate exactly how such efforts can, or cannot, disentangle themselves from these disturbing associations.

With Heidegger's case as a backdrop, how does Schmitt's case look? His ties with Nazism and desire to be an important player, both personally and conceptually, in the political reality being crafted by the Third Reich are markedly stronger than Heidegger's. It is sometimes suggested that Schmitt's active association with Nazism was also brief and relatively minor. Perhaps that take on Schmitt made sense some years ago when Mouffe and others on the left began to borrow from him, but, as with Heidegger, the more information scholars have unearthed, the more difficult it has become to maintain such a position.[12] It has long been

---

11. A sense of the range of controversies that attend future Heidegger interpretation can be gained from Ingo Farin and Jeff Malpas, eds., *Reading Heidegger's Black Notebooks 1931–1941* (Cambridge, MA and London: MIT Press, 2016).

12. See the conclusion reached by the editors of the recent *Oxford Handbook of Carl Schmitt*: "It is difficult to maintain the still-influential argument that Schmitt was just a fellow traveler," 8.

known that Schmitt held important national, administrative, and juridical positions in Berlin (certainly more important than the rectorship of a provincial university), but recent research has also shown that he clearly supported many of its ideals and pursued high-profile policies like continuing to purge all Jews from the German legal profession.[13] Further, he did not resign relatively quickly, like Heidegger who faced growing attacks (from both Nazis and their opponents) over his governance of the university; rather, he was forced out of his high-profile roles, after three years, by his superiors because of direct, ominous threats from jealous SS officials who were determined to replace him with an even more zealous Nazi.[14] In sum, Schmitt's personal connection to the regime was anything but a minor one.

But how does that relate, if at all, to Schmitt's key concepts and writings? The character of one's personal commitments does not automatically taint all of one's philosophical perspective. But can we always entirely separate the two spheres? The answer, we suspect, varies with the facts of a given case, and that can change as research progresses. Schmitt's substantial body of work offers a variety of insights to anyone thinking about political issues, beyond the ones with which we are concerned. For example, if one is a liberal constitutionalist, his specific critique of the foundations of that view through the concept of "legal indeterminacy" is something to be taken seriously.[15] This sort of reception can certainly proceed without the fascist baggage necessarily coming in tow. But it is something quite different

---

13. Reinhard Mehring, *Carl Schmitt: A Biography*, trans. Daniel Steuer (Cambridge, UK and Malden, MA: Polity Press, 2014), 296, 341–346.

14. For Schmitt's chronology, see Mehring, *Carl Schmitt*, 545–546. For Heidegger, see Hugo Ott, *Martin Heidegger: A Political Life*, trans. Allan Blunden (New York: Basic Books, 1993), 149–170, 235–260. Like Heidegger, Schmitt staunchly refused in the postwar period to express regret for his association with Nazism. Finally, at the age of ninety-two, Schmitt did state a preference for the postwar German Republic over the Third Reich; Mehring, *Carl Schmitt*, 346–348, 524–525.

15. Thus we can fully agree, for example, with Sanford Levinson that Schmitt deserves high status as a jurisprudential scholar because the analysis of "legal indeterminacy" can be separated from both his later involvement with national socialism or his later essay on "The Concept of the Political"; see "The Brooding Presence of Carl Schmitt in Contemporary Jurisprudence: Reflections on William Scheuerman's *The End of Law: Carl Schmitt in the 21st Century*," *Philosophy and Social Criticism* 47, no. 2 (Feb. 2021): 178–182.

when a contemporary thinker constructs their essential understanding of politics on the basis of Schmitt's conceptualization of friend/enemy. Having done that, the task of then separating oneself from any affinity with fascism becomes far more problematic. It is simply not persuasive to pretend that constituting political life through the Schmittean existential-ontological categories carries no fundamental framing force. Schmitt certainly had no problem seeing that force. In this context, it is telling that the essay, "The Concept of the Political," in which he first announced his novel perspective, was edited (with specific "National Socialist inflections") and redeployed by Schmitt in 1933 as his speech celebrating his induction into the Nazi Party. Immediately afterward, he took on significant positions in the regime.[16] Moreover, this essay remained central to Schmitt's worldview throughout his life. He repeatedly said: "I consider my essay on the political to be my best work."[17] So Schmitt clearly saw the friend/enemy framing as both expressing the core of his political theory and as smoothly aligning with fascism.

Below, we want to make a specific claim about that compatibility as rooted in "The Concept of the Political." But it is important to affirm that the highlighting of such a relation is not the same thing as claiming that Schmitt's thought as a whole is simply a fascist "glorification" of violence, war, and totalitarianism.[18] That assertion is as one-sided as is the impugning Mouffe offers (cited a moment ago) of the motives of anyone who raises questions about the problem of compatibility.

What does it mean to say that Schmitt's account of the political does not constitute a full-scale glorification of all aspects of fascism? Most notably, it means that the friend/enemy distinction is not explicitly racist, nor does it necessarily glorify violence. However—and this is the key issue—Schmitt's way of making the friend/enemy dialectic the essence

---

16. This inaugural version contains various "National Socialist inflections," see Mehring, *Carl Schmitt*, 183–184, 281, 294–296.

17. Quoted in Mehring, *Carl Schmitt*, 189.

18. Richard Wolin takes this kind of position in "Carl Schmitt: The Conservative Revolutionary Habitus and the Aesthetics of Horror," *Political Theory* 20, no. 3 (Aug. 1992): 436–444.

of politics does implicitly authorize certain reactions in political actors that progressively precipitate outcomes that will likely become violent and racist.[19] For example, although there is nothing necessarily racist about Schmitt's framework in "The Concept of the Political," he does affirm that the people of a successful polity should have a "concrete," homogeneous identity. Thus, when a racial minority gets figured as the "domestic enemy" arrayed against a homogeneous majority—the friends—within the polity, there is no reason not to vigorously pursue racist policies against them, especially if it helps bind together the majority as a "fighting collectivity."[20] Schmitt's own avid pursuit of the elimination of Jews from the legal profession in Germany would seem to follow this logic.[21]

A similar logic of deterioration is evident in terms of violence. In *The Nomos of the Earth* (1950), Schmitt claims that his conception of the political is embodied in the relatively peaceful functioning of the European-dominated international order from the late sixteenth through the nineteenth centuries. That order, Schmitt argues, restrained the sort of violence typical of earlier times, when religious passions overwhelmed political thinking and turned enemies who should be subdued into those who must be "annihilated."[22] Of course, this Schmittean account of a new intra-European restraint must be placed alongside the immense onset of

---

19. The gist of this degenerating logic of justification is grasped by William Scheuerman, "Getting Past Schmitt? Realism and the Autonomy of Politics," in *Politics Recovered: Realist Thought in Theory and Practice*, ed. Matt Sleat (New York: Columbia University Press, 2018), 280; John McCormick, "Teaching in Vain: Carl Schmitt, Thomas Hobbes, and the Theory of the Sovereign State," in *The Oxford Handbook of Carl Schmitt*, ed. Jens Meierhenrich and Oliver Simons (Oxford: Oxford University Press, 2016), 286; and Robert W. Glover, "Games Without Frontiers? Democratic Engagement, Agonistic Pluralism and the Question of Exclusion," *Philosophy and Social Criticism* 38, no. 1 (2012): 96.

20. Schmitt, *Concept of the Political*, 28, 32, 44–45, 72–73.

21. See the summary discussion of Schmitt's behavior during the Nazi era in Jens Meierhenrich and Oliver Simons, "'A Fanatic of Order in an Epoch of Confusing Turmoil': The Political, Legal, and Cultural Thought of Carl Schmitt," *The Oxford Handbook of Carl Schmitt*, ed. Jens Meierhenrich and Oliver Simons (Oxford: Oxford University Press, 2016), 7–9. A fuller accounting is in Mehring, *Carl Schmitt*, 328–348.

22. *The Nomos of the Earth in International Law of the Jus Publicum Europeum*, trans. G. L. Ulmen (Candor, NY: Telos Press, 2003), 140–143.

violence that was authorized in the process of colonization. But, even if we hold aside the question of such "external" violence, the internal dynamics of peace may have actually rested on values that are quite different from those mandated by the stark confrontation of friend/enemy. Here it is interesting to turn to an analogy Schmitt suggests for understanding the restrained behavior of European powers. Those states acted, he says, like equals in a pistol duel between "men of honor."[23] In both cases, conventions of honor and equal status controlled the amount and extent of violence. Interestingly, what Schmitt points to as the ground of restraint, namely, honor and equality among aristocrats, is something that would have given way easily if the European monarchs had in fact fully internalized the primary existential mandate of subduing their enemies. Our point is that whatever conventions exist in political life, they will, in a Schmittean world, give way over time to that prime imperative. Given the uncertainty, danger, and fear endemic to political life, it is hard to see why, *on Schmitt's own grounds*, anyone would ever let a convention of fairness overrule the choice of a more secure way of subduing their enemy. In the real world of Schmittean politics, they should always choose to fire their pistol just a little before the handkerchief hits the ground.[24]

## B. Mouffe's Attempt to Create Distance from Schmitt

In sum then, Schmitt's ontology provides the friend/enemy dynamic with a clear priority over *any* ethical-political norms that might come into

---

23. Ibid., 141–143.

24. The same sort of corrosive logic operates in Schmitt's proffered distinction between "annihilating" one's enemies, such as occurred in the Wars of Religion, versus "subduing" them, which he says would characterize a healthier politics reflecting the restrained violence between friends and enemies. We think it would be hard for anyone who reads the discussion of Schmitt's Nazi affiliations in Mehring's recent biography, cited above, not to see this corrosive logic operating in his own judgments. Jacques Derrida's skeptical comment here is apt: "One wonders what difference [Schmitt] sees between 'physical killing,' whose aim he judges indispensable, and the annihilation which he seems to condemn"; Derrida, *The Politics of Friendship*, trans. G. Collins (London and New York: Verso, 1997), 133. Cf. McCormick, "Teaching in Vain," 277.

conflict with it. Here it is important to stress that Mouffe embraces this foundation thoroughly. As she declares, the struggle between friends and enemies constitutes "our very ontological condition."[25] Hence the Schmitt-Mouffe position may at times seem to allow for the affirmation of things like the rule of law, and yet that affirmation will effectively dissipate whenever our appeal to it runs afoul of what is necessary to aid our friends and smite our enemies. Whenever democratic norms align with our friends' and our interests, we will behave in a fashion that affirms them, but when such constraints hinder what we truly desire, we will, with clear-eyed realism, grind our opponents into the dirt of history. The friend/enemy dynamic—because it embodies the ontology of political life—thus exerts an imperializing force in relation to other values.

Now Mouffe clearly does not want her perspective to manifest this sort of corrosive logic. She desires to avoid the dangerous implications carried by a Schmittean stance, so that the struggle of friend and enemy does not undermine her commitment to social democracy. When she declares that she will turn antagonism into agonism, she means mutually respectful struggle in which imperial hostility is subordinated to a "shared adhesion to the ethico-political principles of liberal democracy: liberty and equality."[26] But why should we expect such subordination to manifest in the minds and actions of those who have defined themselves politically in the way Schmitt recommends? Why would someone whose basic, existential-ontological comprehension of the world is cast in terms of friends and enemies not violate norms of liberty and equality whenever protecting one's "friends" seem to call for it? Clearly, one would expect a careful, sustained argument at this juncture from Mouffe as to why people who followed her recommended fundamental commitments would not behave in such a fashion. As we argued above in regard to Heidegger's work and its anti-Semitism, interpreters who now wish to rely on his thought have a central obligation to show how they can employ Heideggerian ideas *without* implicitly involving themselves in that problematic. Mouffe has

---

25. Mouffe, *The Return of the Political*, 3.

26. *The Democratic Paradox*, 99, 102–103; *On the Political*, 19–20; and *For a Left Populism*, 90–93.

shown herself to be surprisingly uninterested in the comparable task that presents itself in Schmitt's case.

What is at issue here is hardly an arcane philosophical matter. There has been an "Agonist-in-Chief" of this imperializing sort in the White House. Donald Trump's world is one of political friends and enemies. Of course, he also frequently affirms his support for basic democratic norms—until, that is, they grate against his and his friends' interests. While it became increasingly clear that Trump himself disdains such norms, many of his supporters don't think of themselves that way: rather, they are upstanding supporters of democracy and the rule of law. What interests us then is how imperializing agonism implicitly encourages a corrosion of those norms, such as we see in recent efforts to restrict voting rights or flagrantly overturn fair election results. What we call a tempered agonism can affirm all sorts of contentious political activity and partisanship, but it would also recognize a clear distinction between that, on the one hand, and the illegitimacy of wholesale efforts to undermine the integrity of voting and elections, on the other hand. Imperializing agonism, however, corrodes such lines of demarcation with a clear conscience.

If this danger would seem to attach to Mouffe's attempt to rely directly on Schmitt, how does she imagine herself remaining free of it? She presents two strategies for warding it off. First, Mouffe claims to have identified a point in Schmitt where the conceptual coherence of his friend/enemy framework breaks down on its own terms and thus creates a plausible opening for thinking in a different direction. She argues that Schmitt sometimes speaks as if "the people" in a country like Germany in the 1930s were already "a concrete unity," and thus the category "friend" and "enemy" was really being mapped onto an empirical situation, "merely a recognition of already-existing borders" between countries.[27] Mouffe contends that Schmitt here clearly overlooks the fact that plural elements are always empirically present within a given polity. To be consistent, Schmitt would have to accept that "the people" he extols actually embodies plural elements (ethnic, racial, etc.). And if plural elements are always present,

---

27. "Carl Schmitt and the Paradox of Liberal Democracy," 49–50.

then we should "refuse" Schmitt's own explicit anti-pluralist claims because they result in a self-contradiction, and we can instead accept the idea that one can have an agonism that accepts pluralism.

But this is a remarkably strained reading. For one thing, Mouffe cites no work of Schmitt's when making her claims. And even if she could come up with some citations in which Schmitt seemed to speak as though Germany was at that time "a concrete unity," it would be simpler to interpret such comments as aspirational, rather than reflecting a patently false claim about existing empirical reality. Moreover, it is precisely that aspiration that makes the "political construction" of "the people" a central, ongoing task within a Schmittean polity, and carrying out that task is where the hostility and corrosiveness of the friend/enemy dynamic manifests. Our reading of Schmitt in this context is simpler and more consistent with his underlying ontology and the framework of concepts that surround it than the one Mouffe offers. If this is so, then her attempt to judge Schmitt to be "ultimately contradictory," thereby supposedly opening up a more pluralist democratic interpretation of the trajectory of his agonism, comes up short.[28]

Mouffe's second strategy for avoiding being drawn into the imperializing logic of Schmitt's political world is a rather surprising one: she invokes the saving power of political institutions. Despite her tendency to look quite critically upon liberal democracy, she nevertheless suggests that "the great strength of liberal democracy, *pace* Schmitt, is precisely that it provides the institutions that, if properly understood, can shape the element of hostility in a way that defuses its potential."[29] In short, the task of preventing democratic norms from corrosion rests with the existing institutions of liberal democracy. They are supposed to function as impermeable walls that hem in any citizens whose motivations are deeply at odds with them.

But why wouldn't agonistic, Schmittean citizens try to undermine such obstacles? And why would we expect those who staff political institutions not to share the same ontological orientation as the rest of the citizenry? It

---

28. Ibid., 50.
29. *The Return of the Political*, 5.

appears that the agonistic nature of political life mysteriously stops at the threshold of institutions. Recent political events in the U.S. and elsewhere again provide vivid grounds for deep skepticism about Mouffe's way of keeping her Schmittean agonism from undermining democratic norms. Consider how Trump and many of his supporters have tried to subvert every democratic institution that seemed to them to stand in the way of his and his friends' path. These folks seemed to have fully internalized a Schmittean logic and thus had no qualms about trying to overturn—for no evidence-based, democratic reason—the unwanted outcome of the 2020 presidential election. Moreover, this stunning effort to undermine electoral institutions merely continued the ongoing Trumpian war on democratic institutions generally, carried out according to the strategy of a politics of friend and enemy. The litany of violations was extremely long: politicizing the Justice Department; firing multitudes of institutional personnel who objected to assaults on normal legal processes and restrictions; allowing unchecked official corruption, as long as the perpetrators were "friends;"; and on and on.

Few observers of American politics before and immediately after the 2020 election would likely share Mouffe's naïve faith in the automatic saving power of institutions. Many were, no doubt, pleased that institutions, such as the judiciary and state election apparatuses, held their ground against the Trumpian onslaught, manifesting an admirable refusal to see the political world in simple friend/enemy terms. But many Americans were also quite legitimately concerned about how close we came to having our institutions overpowered. And, if this level of institutional threat could emerge so quickly in a polity with a constitutional tradition of almost 250 years, then the idea that institutions are magic saviors in a world thoroughly redefined in Schmittean terms will sound especially hollow to people in other countries with less-established democratic traditions.

If Mouffe's efforts to tame Schmitt are ineffectual, then we seem to be left finally with only one salient characteristic of her turn to his work: her determination to take full advantage of the initial knockdown power Schmitt provides against the likes of Habermas and Rawls, without accepting, as well, any real responsibility for adequately grappling with the potential ethical-political drawbacks that attach to such a strategy.[30] Mouffe simply does not take seriously the fact that her full commitment to a Schmittean ontology—something she has never renounced—creates real problems for any subsequent affirmation of democratic norms.

In addition to the unsuccessful explicit attempts to reduce the effect of her embrace of Schmitt, might there be other avenues that implicitly offer such a possibility? For example, she has turned to Wittgenstein as a resource. She draws on that thinker's notion of "language games" to help illustrate the sense of agonism. Wittgenstein asserts the idea that games frequently involve moments of flux where players, in unanticipated situations, may offer varying answers as to how they think a game's rules should be applied to new circumstances. There is no master, authoritative rule book that lays down the invariably right answer. The analogy would be that in politics there is also no set of authoritative, "foundational" moral rules that can satisfy our "craving for certainty," only different ways of "going on from here," as Wittgenstein put it.[31]

How exactly should we understand this use of Wittgenstein as it relates Mouffe's grounding in Schmitt? Does the appeal to Wittgenstein's game analogy fundamentally shift Schmitt's ontology of politics out of its central role? On Mouffe's own terms, this does not appear to be the case. One might say that Schmitt constitutes her landscape of politics, and Wittgenstein then provides her with the best "style" (Mouffe's word) of thinking in order to felicitously negotiate that landscape after giving up on any idea that there is a master moral map.[32] If this is indeed Mouffe's position, then there is nothing in the turn to Wittgenstein that displaces

---

30. Even a sympathetic reader of Mouffe like Arletta Norval finds the attachment to Schmitt problematic. She astutely notes that without that attachment "there is little left to distinguish between Mouffe's . . . approach" and what we identify as "tempered" agonistic ones; *Aversive Democracy: Inheritance and Originality in the Democratic Tradition* (Cambridge: Cambridge University Press, 2009), 158–160.

31. Cf. Tully, *Public Philosophy in a New Key*, 1:135–159. Mouffe acknowledges borrowing from Tully in *The Democratic Paradox*, 61.

32. Mouffe, *The Democratic Paradox*, 61. This prioritizing of the Schmitt's position in relation to Wittgenstein's is also indicated by the placement of the key Schmitt chapter before the one on Wittgenstein (the volume is composed of pieces previously published).

the priority of the Schmittean framework. In short, the unconditioned cleaving of others into friend and enemy dominates the Wittgensteinian idea of openness in regard to how the game is to be played at any given point.[33] Our reservations here in regard to Mouffe should not be mistaken, however, for a broader one denying Wittgenstein's usefulness in thinking about politics from a perspective that embraces a *tempered* agonism.[34]

After our survey of Mouffe's unsuccessful efforts to, as she puts it, "think both *with* and *against* Schmitt," it is evident that she does not manage to extricate herself from the force of his conceptualization of the political world. Moreover, it is difficult not to be a little perplexed as to why she manifests so little concern about this problem. But perhaps that just reflects the way she defines her vocation. Despite her years of academic affiliation as a professor specializing in political theory, she resists being identified as such. Rather, she refers to herself as "an activist, but through ideas."[35] Given that self-understanding, it should perhaps not be surprising that Mouffe's writing often seems to be focused on motivating an audience to move in her proposed political direction without worrying overmuch about ways her framework might be open to encouraging less democratically palatable orientations. She exhibits a tendency to ignore things that cast doubt on her central claims. For example, in a recent book expressing enthusiasm about the potential for a future, left-wing populism, all she focuses on is the claim that the only task such a movement faces is transferring hostility from its current right-wing focus on nonwhite targets to a future focus on the "oligarchy." For her, any worries about the deep-seated racial and

---

33. Arletta Norval, even though sympathetic to Mouffe, nevertheless finds questionable her claim to be able to join a Schmittean ontology of agonism to a Wittgenstein orientation; see *Aversive Democracy*, 160–162. The way Norval interprets Wittgenstein, his ideas would have more resonance with Connolly's tempered agonism rather than Mouffe's variant.

34. See Norval's creative use of Wittgenstein's idea of "aspect change," in *Aversive Democracy*, 105–140. See also footnote 17 in our Chapter 6.

35. See Morgan, "Chantal Mouffe."

ethnic hostilities within current populism are simply brushed aside. We merely need to develop "a different language" to transform that hostility into a positive force.[36] Now many on the democratic left would certainly support strategies to try to woo populist rank and file away from their undemocratic orientations, but Mouffe's determined refusal to recognize the deep difficulties involved in this effort—especially while maintaining her Schmittean foundations—only betrays a willful blindness to the seriousness of the dangers that current variants of populism represent.

Our underlying concern with Mouffe's engagement with Schmitt is that she manifests a persistent disinterest in taking seriously what we have called the corrosive logic that attaches to the embrace of his ontology. At this point, however, a Mouffe defender might respond with one further claim that we are unfairly overstating the difficulties she takes on with this embrace. Why, it might be asked, can't she just depart from that ontology at will without any systematic conceptual explanation?

It is important to clarify at this point that the validity of our critique does not have to rest on a claim that the embrace of an ontology will necessarily determine everything about how one perceives public life. But an ontology should at least be broadly congruent with the normative orientation one affirms. To be sure, the usage of "ontology" has become looser in recent years, so that some use it almost interchangeably with terms like "conceptual framework" and speak of an ontology being "deployed" for a variety of purposes. We might think of this as a reaction against what "strong" ontologies (whether Aquinas's or Schmitt's) traditionally claimed, namely, that they fully capture the essential entities, values, and interactions embedded in the world and thus that our lives should manifestly conform to the normative shape they dictate. The looser use of "ontology" obviously rejects that notion wholesale; however, it also pretty much empties the concept of any philosophical distinctiveness.

---

36. Mouffe, *For a Left Populism*, 22–23. McKean deftly exposes the problems with Laclau's and Mouffe's approaches to this whole question; "Toward an Inclusive Populism," 797–782.

But there are not just two options here. The idea of "weak ontology" opposes strong ontology's absolute truth claim; it sees our ontologies as fundamental but still contestable.[37] This alternative does not simply reduce to the other, looser usage, however. To speak of weak ontology is to argue that an ontology is not something we deploy or not, as we might a hammer or a conceptual frame. Rather, it is at least partially embedded in our lifeworld, the background upon which we draw to make coherent ethical-political distinctions. Here we agree with Charles Taylor about the centrality of our ontological sources to a coherent life.[38]

But, as Taylor also admits, this does not mean that there is a complete, unchanging fit between one's ontology and one's ethical-political orientation.[39] Once we see ontologies as weak, we also must admit there is always some play between them and our actions. While ontologies are not determinative of our ethical-political orientations in an absolute sense, neither are they entirely up to us. We are continually engaged in bringing the depth interpretations that our ontologies embody into engagement with specific life problems, and in that interaction, gaps open up and modifications can occur on both sides. This process of cultivation includes the possibility that one, over time, may reject an internalized ontology, slowly allowing another to gain traction in one's life. There are certainly plenty of people who were born into an environment suffused with an ontology different from the one they later came to affirm; over time, they have rearticulated their basic orientations to the world.

---

37. Stephen K. White, *Sustaining Affirmation: The Strengths of Weak Ontology in Political Theory* (Princeton: Princeton University Press, 2001).

38. Taylor, *Sources of the Self: The Making of Modern Identity* (Cambridge, MA: Harvard University Press, 1989), Part I.

39. For Taylor, the relation between one's onto-ethical sources and one's actions is not like my shining an ontological flashlight that allows me to simply discover how the social world ought to look. Rather, in the "articulation" of an ontology, "discovering . . . depends on, is interwoven with, inventing," ibid., 18.

In short, a weak ontological perspective can accommodate the ideas of cultivation, gaps, and modifications in the relation between one's ontology and one's ethical-political affirmations. But none of this helps lend coherence to Mouffe's unequivocal embrace of a strong ontology followed by an unrelated ethical-political affirmation that points us in a distinctly different direction.

One final reflection on Mouffe: What if her defenders were to simply accept our argument that her framework is not coherent and decide to declare allegiance to Mouffe without the Schmittean foundation? Where would that leave things? The answer is that she would end up with an account that is not significantly different from those offered by the "tempered" agonists we consider below; in short, she would be left with the same sorts of problems they have.

## II. TEMPERED AGONISM

"Tempering" does not equate to "softening." Rather, the tempering of a piece of metal refers to a process by which it is strengthened and made more resilient than an un-tempered one. Accordingly, we want to consider other formulations of agonism that are robust but not as corrosive for democracy as the Schmitt-Mouffe variant. The best come from Connolly and Honig, whose contributions, like Mouffe's, emerged in the 1990s.[40] Although we will argue that they begin to move us toward a cogent agonism, there nevertheless remains a crucial problem. Tempered agonism is animated by affirmations of equality and autonomy, but their role remains underarticulated. We will show that proponents fail to provide an understanding of these values that persuasively integrates itself with their agonism.

---

40. Another notable contribution, slightly later in the 1990s, is David Owen, *Nietzsche, Politics and Modernity* (New York and London: SAGE, 1995).

## A. Otherness and Hostility as Existential Problem, Not Ontological Fate

Connolly's *Identity\Difference* (1991) develops an ontology with agonism at its center.[41] He argues that the process of constituting the identity of anything can only proceed by progressively contrasting it, even if only implicitly, with that which is different. Identity is ontologically dependent on difference. Distinctive here is not just that the identity of human agents emerges in this persistent dynamic of "identity/difference," but that this dynamic has ethical-political implications. This is where the significance of agonism comes in. Humans, as consciously mortal creatures, are perpetually anxious and insecure about "owing" their identity to that which they cannot control, whether other humans or events in nature, and hence, they are deeply liable to existential resentment, reflecting their constitutive lack of untrammeled freedom and sovereignty in relation to what is different from them. The propensity of each to feel that she owes too much of herself to what is "other" embeds an underlying agonism in life.

This tendency to proto-hostility in engagement with the world is, however, just that—a tendency, a possibility, not an iron necessity. Our mortality and the ontology of identity/difference do not cast us automatically into a political world of unrelenting conflict between friends and enemies. How humans understand and negotiate their mortality can vary. One may give in wholeheartedly to resentment of the other and cast them as an "enemy." This, for Connolly, is a continual propensity of all social life, but it is not the ontological fate of specifically political interaction that we get with Schmitt.[42] As the former says, the challenge is that we are always

---

41. William Connolly, *Identity\Difference: Democratic Negotiations of Political Paradox* 2nd rev. ed (Ithaca, NY and London: Cornell University Press, 1991; University of Minnesota Press, 2001).

42. Arash Abizadeh has argued that Schmitt and Mouffe are wrong in their claims that an ontology of us/them demonstrates "the metaphysical impossibility of a shared global identity." We think he is correct in that argument but incorrect in thinking that Connolly's position also involves such an impossibility claim. See "Does Collective Identity Presuppose an Other? On the Alleged Incoherence of Global Solidarity," *American Political Science Review* 99 no. 1 (Feb. 2005): 45 and fn. 13. Connolly's position could justify working toward a future shared global

confronting an agonistic relation with difference; however, we can cultivate resistance to the temptation to transform that contestation into a war of self and other-as-enemy. Connolly's ontology, unlike Schmitt's, thus leaves some conceptual and ethical space within political life in which one is able to imagine a robust role for norms that can align with liberal democracy. In short, it gives us what Mouffe desires, but what her prior, and continuing, embrace of Schmitt's ontology forecloses.

As we have indicated, Connolly imagines human interaction as suffused with the dynamic of identity/difference. This dynamic is one manifestation within a broader sense of being that is captured by the Nietzschean notion of "being as becoming," in short, being that is always in the process of transformation. Connolly urges us to cultivate an attitude of "protean care" for the perpetual movement of becoming and "agonistic respect" for the difference such becoming continually presents. This responsiveness best enacts our role as witness and participant in this ongoing drama.[43] Connolly's onto-ethical scene is thus one in which we cultivate restraint on what might be our initial reaction to the other and show openness to their expressions of self. We temper how the inevitable agonism that emerges between self and other expresses itself, respecting its persistent reality but also not allowing it to manifest as a preemptive hostility that attempts to secure my present world by freezing the process of becoming.

Thus, Connolly makes vivid for us what we will call an "exemplary scene" of agonism in social interaction, portraying both how one is tempted by a deep-seated propensity to frame the other actor as an object of denigration and hostility, as well as how one can begin to cultivate attitudes that slacken that propensity. This onto-ethical scene is meant to help

---

identity rooted in a perception of the difference constituted through contrast with nationalized identities of the present versus the past.

43. Connolly, *Identity\Difference*, x, 166; *The Augustinian Imperative: A Reflection on the Politics of Morality* (Newbury Park, London, New Delhi: SAGE, 1993), 155–157; *The Ethos of Pluralization* (Minneapolis and London: University of Minnesota Press, 1995), xxiii, 28, 40, 93, 180–184; *A World of Becoming* (Durham and London: Duke University Press, 2011), 6–8; and *Aspirational Fascism: The Struggle for Multifaceted Democracy Under Trumpism* (Minneapolis: University of Minnesota Press, 2017), 75.

orient us to the concrete challenges of political life in pluralistic societies in which there is a continual tendency for majority populations to categorize minorities—racial, ethnic, religious, national, sexual—as threatening "others." In general terms, then, Connolly intends for the scene to be a continual source of insight and motivation for orienting ourselves in ways that unsettle relations of inequality that are too often insufficiently foregrounded by theories of justice. Thus, for Connolly, agonism is a way of focusing attention initially not on the theorization of justice but on the persistent occurrence of inequality and injustice.[44]

For anyone acquainted with contemporary variants of agonism, an emphasis on equality is one of its hallmarks. This is certainly true of Honig's work as well. In *Political Theory and the Displacement of Politics* (1993), Honig, like Connolly, draws heavily upon Nietzsche, and yet she also does not try to ontologize politics as essentially agonistic. Further, she affirms that the "substance" of agonism is a "commitment above all to equality."[45] It emphasizes the condition of those to whom existing political orders accord "'no right to be counted.'"[46]

But exactly how is the commitment to equality rooted? Connolly's and Honig's indebtedness to Nietzsche certainly sharpens the point of this question, given the latter's general aversion to that value. And yet, despite Nietzsche's well-known attitude toward equality, might there be places in his work that create a plausible connection between that value and agonism, thus opening a path to affirming the kind of equality desired by both Honig and Connolly?

Honig has offered some specific direction here by referring us to Nietzsche's essay "Homer's Contest." There he discusses the ancient Athenian practice of ostracism, whereby the citizens could vote to exile political leaders who were becoming too prominent, assertive, and

---

44. *Ethos of Pluralization*, 75–104; *Identity\Difference*, 33–34.

45. "What Is Agonism?," in Maxwell, ed., "The Agonistic Turn," Special Section, *Contemporary Political Theory* 18, no. 4 (Dec. 2019): 662.

46. This line comes from Jacques Rancière and appears as part of the epigraph Honig has at the start of *Democracy and the Foreigner* (Princeton: Princeton University Press, 2001), vii.

powerful. This shows, Honig argues, how an appreciation of agonism was embedded in institutions and laws that prevented any overly dominant figure from displacing the ongoing, healthy struggle of leaders for greater eminence.[47] Thus, agonism was tied, in at least one historical instance, to a rough norm of mutual citizen respect and fairness—and hence some sense of equality—designed to restrain antagonists to some degree.

But this argument only takes us so far. A key question remains: Although agonism of this sort might preclude a Schmittean variant that affirms a single, supreme leader who suppresses all opponents, does it encompass, on its own, a strong enough sense of equality to satisfy modern democrats? Agonism in Athens obviously remained compatible with slavery and the non-enfranchisement of various categories of adults. Thus, for defenders of agonism to look to a Nietzschean image of a fair agon still does not yet fully address the problem of conceptualizing equality in a fashion convincing today.[48] In short, the appeal to ostracism does not really get us any further than Schmitt's appeal to the fair agon represented by "men of honor" engaging in a duel. This circle of the "worthy" is always conceived against the background of a broader category of the "less worthy." What is needed, rather, is an account according to which *all* others are accorded worth, in short, a status entitling them to contest norms to which they are subject, especially those that would assign them, explicitly or implicitly, the status of being somehow "unworthy" or not among the "honorable."[49]

---

47. Honig, *Political Theory and the Displacement of Politics* (Ithaca, NY: Cornell University Press, 1993), 69–74. See also the discussion of Honig's appeal to Nietzsche here in Miriam Leonard, "Theater and the Dispersal of the Agon," *Contemporary Political Theory*, 658–659.

48. Another possible source for conceptualizing the idea of maintaining a fair agon would be Machiavelli. Honig draws partially from him, as well as Nietzsche. On Machiavelli in relation to these issues see, e.g., John McCormick, *Machiavellian Democracy* (Cambridge: Cambridge University Press, 2011). But, as with Nietzsche, Machiavelli does not provide us with a perspective on equality that is adequate for the kind of tempering of agonism we argue for here.

49. The effort by Owen to bring equality into Nietzsche's agonism has a comparable problem. He uses the ostracism example to show that agonism is constituted in community norms, and this relationship secretes a sense of equality implicit in the very intersubjectivity of community. But we would object that the sense of equality present in some given community (like Athens) is not the same as the strong, modern sense of equality that a tempered agonism needs today. Owen does not provide sufficient argument to justify his assertion that Nietzschean agonism "commits us" to equality in "agonistic dialogue . . . in which we test our claims against the claims

If the appeal to Athenian ostracism does not open up much hope for a way that Nietzschean-based agonism can embrace the robust sense of equality that Honig and Connolly tacitly affirm, is there another possible approach through Nietzsche that might provide a more promising path? In this context, *Thus Spoke Zarathustra* might be seen as offering just such an opening. In it, there is a scene where Zarathustra, having traveled a long distance, comes to a city where a would-be disciple of his teaching meets him at the gates. This "fool," who clearly has only a superficial understanding of that teaching, is adamant that Zarathustra not enter the city because the inhabitants are heedless of his views and thus should be "despised." Zarathustra refrains from entering the city, but this is not because of the fool's warning. The former does not believe the inhabitants should be hated, because such vehement emotional investments should be saved for contestation only with those who are worthy. Rather, Zarathustra says to the fool, "I contemn your despising."[50] The inhabitants may disturb Zarathustra, but that should not be allowed to evince any great negative passion. The town inhabitants are not worth any investment of thought or strong hostility. He expresses rather an estranging emotion, namely,

---

of others," *Nietzsche, Politics and Modernity*, 139ff, 146–162. With the exception of this crucial flaw, Owen provides a quite powerful rendering of Nietzsche's agonism.

50. Nietzsche, *Thus Spoke Zarathustra: A Book for All and None*, ed. Adrian del Caro and Robert B. Pippin and trans. Adrian del Caro (Cambridge: Cambridge University Press, 2006). We have changed the translation of this sentence. The German exhibits a typical Nietzschean playfulness: "*Ich verachte dein Verachten.*" The standard English translation is "I despise your despising..." 142. The key German word here is semantically rich enough to play across several meanings. The standard translation seems to us to reverse Nietzsche's philosophical point when he directs the remark to the fool. Presumably he would not want to use the intense term "despise" for his attitude toward the fool; rather, he is calling out the fool precisely for his inappropriately intense feelings toward the townspeople. Accordingly, we have translated this passage as "I contemn your despising," since "contemn" connotes more of a sense of scorn or contempt, and that is the kind of distancing emotion Nietzsche is encouraging in situations where one encounters people such as either the "fool" or the town dwellers. See "Also Sprach Zarathustra," in *Friedrich Nietzsche: Sämtliche Werke*, ed. G. Colli und M. Montinari, Band 4 (Berlin and New York: De Gruyter, 1999), 224.

contempt. Accordingly, the city folk should simply be "passed by."[51] Zarathustra then departs from the city gates.

In a perceptive essay, Shalini Satkunanandan has interpreted this scene of "passing by" in an intriguing fashion. She suggests that passing by the unworthy may be an important mode of agonistic interaction to engage in, as opposed to some act of vehement denigration that leaves the object of that judgment ripe for abuse. In effect, passing by constitutes a "negotiating [of] space," with the other, a "mode of responding to difference" and of "dwelling together *in light of* and *despite*" our conflict.[52]

Satkunanandan's reading of the Nietzschean scene of "passing by" opens up a provocative possibility. We might see the interaction as enacting, at least implicitly, a significant way of comprehending equality. Although Nietzsche emphasizes the *strategic* value—for Zarathustra's psychological health—of passing by, one wonders whether perhaps there is an understanding of equality that might be implicitly involved here. Could this Nietzschean scene perhaps represent an acknowledgment that any particular other, even an apparently unworthy one, is always a potential source of new, unexpected—and possibly worthy—value creation? Even though Zarathustra is judging the town dwellers to be unworthy of engagement, this is not the same psycho-political judgment of them as unworthy in the stronger sense of "others" or enemies in a Schmittean sense.

On this interpretation, Zarathustra's stance could imply a figuration of agonistic respect based on something like the equality of potential value creativity. The city's inhabitants may not at this moment appear to be great

---

51. The title of this chapter is "Of Passing By," *Zarathustra*, 195–198. Connolly at one point refers to Nietzsche's idea of passing by such people, but he quickly transfers his attention to the latter's idea of contestation with those who *are* worthy of our passionate engagement and who deserve that "generosity" and "respect" that are the core of a tempered agonism; *The Augustinian Imperative*, 88. But, as noted above, this orientation implicitly leaves in place sovereign acts of existentially distinguishing between worthy and unworthy. Connolly clearly does not want to follow Nietzsche in this direction, but one is thus left a bit un-oriented here in regard to the treatment of possible unworthies. This is a key point at which the lack of a strong sense of equality shows its effect.

52. Satkunanandan, "Beyond Belief: Passing by Others in Nietzsche's *Zarathustra*" (paper delivered to Political Theory Colloquium, University of Virginia, November 2019, 1–3, 5, 12).

sources of creativity—far from it—but in time perhaps they will be. The choice to pass by, instead of either engaging in an argument driven by a motive of revenge upon these "unworthies" or in actual violence against them, leaves the city dwellers to a possible future of more creativity than shown in their past behavior. Unworthy people may eternally recur, but particular ones may later blossom with creativity.

Such an interpretation does not seem to necessarily conflict with at least some of Zarathustra's other core convictions. If so, then might this approach to equality be just what is needed to support a tempered agonism? Our reservation is that even if this might capture an admirable dimension of equality, it cannot by itself produce the tempering effect that is needed. The difficulty arises from the fact that the scene in which Zarathustra's actions are portrayed is one in which equality functions in an essentially privatized manner. Zarathustra, on our interpretation, embraces this sense of the equality of the inhabitants as a private judgment, and he accordingly acts to personally avoid these people altogether, at least for the foreseeable future. He summarily leaves not only the city but also its possible public, normative entanglements, and associated demands for justification. Above, we quoted Satkunanandan suggesting that this is a portrait of "dwelling together." But there is really no "together" here; rather, there is an explicit departure from possible constraint by any social-political norms in which Zarathustra and the inhabitants might be mutually embedded. This, in effect, is an opting out of a public world constituted by multiple obligations and contestation between normative assertions about how we ought to dwell together in a mutually acceptable way.[53]

What is needed is not just a scene in which the other is privately judged valuable, because she is a potential site of creativity and continually

---

53. A private decision to back away from another, operating as a way of dampening hostility and thus showing an openness to a kind of equality, can certainly be an admirable strategy. But without its being connected to a stronger moral-political notion of equality implying something intersubjectively owed, this orientation is open to being revoked whenever my interests conflict with it. This same concern applies to other comments that Nietzsche makes about equality; see, e.g., Nietzsche, *Human, All Too Human: A Book for Free Spirits*, with an introduction by Eric Heller, trans. R. J. Hollingdale (Cambridge: Cambridge University Press, 1986), 136.

emergent difference, but also one in which some context of social-political norms is always already in play *and* in which the other is accorded the status to contest both those extant norms, as well as assess possible new ones. It is only in a scene of this sort that the core sense of equality needed by a tempered agonism can fully come to life.

## B. Equality and Autonomy in Tempered Agonism

If Nietzsche offers little in the way of footholds for conceiving an agonism robustly animated by equality, then the task of creating such a connection falls more directly on Connolly and Honig. The former clearly sees his ontology as moving us in that direction by exposing how social difference metamorphoses into categories of political otherness, a process that helps constitute and solidify the domination of those whose identities make them liable to this treatment. But there is a significant difficulty that attaches to this way of highlighting injustice and calling for an agonistic respect of those who are subject to this operation of denigration backed up by power. The problem appears if one asks: What exactly is the *object* of Connolly's agonistic respect? It might seem as though it is the status of the other human being who is being denigrated. But that is not correct. The object of respect is, rather, *becoming itself* in its manifold presencing. This is an ontological quality of the world; humans are merely one manifestation of it. When the object of respect is so conceived, humans lose their special place in the world, traditionally assigned to them by God or because of their capacity for language. For Connolly, that status or capacity has too often become part of a narrative of domination over both other humans as well as nonhuman nature.[54]

For present purposes, we want to focus just on how this ontological stance bears on humans as language animals, especially in their capacity to create frameworks of justice. Connolly's desire to keep his perspective

---

54. Connolly's later work has been especially animated by the need to move us away from anthropocentric thinking and toward "interspecies pluralism"; *Aspirational Fascism*, 95.

unattached to the centrality of human-language capacity is grounded in his conviction that no "discourse of justice" can adequately sensitize us to the range of harm generated by the dynamic of identity/difference. The force of this claim is evident in his declaration that the receptive attitude animating agonistic respect "is more fundamental than justice."[55]

Our concern with Connolly's orientation is that when respect is cut loose in this fashion from a distinctive attitude to persons, their status is submerged into a generalized equality of all appearance, and they take their place as simply one among many manifestations of the flux of becoming. Human communicative capacity no longer constitutes any qualitative distinctiveness in this flux. My role as affirmer of becoming entails resisting the temptation to freeze difference into the role of otherness. This mandate applies to other humans but just as essentially to nonhuman nature, for example, to my not seeing a rain forest first and foremost as a resource to be manipulated in order to serve certain patterns of human consumption.

Despite the many admirable qualities of Connolly's portrait of generalized agonistic respect for the world, there emerges here, as well, an unintended drawback. In exercising this respect without recognizing the distinctiveness of human speakers, individuals accord to *themselves the exclusive role of sovereign interpreter* of how this attitude should unfold. One's human counterpart carries no special capacity to contest the legitimacy of another's framing of what constitutes an acceptable interpretation of agonistic respect in a given case, any more than a rain forest does. A significant, unintended implication of this is that Connolly's framing is not able to disqualify some undemocratic ways of cashing out agonistic respect. We can imagine a warrior ethic that exalts those who distinguish themselves as superior in ongoing violent conflict and who are also continually willing to engage in it and re-prove that superiority. Here a person's role as successful warrior is not boosted by any petty psychodynamic of freezing opponents into a denigrated status; it rests simply on subduing them in battle. This is a world that extols a certain kind of continual becoming, and

---

55. *Ethos of Pluralization*, 187.

it does not exhibit any tendency to transform difference into otherness. Thus, it technically satisfies the criteria of Connolly's exemplary scene.

He would not, of course, endorse such an interpretation; the question is can he preclude it within the terms of agonistic respect as he has conceptualized them? When he declares that agonistic respect is "more fundamental" than justice, he is stating that the specific affirmation of equality that he sees himself defending is not adequately acknowledged within discourses of justice. And yet, it seems now that the only way he can fully support his own affirmation of equality—and disqualify a warrior ethic—is by unexpectedly and tacitly drawing from that kind of discourse. At one point, Connolly suggests that we should understand the relationship between the discourse of agonism and that of justice as one of "dissonant interdependence" between two "valences" of our sensibility.[56] But that portrayal does not seem to acknowledge adequately how deeply what is declared to be "more fundamental" is actually dependent on the supposedly less fundamental.

For Honig, politics is also posited as a bipolar world of two "recurring impulses": one toward the ordering of justice and one toward the agonistic unsettling of order, highlighting who gets suppressed or marginalized in such orders. Unlike Connolly, though, Honig does not posit the agonistic impulse as necessarily more fundamental.[57] Nevertheless, it remains unclear in her work exactly how the two impulses are entwined and thus mutually limit one another. What both Connolly and Honig need from the justice "valence" or "impulse" is an abstract universal, without which the sense of equality that clearly animates their perspectives has insufficient traction. But agonists generally want to distance themselves from such moral universals, since they are seen as functioning so as to implicitly privilege certain characteristics of humans in ways that deny the

---

56. Ibid.

57. Honig merely refers to the need to "negotiate" between the two; *Political Theory and the Displacement of Politics*, 2–3, 6. Recently, she has suggested that the difference is a "staged clash," "What Is Agonism?," *Contemporary Political Theory*, 661. Thus, what appears to be quite a surprising deus ex machina enactment in Connolly is perhaps a less abrupt shift in Honig, but if it is less abrupt, the precise rationale for it remains rather underdetermined conceptually.

persistent significance of the identity/difference dynamic. Through this effect, universalization enacts, as Honig puts it, a powerful "displacement of politics," a reductive stabilization of meaning that hides the inevitable "remainders."[58]

We want to argue, however, that one universal, the idea of a moral equality of voice, is needed in the sort of political world Connolly and Honig imagine, and it is better to affirm that from the start than draw it in awkwardly from a source that has been designated as less fundamental or at least deeply impaired.[59] The richer exemplary scene that we develop in Chapters 5 and 6 both relinquishes the priority claims of either impulse and begins instead by foregrounding the communicative capacity of human beings. That, as we will show, provides the best path toward a tempered agonism that better embodies equality while emphasizing the significance of identity/difference and agonistic respect.

Without better clarification of how their frameworks conceptualize equality, Connolly and Honig end up with deficiencies in their accounts of agonism's political implications. We have already noted how this problem emerges in Connolly, but a comparable one appears in Honig's approach as well. Consider one of the illustrations she offers regarding an agonistic reading of the history of democratic politics. She writes eloquently and convincingly about how oppressed groups have often gone outside normal institutional procedures of liberal political orders and engaged in democratic "taking," that is, a "transgressive," sometimes violent "enacting [of] the redistribution of . . . powers, rights, and privileges."[60] In effect, they seized what should have rightfully been accorded to them, thereby enacting their equalization. But Honig leaves this sense of rightness implicit, and thus it is accorded no clearly justified role in this picture of the employment of force.

---

58. Honig, *Political Theory and the Displacement of Politics*, 2, 208.

59. Although in the present context, we emphasize the role of the moral equality of voice as a universal, it is important to note that the identity/difference dynamic is itself a kind of universal.

60. *Democracy and the Foreigner*, 8, 39, 99–100.

Our concern is whether this lack leaves the recourse to force underdetermined and thus open to being deployed to justify clearly undemocratic practices as well. "Taking" as a conflictual strategy can be enacted by all sorts of actors who perceive themselves to be aggrieved. In the summer of 2020, in the U.S., heavily armed groups supporting Trump tried to "take" back the streets of some cities from groups engaged in protests over deep racial injustices. Are the former's claims distinguishable—on purely agonistic grounds—from the groups Honig admires? Certainly, she intends them to be, but the question again is how do the criteria of differentiation emerge? We would argue that those criteria would seem to have to emerge from an abrupt recourse, just as in Connolly, to the impulse/discourse of justice. If this is so, then equality remains curiously external to agonism; it must be inserted abruptly into agonistic scenes like a deus ex machina.

So far, we have been tracking the tempered agonists' failure to adequately conceptualize equality. But a similar problem occurs with autonomy. Consider again Honig's use of the idea of "taking." She uses it to thematize a sort of basic impulse to resist on the part of the dominated that implicitly invokes a right to both equality and autonomy. But, just as with equality, there is a comparable underdetermination as to how autonomy should function here. In this case, the problem is insufficient clarity about autonomy's being not just any demand a person makes about the space or possessions they see as properly theirs but also an intersubjectively shared and mutually binding value that is tied to how we determine normative rightness. Without the latter valuation, which relates our claim of "taking" to the idea of a community in which its validity is assessed, this "taking" remains automatically self-justifying. In Connolly's and Honig's tempered agonism, autonomy is left at the level of something like the sheer appearance of insurgent difference, without sufficient reference to the specificity of the normative claim raised by that resistance voice.[61] And, as was shown above with equality, such a perspective ends

---

61. In Chapter 6, we will show how our originary exemplary scene brings to life both sides of autonomy: its character as both resistant and appellational.

up being deeply problematic in terms of its inability to differentiate cases on normative grounds, unless criteria are implicitly drawn in. The danger here is that the failure to give clearer normative shape to what autonomy means in the tempered agonists' perspective allows that value to be turned in undemocratic directions.

The Schmitt-Mouffe version of agonism boldly endorses such a turn in the sense that it ontologically authorizes the elevation of "my" demand into a solidaristic, unquestionable demand of "our" "fighting collectivity" versus those who threaten us. "We" stand autonomous against our enemies. Tempered agonists, while not explicitly authorizing such a justification, nevertheless do not deploy sufficient ontological resources to point us in a distinctly different direction in regard to how resistance is conceptualized and valorized. In the current political environment, this is hardly a remote, hypothetical issue. In liberal democratic societies that claim to highly regard individual autonomy, this value can slide relatively easily into a frame in which actors style their protest and resistance simply as an expression of an absolutized sovereignty: their being as entities immaculately prior to any structure of social normativity. This picture of individuals bearing protean rights and arms has been embodied in those statutes recently passed in multiple U.S. states that are generally referred to as "Stand Your Ground" laws. These essentially give the heroized individual the right to shoot someone who—in their exclusive judgment—appears to endanger them at any place or time.[62] Such heroes stand sovereign against a threatening world, proudly aloof from any voice that might challenge their interpretation of what constitutes a serious threat and the most reasonable response to it.

Contemporary social media technologies can easily accelerate and help morph what starts as an apparently individualistic stance into something that increasingly looks rather Schmittean. In effect, you don't start with an explicit friend/enemy partitioning of the world, but you begin

---

62. See the discussion of this phenomenon in Stephen K. White, *A Democratic Bearing: Admirable Citizens, Uneven Justice, and Critical Theory* (Cambridge: Cambridge University Press, 2017), ix–x, 32–33.

to progressively reinterpret things in that way. You may connect your individual stance to a community, but it is not a community with voices that might seriously resist your interpretation. Your online world is composed of the like-minded who create, as has often been suggested, an echo chamber in which perceived threats grow exponentially for these communities that thrive on conspiracies theories. Thus, a world of friend and enemy is not presumed from the start; rather, it takes shape through a mutually reenforcing blend of technology and the social-psychological dynamics of resentment, self-righteousness, and a sense of being persistently threatened.[63]

So, just as with equality, tempered agonists leave us with appeals to autonomy that are insufficiently differentiated and thereby unable to distinguish moral-political stances they affirm from ones they would clearly wish to reject. Might there be an alternative way of better integrating equality and autonomy into agonism, one that more coherently figures an opening toward what Honig calls our two "impulses"—the one toward resistance and the other toward justice? Chapters 5 and 6 will take on this issue. For the moment, we simply want to ask a preliminary question: Why are equality and autonomy, concepts so central to agonism, left so underarticulated by the tempered agonists? One reason, we suspect, is that initially both Connolly and Honig sought to articulate their positions as boldly as possible, without entangling them from the start in the discourse of justice, with its tacit demand for order, for a moralized code or command that persistently undermines a deeper respect for difference. Both want to maintain distance from what they see as the compulsion manifested in determinate, comprehensive theories of justice.

In short, both authors present us with a bivalent world, but one of those valences demands our attention more than the other. It is

---

63. The sense of precarity here is different from a sense that we will argue, in Chapters 5 and 6, is necessary to a democratic ethos. For the moment, the distinction can be described this way. For the imperial agonism of right-wing populism, a feeling of precarity is an experience to be overcome by subduing one's enemy; within a democratic ethos, however, that feeling is part of political reality, to be accepted and even cultivated.

important to emphasize here that this preference for an agonistic orientation is not, however, the same as the categorical, ontological priority assigned to it in the Schmitt-Mouffe position. Even though Honig and Connolly emphasize agonism more than its counterpart, this does not create for their positions the same sort of bind we ascribed to Schmitt-Mouffe, in the sense that the former do not affirm from the start an exclusively one-dimensional ontology of politics that posits an essential struggle of friends and enemies. Such a monological, strong ontology, as we argued earlier, defines a world in which norms of democracy are destined to become mere pawns in a deadly conflict. Honig and Connolly express something closer to a temporal preference for the agonistic impulse; in short, *start* your interpretation of any given political situation with insights generated by that impulse. Later you can correct it with a justice orientation.

This kind of preferential ordering clearly made good sense in the early 1990s when models of agonism first made their appearance. That period was dominated by the justice frameworks of Rawls and Habermas.[64] So, if one portrayed political theory then as pursuing too exclusively themes of justice (which determines a particular conceptualization of equality and autonomy), that could certainly be affirmed as a rhetorically justifiable strategy aimed at dislodging unexamined commitments with bracing agonistic assaults. But part of our thesis is that we are now in a different era, one in which agonism has become ascendant, and, more disturbingly, one in which a virulent, imperializing version is flourishing. If this is so, then it makes sense to partially adjust our conceptual strategy toward reconceiving how the values of equality and autonomy might be more vividly situated within a tempered agonism that no longer tries to prioritize or too sharply separate one impulse—toward either resistance or justice—in relation to the other.

---

64. We will complicate this standardized reading of Habermas in Chapter 5.

## III. CONCLUSION

Contemporary agonists have been worried that theories of justice and rationality dominating the intellectual landscape subtly draw attention away from the realities of persistent and multifaceted injustices. And they have been admirably successful in disrupting this situation. But the political world has changed in the last few years. Of course, the injustices are not gone; what is novel today, however, is the degree to which some national leaders in generally democratic countries rather boldly deny the seriousness of the problem.

Claims of injustice by those who are not part of my "concrete" identity order of friends are now interpreted as merely the hostile cries of my political enemies. This turn of events should encourage a careful reexamination of exactly how one frames an affirmation of agonism.

Mouffe's original, high-profile embrace of Schmitt as an effective siege engine against Rawls and Habermas may have had a salutary, performative effect initially in shifting theoretical attention. But achieving a full reconfiguration of the conceptual space of democratic norms, while continuing to adhere to Schmitt's ontology, is a more difficult task, and her failure to adequately acknowledge the difficulties involved here is disappointing. As we noted earlier, the embrace of an ontology may not have to determine everything in how political life is subsequently imagined, but the affirmation of a normative political world that is fundamentally incongruent with one's ontology does not provide coherent orientation.

Connolly and Honig offer admirable attempts to think toward an ontology that prefigures a more democratic agonism.[65] Unlike Schmitt's

---

65. Mouffe has briefly commented on the agonism of Connolly and Honig. They provide us, she argues, with an unsatisfactory version that really only gives us an *ethos* of agonistic respect. They fail to see the necessity of also accepting the Schmittean political "moment of decision," in which one sharply separates friend from enemy, thereby forming a "democratic hegemony." But this critique would only carry force if Mouffe could find a way of separating her own perspective from the imperializing logic of a Schmittean world; precisely what we have argued she has not done. Otherwise, her emphasis on the necessity of a sovereign, norm-free decision has no way of condemning orientations grounded in all sorts of disreputable modes of "concrete identity," such as white nationalism; Mouffe, *Agonistics: Thinking the World Politically* (London and New York: Verso, 2013), 11–15.

monological account, they seek ontological pictures that retain a bi-dimensionality: in short, ones that have space for both conflict and justice. With this stance, they offer openings to a tempered agonism, in which an ontology cogently structures an admirable normative orientation. But we have also argued that these openings remain insufficiently developed because they do not portray the concepts of equality and autonomy in an adequate fashion. The difficulty resides in discerning how to persuasively figure two sides of these values: both as touchstones for highlighting injustice and initiating resistance and disruption, on the one hand, and as a frame for highlighting a universal moral status, on the other hand. In other words, we need a way to conceive of equality and autonomy that can do justice to both faces of democracy. In the next two chapters, we will argue that we best navigate this problem by sketching an exemplary scene whose figuration of the moral equality of voice draws both on the impulse of justice and yet also encompasses what agonists want to see emphasized: a conceptualization of equality and autonomy attached to resistant voice rather than to one's status within a determinate theoretical vision.

#  5

# Re-envisioning the Core of Democracy

A full comprehension of democracy must encompass what we have called its two faces. As we have shown, however, neither the deliberative nor the agonistic approaches seem capable, by themselves, of accommodating the full range of values that emerge from the intuitive draw of these two faces. A more adequate approach must clarify the value of reason and civil discussion, on the one hand, and contention and conflict, on the other hand, as well as show how they are interwoven. In order to move toward that goal, we will have to think in a fashion that substantially decenters the claims of both deliberation and agonism. In the former case, the need for rethinking arises from the accumulation of serious challenges, both internal and external, to its prevailing self-understanding of the character and role of deliberation in political life. In the latter, a comparable deficiency arises from a failure to provide a better accounting of the values of equality and autonomy to which it tacitly appeals as sources for the moderation of the slide toward unmitigated conflict. In both cases, rectifying these deficiencies requires a better account of the moral core of democratic life.[1] Only after that has been provided will we have an adequate

---

1. In referring to this "moral core," we use the term "moral" in a broad sense that does not follow the tradition (in much German philosophical thought, including Habermas) of understanding "moral" as only referring to what is right, on the one hand, and "ethical" as referring to what is

grasp of why we feel the orienting force of *both* faces of democracy: the one displaying the hold on our intuition of scenes of speaking, listening, debating, arguing, and voting; and the other displaying the hold of scenes of protest and resistance to undemocratic forces.

What would a better articulation of the ethical-political core of democracy look like? An effective answer to this question must proceed on two levels. Obviously, it requires an account of exactly what we take this core to be. But for that sketch to be plausible, we must first clarify what the very idea of such a foundation in our present "post-foundational" world can mean. In short, what sort of character and validity could it have? How should political reflection today understand its most originary gestures both in regard to their conceptual claims and to their sources of affective force? Only after such general questions have been addressed, can we then proceed to tackle the specific one of sketching a basis for our communicative model of democracy. In this chapter we take on the former task, while in Chapter 6 we tackle the latter.

There exists today a distinct presumption, often operating implicitly, that reflection on political life must proceed in a "post-foundational" sense; that is, there is no longer a universal belief in a strong ontological, moral-religious basis for political life, such as the one that sustained Locke's thinking. The prefix "post" implies for many today that we are somehow beyond such matters, in the sense that we no longer need to be bothered with carefully discussing things on this terrain of what used to be called "foundations." This aversion, avoidance, or reticence in regard to foundational issues can be seen in a variety of maneuvers. Consider, for example, how the moral core of deliberative democracy is presented by the coeditors of the recent and influential *Oxford Handbook of Deliberative Democracy*:

> Deliberative democracy is grounded in an ideal in which people come together, on the basis of equal status and mutual respect,

good, on the other hand. The content of the originary exemplary scene and the orientations of actors within it do not conform to that strict distinction.

to discuss the political issues they face and, on the basis of those discussions, decide on the policies that will affect their lives.[2]

This foundational declaration is made with no further explication of the ideal or what it means to "ground" a perspective. It is casually and tersely presented almost as if this matter is a minor burden to be dispensed with quickly and easily before moving on to issues of conceptual elucidation and operationalization—in short, issues related to the further development of a deliberative democratic research program. A different "post" strategy is represented, as we have shown, by some agonists and other realists, who suggest that one can simply dispense with any underlying "moralization" of political life or treat it as a secondary add-on. Even among agonists who seek a tempered version, there is some reluctance to reflect in a sustained way about their implicit, core values of equality and autonomy. In sum, many scholars seem to be somewhat dismissive of, or uncomfortable with, discussion of such foundational matters.

In what follows, we resist this tendency. But doing so effectively, without reverting to a traditional notion of foundations, requires a persuasive answer to the question of how political theory can comprehend and represent its most basic moral sources in what we have called a weak ontological sense.[3] These sources provide us with our most basic figuration of ethical and affective orientation. But there is an initial problem: any appeal to moral sources in this sense would seem to involve deep disagreements at the outset. On some level, this is no doubt true; our task, however, does not involve all ethical issues, just the ones crucial to a democratic political order: equality and autonomy. Importantly, these values are shared by both deliberativists and agonists.

---

2. André Bächtiger, John S. Dryzek, Jane Mansbridge, and Mark Warren, eds., *The Oxford Handbook of Deliberative Democracy* (Oxford: Oxford University Press, 2018), 2.

3. We use the notion of "moral sources" in a way that is broadly similar to that of Charles Taylor in *Sources of the Self*. But whereas he speaks of the sources that ground my identity in the fullest sense, we are only speaking of the sources that ground my sense of myself as a democratic citizen.

With this goal in mind, we start by arguing for the value of keeping our political reflection in touch with an "originary exemplary scene" that portrays our moral sources in an interconnected and persuasive way.[4] The term "scene" is meant to be broadly construed as the setting in which some sequence of imagined action unfolds. Such a scene involves staged characters portrayed in interaction, thus creating a proto-narrative. All of this is intended to evoke certain images, ideas, and emotions that reflect our democratic sense of ourselves. The notion of an *originary* exemplary scene is meant to be a replacement concept in situations where in the past one would have talked about recourse to "foundations." The reasons for this major terminological shift will be clarified as the chapter progresses. In Section I, the ground for our project is prepared by situating the idea of an originary scene in relation to more traditional ways of providing foundations for moral-political thinking. This comparison and contrast should allow the sense and function of such a scene to come into better focus.

Section II continues to elucidate the intentions behind our referring to scenes rather than foundations in the traditional sense. It also takes on a significant problem that arises in the wake of relinquishing all

---

4. Some terminological clarification is required at this point. We are attempting to illuminate the weak ontological foundations of our ethical-political world, and how the contents of that foundation orient one, cognitively and affectively, to that world. In exploring this topic, we refer to three related concepts: ontology, moral sources and originary exemplary scene.

The term "ontology" attends to the status of concepts, which are fundamental within a framework. To use Connolly's framework as an example, ontologically his world is fundamentally characterized by the relation of identity/difference and by a quality of being as becoming.

Second, the term "moral sources" thematizes, as does Taylor, how the core values embedded in an ontology provide actors with a resilient source of identity and motivation. For Connolly, these sources are the values of "agonistic respect" and "presumptive generosity," functioning as appropriate manifestations of our freedom and equality in a world of becoming.

Finally, the term "originary exemplary scene" attends to how those core values are arrayed with one another in a proto-scene of interaction. For Connolly, this would be his scene of an actor confronting difference in others and trying to resist the temptation to reduce what is different to what is other, thereby rendering it as an object of incipient hostility.

In this chapter and the next, we will flesh out what each of these three concepts refers to within the portrait of weak foundations we are offering.

rational-transcendental anchors. Against that background, an originary scene must accept the fact that its force now rests more heavily on what we imagine ourselves and our traditions to be, and how that should orient and animate us in relation to the challenges of political life. But when affect and imagination are given such a central role, there is no avoiding an acknowledgment that one's constructions cannot be kept entirely free of certain qualities usually associated with myths. Along with our more aesthetic, imaginative language of "scenes" comes a partial decentering of rationality in the process of political reflection. Does this not carry problematic normative implications, given that trafficking in myths has typically been associated with distinctly antidemocratic regimes over the last century?[5]

There is indeed a danger in appeals to imagination in political contexts, but if such recourse appears unavoidable, then perhaps the real question is as follows: Can the dangers involved be effectively mitigated? We think this is possible, but it requires a careful articulation of how an originary exemplary scene animates a democratic "mythic." This task is begun in the present chapter and carried further in Chapter 6. In the latter, we elaborate our portrait of a particular originary exemplary scene that can provide the sort of foundation we see as necessary, which includes showing how it can open into the idea of a democratic mythic.

## I. MORAL SOURCES AND FOUNDATIONAL SCENES

How should we begin to think about the relation between the moral sources configured within our ontological frame and our actions? Political

---

5. These concerns have led to "a deep aversion to myth in political theory"; Tae-Yeoun Keum, *Plato and the Mythic Tradition in Political Thought* (Cambridge, MA: Harvard University Press, 2020), 15. This worry about myth haunts current attempts to reflect anew on myth and political life today. In his introductory comments to a recent conference, Shai Lavi, posed the opening question this way: "Should we de-mythologize politics?" A recording of the conference, "The Force of Myth: Authority, Illusion, and Critique in Modern Imaginaries," June 2021 sponsored by the Van Leer Jerusalem Institute is available from the institute.

matters often become vivid and pressing when a wrong or injustice is experienced; that is, when one confronts, conceptually and affectively, some violation of normal expectations and says "no."[6] Phenomenologically, this is the core experience that underlies our sense of the second face of democracy, involving some sense of violation and a desire to resist or contest the source of that perceived harm. One may immediately react with protestations or active resistance against those held to be responsible. And this may result in immediate corrective action that resolves the perceived injustice. But more often things are not so simple; situations of friction expose their entanglement with larger action frames, prompting questions such as: What is the full character of the issue being contested? Who exactly is responsible for the wrong? And how might our cause be persuasively represented and defended? These are questions that involve the virtual or actual appeal to a "we" who might acknowledge and perhaps help redress that wrong. Here the experiential sense of resistance against injustice begins to open into the first face problem of specifying more persuasively how a vaguely shared sense of justice might be given more coherence as we try to imagine a corrective path forward.

A. Resistance and Recourse

As one is initially pulled into this process, to what does one have recourse? This is where, in political situations, we begin drawing on a greater range of commitments, conceptions, values, and norms. If we reflect on the moment of resistance and what that evokes, we usually see it as involving some effort on the part of the person involved to clarify what motivates and justifies the "no-saying." And that means having recourse at some point to sources of one's conception of self, as well as conceptions of the proper shape of moral, economic, and political life that one sees as under some assault. The sources people appeal to are, as we said earlier, quite

---

6. This was the simple but crucial point that Judith Shklar grasped in *The Faces of Injustice* (New Haven and London: Yale University Press, 1990).

varied, but for our purposes—elucidating the core of democracy—we will focus on freedom or autonomy and equality.

We want to attend to how these sources can be embedded in scenes that orient us conceptually and provide motivation through their capacity to engage our imagination and sense of appropriateness. In the past, foundational claims in politics were often set in scenes, such as the state of nature, but attention traditionally focused not on the imaginative aspect so much as on how firmly those scenes anchored strong ontological claims. Our intention, however, is to explore the possible role of core scenes after one has relinquished such anchors. Of course, once that is done, the role of imagination moves more into the foreground.

In recent years, reflection on the orienting background of social and political life has often invoked the term "social imaginary." Although its use has become common, its exact meaning and implications for normative political theory are not very clear. For our purposes, the best account of the concept is offered by Charles Taylor.[7] In the present context we need to explain how this idea of a "social imaginary" is related to claims about the status and importance of our notion of an imagined exemplary scene.

Social imaginaries, Taylor suggests, provide the conceptual lens for how you "see" your political world, and thus how your actions are oriented. In situations of what we call "no-saying," these lenses would likely include, according to Taylor, such modern notions as rights-bearing individuals and the democratic public sphere—in short, ones that have become part of how we imagine the political world. And these notions are typically "carried in images [and] stories."[8] Such carriers would include the two sorts of scenes we referred to under the rubric of the two faces of democracy.

If recourse to *specific* aesthetic or historical exemplary scenes is entangled with a social imaginary in the sense that the former embody the constitutive meanings made available by the latter, what is the relationship

---

7. Charles Taylor, *Modern Social Imaginaries* (Durham and London: Duke University Press, 2004). Taylor was not the first to deploy this term, but his particular usage has been especially influential.

8. Ibid., 49, 115, 172.

between what we have called an *originary* exemplary scene and a social imaginary?[9] When Taylor introduced the notion of such an imaginary, it was deployed in the context of a larger project of showing how the "moral order" of the modern Western world differs from that of medieval Europe. Thus, he was mainly concerned to show how modern Western individuals began to imagine the social world differently than their predecessors. And that figuration operates through the constitutive relationship between a novel social imaginary and how those individuals came to see the world and thus orient their actions in it.

Taylor's framework is generally quite helpful, but it can nevertheless be slightly misleading in the present context, namely, when we try to understand how an originary scene functions. He draws a distinction between the role of a social imaginary operating implicitly in the everyday lifeworld shared generally in a society, on the one hand, and the role of explicit ideas and values carried in instances of "theory" propagated by intellectuals trying to consciously refigure the conceptual, normative, and aesthetic-affective shape of the world experienced by those people, on the other hand.[10] Thus, unlike medieval Europeans, modern Western individuals tacitly share the general idea of individuals as rights' bearers, although we may also react differently to specific theories about how, say, the right to property ought to be normatively weighed against the right to free speech in given situations. Taylor is relying here on a familiar distinction between rules that are constitutive versus ones that are regulative.[11] He discusses how Locke's idea of a state of nature was originally, in the seventeenth century, a "theory" proposing new rules to regulate political life, but by the eighteenth century it had evolved to become an implicit, constitutive part of our Western social imaginary. Taylor's distinction is analytically and historically illuminating, but problems can emerge when

---

9. In a moment a more adequate characterization will be offered for the distinction between "specific exemplary scenes" and "originary" ones.

10. Taylor, *Modern Social Imaginaries*, 6–8.

11. On the distinction between the two types of rules, see John Searle, *Speech Acts: An Essay in the Philosophy of Language* (Cambridge: Cambridge University Press, 1969).

we speak of the components of a social imaginary as they are being drawn upon in situations of "no-saying." In that context, the actual distinction between what is constitutive and what is regulative (in the sense of normatively binding) reveals itself to be more porous and contestable than the bi-fold evolutionary story above implies.[12]

To unpack what we want to highlight here, consider how regulative rules are typically distinguished from constitutive ones. The difference is often clarified by reference to the rules that regulate or prescribe what moves in a game like chess are likely to help you win a given match, on the one hand, versus the rules that constitute the game itself (e.g., that define what a "pawn" is), on the other hand. This distinction is clearly relevant to all sorts of social and political situations. For example, understanding what it means to vote (constitutive) is different from arguing for one political party always being the right one to vote for in elections (regulative). But it is important to realize that these sharp analytic distinctions do not always map onto social reality in entirely fixed, clear-cut ways, and this is especially important when we are talking about political imaginaries and their originary role. Our modern Western political imaginary is not just a general figuration that gives sense and coherence to our thoughts and actions, it is also replete with figures that are not clearly or unproblematically related to one another in a normative sense—just what we have suggested is the case with the two faces of democratic life. Thus, the "map" constituted by the imaginary often provides only partial coherence and orientation for actors in particular situations.[13] For example, the sense and significance of voting as a constitutive part of democracy is taken for granted generally, but what that actually means in a specific situation is frequently subject to significant differences of interpretation that are deeply entangled with normative (regulative) disagreements about what is legitimate or illegitimate. In the wake of the 2020 presidential election, for

---

12. Although Taylor uses this neat bifold picture, he seems quite aware that, in reality, our basic political discourse continually interweaves the constitutive and regulative; *Modern Social Imaginaries*, 8–9, 23–24.

13. Ibid., 25–26.

example, a plausible interpretation of what precisely constitutes bona fide voting in the U.S. became a matter of substantial controversy. The actions of some on the political right to stop "voter fraud" and ensure that only "real" votes count by means of effectively restricting access to the ballot box—on the basis of no legitimate normative grounds—seem to be deeply corrosive of familiar parts of our democratic political imaginary.[14]

Our point in drawing attention to the foregoing is simply to indicate that if one sees our political imaginary as simply a general conceptual "map" that reliably provides us with coherent orientation, one has radically oversimplified what is going on when recourse is had to moral sources. Such recourse is rather entangled in a much more contentious process in which the boundaries between what is constitutive and regulative are periodically blurred and made the subject of efforts to redraw them. And this should not really be surprising. The distinction between constitutive and regulative is, as noted a moment ago, often illustrated by reference to a game. However, when we try to map the distinction onto political life, rather than a board game, things become more complex. In the present context, one important difference is that constitutive rules in politics are sometimes neither as unambiguous nor as stable as in many games. In our political imaginary the border between constitutive and regulative is more porous, and it gets drawn and redrawn; further, these issues become continual subjects of political strategies aimed at figuring and refiguring our imagination.[15] For example, after the Civil War, political and literary

---

14. The idea that "voter fraud" allowed the 2020 presidential election to be "stolen" constitutes a breath-taking inflation of a long-standing tendency in the Republican Party. The myth became so egregious under Trump that it caused perhaps the most prominent expert on election integrity in the Republican Party, Benjamin Ginsberg, to break ranks in 2020, declaring that the recent claims of fraud had developed into pure fantasy. He called this phenomenon the "Loch Ness Monster of the Republican Party." See Benjamin L. Ginsberg, "My Party Is Destroying Itself on the Altar of Trump," *Washington Post*, November 1, 2020, https://www.washingtonpost.com/opinions/2020/11/01/ben-ginsberg-voter-suppression-republicans/. The more that facts are simply ignored in issues like this and faith is blindly placed in the leader who makes such claims, the more there is a slide from a simply antidemocratic mythic to a palpably fascist one.

15. The point here is not that the constitutive rules of games never change. Wittgenstein has given a rich analysis of this process. However, in political life, the *point* of much of the action is precisely to change many of the rules.

authorities in the southern U.S. worked to configure a political imaginary in which the cause of the Confederacy was constituted as an essentially reasonable defense of states' rights, a picture that implicitly removed slavery and its legacy from the foreground of historical vision. That imaginary carried constitutive force for generations of white southerners, but this force cannot be disentangled from the normative regulations that accompanied its rise and policed its continued existence. In short, it was intended to constitute reality (the Civil War just *was* about states' rights), as well as reflect and further promote a structure of normativity (involving a determined inattention to the legacy of the wrongs committed against blacks). This whole background became a more intense and fluid field of contestation in 2020 in the U.S., when, in the wake of George Floyd's murder by police, the political consciousness of many whites began to shift noticeably.

The implication of the foregoing is that when one refers to a "social imaginary" of modern politics, it should conjure up partially stable but also persistently contested terrain where sensemaking, legitimacy and aesthetic-affective orientations are complexly intertwined and appear as matters of recurrent struggle. How then should we understand the place of an originary scene and the role of having recourse to it? Such a scene is located precisely in the porous and contested borderland in which what is constitutive and what is normatively regulative are closely intertwined. It presents us with a particular arrangement of our crucial sources that provides aspects of conceptual coherence, normative justification, and aesthetic-affective force to our perceptions and judgments. Thus, it helps us navigate and find cogency among the often disparate, only partially coherent, and contested figures present in our political imaginary.

Even if the foregoing analysis has helped clarify, in relatively abstract terms, the idea of having recourse to an originary scene today, the notion of such an appeal is still likely to seem highly abstract and somewhat forced. In the face of this skepticism, it might be helpful to point to other work in which something like the idea of an originary scene appears. One such scene is clearly deployed by Connolly in the form of his portrait of actors mutually negotiating their relationship in the context of the perpetual tension between identity and difference. Further, the above-noted quotation from the *Handbook*, even though it is presented by the authors as a straightforward statement of an "ideal," is intended to be an attractive and meaning-generative scene of people coming together with certain assumptions and intentions that animate the idea of democratic deliberation.

The most self-conscious recent effort to sketch an originary scene that is structurally similar to ours has been made by Judith Butler. Proceeding at the most elemental level of reflection regarding how our ethical-political thinking and imagination should be portrayed, Butler has attempted to ground a novel perspective on the justification of nonviolent political action. She begins by critiquing the traditional "scene" of the state of nature with its sketch of the emergence of a social contract among essentially unconnected individuals. In that scene, our original social "dependency is . . . written out of the picture."[16] Butler proposes that we start instead with a "description of [the] social bonds without which life is imperiled"; in short, a scene in which "embodied" "social interdependency" and "vulnerability" constitute the condition of the possibility of social life, thus establishing the context in which we then frame issues of political violence and nonviolence. But this bare ontological landscape is too sparse to provide the rich background she imagines; the scene is thus infused as well with an "aspirational" "egalitarian imaginary" that portrays our world as one in which we can see that "all lives are valuable, grievable" and thus worthy of protection.[17]

It is not necessary to follow Butler's account further to establish the point we wish to make. She is offering an originary counter-scene to the state of nature; more particularly one that "takes place at the level of a social ontology, to be understood more as a social imaginary than as a metaphysics of the social" (the latter being what we refer to as a strong ontology).[18] Her ultimate aim is to have us embrace this scene as the basis for

---

16. Judith Butler, *The Force of Nonviolence: An Ethico-Political Bind* (London and New York: Verso, 2020), 16, 35–39.

17. Ibid., 16, 24, 28, 40, 46, 147.

18. Ibid., 16.

our ongoing interpretations of how to engage crucial challenges in ethical-political life today.

We see the character and appeal of Butler's perspective as structurally similar to ours. It presents a social ontology that deploys certain core concepts and animates them with distinct moral sources, all with the intention of generating significance for individuals, in a conceptual, aesthetic, and motivational sense that can orient them in action contexts. What she offers then is not a particular exemplary scene, such as offered by a piece of literature, but rather an originary exemplary scene. Thus, we imagine Butler hoping that readers of, say, her influential treatment of the specific exemplary scene offered in Sophocles's *Antigone* will bring the "political imaginary of the radical equality of grievability" into play as a basis for interpreting the former's significance.[19] We would want someone who was initially inspired by a particular historical or literary exemplary scene to have recourse to our originary exemplary scene in a comparable way.

One might still object that such scenes, even if they are common among academics, are too far removed from the sphere of the average person—too exclusively philosophical—to be worth paying attention to. But perhaps such skepticism is overstated. In teaching political theory, one of us (Stephen) has discovered that one traditional originary exemplary scene remains quite deeply embedded in American political culture. Over many years, I have found that the most effective way to start teaching "Modern Western Political Thought" to undergraduates, many of whom suffer initially from the much dreaded "theory angst," is to begin not with Machiavelli or Thomas Hobbes, as do many political theorists (for good scholarly reasons), but rather with John Locke. I do this for the simple reason that the idea of a state of nature, as he portrays it (versus Hobbes), continues to have remarkably powerful constitutive and

---

19. Ibid., 74. See also Butler, *Antigone's Claim: Kinship Between Life and Death* (New York: Columbia University Press, 2000), 22–24, 29, 55, 78–79. In her reading of the play, she suggests that Antigone raises, in regard to kinship and gender, an exemplary question regarding the losses that are publicly grievable versus ungrievable. In *The Face of Nonviolence*, that issue receives a more generalized philosophical treatment. The connection between the two is what we call a relation between a specific exemplary scene and an originary one.

normative force for students (just what Butler worries about). Starting in this fashion makes vivid to them that they are already entangled in this tradition of modern political thinking, even before they have consciously thought about it or confronted any of its complexities or problems. In a survey conducted at the beginning of the course, before students do any reading, they are asked: "Do you believe that people have natural, God-given rights?" The percentage answering "yes" has been around 80 to 85% through the first two decades of the twenty-first century. And when, immediately afterward, they read Locke's *Second Treatise*, with its state of nature embodying that idea, they plug into its central features quite "naturally"—even if they often do not really comprehend exactly what they have affirmed. Students initially find the scene/proto-narrative of his state of nature and social contract vaguely familiar and significance generative in relation to the political world around them. In short, they are implicitly attached to an originary scene as a vivid embodiment of their core ideas about ethics and politics. It is already part of how they imagine their social and political world.[20]

But we can see something else important—touched on a moment ago—in the fact that Locke's exemplary scene is embedded in contemporary consciousness in a somewhat conflicted way. This is because the scene, in its original Lockean version, was still fully grounded in a transcendent authority, insofar as the entire normative frame rested on divinely sanctioned natural law. Based on my survey, one might assume that this affirmation is shared by contemporary students, given the evidence cited above about the high percentage of them who believe in "God-given natural rights." But that apparent affirmation, for most of those students, does not really imply an acceptance of divinely grounded natural law, but rather, I would argue, something more like an investment in a mythic expression of the

---

20. One can also see this, for example, in how Locke's story has embedded in it rough, early prefigurations of the two faces of democracy. The first, more deliberative face, oriented toward the opinion of the political community, is at least partially thematized in the broad notion of political legitimacy grounded in what the majority judges to be right; and the second face, oriented toward potential resistance, is animated by both the idea of political power not being natural and the idea of the right to resist unjust exercises of power through revolution.

idea of individual rights. "God-given" thus functions as a kind of symbolic exclamation point, more than an explicit belief.[21] My interpretation of the students' frame of mind here reflects an insight arising from how they answer a second question, one that is placed as far away as possible on the survey from the query regarding divinely authorized natural law. They are asked whether they think individuals should have the right to decide to end their own lives. Students answer in the affirmative more than 80% of the time. Of course, they don't realize—as Locke would have immediately—that their affirmation of suicide runs directly contrary to the tradition of natural law.[22]

If what we have said is correct, it shows that although initially an originary scene may not be fully describable by ordinary people, it may be tacitly animating their thinking; and, in subsequent processes of reflection and argumentation, it can also become more explicitly affirmed or contested. Fleshing out a scene helps in gathering and vivifying implicitly operative components of their political imaginary, as well as in making apparent how that imaginary is interlaced with normative elements that may be conflicted. In this context, one function of an originary democratic scene will be to help individuals understand which paths through that conflict are more likely to affirm a democratic way of life.

A political imaginary is especially subject to being pulled in contradictory directions, and it is often the subject of conscious efforts at normative reinforcement or refiguration, whether by ordinary people, political elites, or theorists. There is a continual struggle to manage whether we see certain aspects of political life as unquestionable and thus legitimate, on the one hand, or as illegitimate or arcane matters for theorists alone to argue

---

21. Some might assume, contrary to what we are arguing, that students at a southern school like University of Virginia are quite conservative, thus explaining the high rate of religious affiliation. But, in fact, in the same survey the number of students self-identifying as "conservative" versus "liberal" or "moderate" was only around 25%.

22. The venerable, normative force of that prohibition is testified to by the fact that it continues to be embedded in the laws of a number of states in the U.S. In Locke, killing yourself or others is prohibited because doing so substitutes your purposes for whatever ones God might have for you and others. See Locke, *Two Treatises of Government. Second Treatise* (Cambridge: Cambridge University Press, 1960), Ch. 4, para. 23.

about, on the other hand. The class example above regarding the Lockean framing is instructive here. The discovery of a self-contradiction in the students' affirmation of the Lockean originary scene exposes an opportunity to manage the direction of their thinking in the sense of trying to take something deeply embedded and direct it toward certain explicit normative political affirmations. From opposing political perspectives, one could try to manage the uncertainty of this scene by different strategies: for example, a secular liberal might just skate over the "unfortunate" reference to God's role, preserving a tidy (if rather deceptive) image of Locke, or, from a more conservative perspective, one might press the theism issue energetically, arguing that students should realize that God is already deeply embedded in their political imagination, and that they should consequently acknowledge that more fully.

In general, then, when we have recourse to what is most basic to our political world, we enter a domain where the border between constitutive imaginary and explicit normativity is open to uncertainty and relocations. *We see our originary exemplary scene as residing precisely in this uncertain and disputed borderland where both "imaginary" and "theory" are entangled.* The scene will embody and make conscious compelling aspects of our imaginary, as well as provide direction for how we interpret and act in our political world.

Of course, to say this is to admit that such orienting force in this borderland of the conscious and pre-conscious involves actively arranging and rearranging the fundamentals of people's political imagination. In political life this kind of work is, for good reason, often looked at with suspicion, as something that reason cannot fully track and thus as entangled with the creation or perpetuation of myths. In short, work on the imagination has usually not been considered healthy for democracy. Given the history of the twentieth century, with its experience of the racial myths of fascism and the "enemy of the people" myths of totalitarian communism, this is not a danger to be taken lightly. We will keep this significant issue in the foreground by referring to an originary exemplary scene as being at the core of a democratic political "mythic."[23] But there is not just danger here, there is also opportunity for thinking creatively about the role of imagination in politics. In this vein, we acknowledge that part of the task of justifying an originary scene involves showing how it works in tandem with a democratic mythic.

## B. Originary Scenes and Myth

The association of myths with deceptive, antidemocratic work on the imagination is a familiar one. A classic example is the myth of the metals that Plato creates in *The Republic*. This "noble lie" recounts how at birth different grades of metals are mixed in the souls of different people; a few get gold, a few more get silver, but most people get iron and bronze, the last allocation implying that the many are not capable of any political role.[24] But myths can also carry meaning in a more democracy-friendly way. Consider here the views expressed by Protagoras in the Platonic dialogue

---

23. Our unusual use of the adjectival form "mythic" as a noun follows the comparable use of the adjective "imaginary" in the idea of a "social imaginary." We have more to say about our reason for this usage below.

24. Plato, *The Republic*, Bk. 3, para. 414c–415d. Our criticism here of Plato's myth of the metals does not entail the sort of extreme view offered by someone like Karl Popper who sees a strong connection with fascism; see Tae-Yeoun Keum's critical analysis of Popper in *Plato and the Mythic Tradition in Political Thought*, 37. One can accept a much more nuanced notion of how myths broadly operate in relation to philosophical reason than Popper, without thereby relieving Plato completely of the antidemocratic force of this particular myth.

Sometimes efforts to mitigate Plato's suspicion of democracy seem to try a bit too hard. For example, Elizabeth Markovits calls attention to Plato's efforts to soften the force of the political inequality he proposes by offering an accompanying myth. The myth of the metals is preceded by one about autochthony, according to which Athenians are all commonly born in the earth, implying thereby that citizens are equal in the sense of being "brothers" (414e). Markovits suggests that this should be interpreted as undermining the inequality implied by the myth of different metals. Possibly, but many antidemocratic arguments historically have been accompanied by ideas that simultaneously extol a sense of community among citizens. The point is usually that citizens should just focus on the need for community and not worry about minor matters like political inequality. See Elizabeth Markovits, *The Politics of Sincerity: Plato, Frank Speech, and Democratic Judgment* (University Park: University of Pennsylvania Press, 2008), 137–145.

of that name. When challenged by Plato's Socrates to explain how ordinary people could possibly have the capacity for political judgment, Protagoras announces that he will start with a "myth" (*muthos*) rather than a rational argument.[25] Plato may be staging things this way to indicate that a sophist like Protagoras prefers to avoid reason in his attempts to manipulate his audience. But there is another way to comprehend what Protagoras is doing. Here it is important to recall that, for the ancient Greeks, *muthos* had a broader meaning than we tend to give it today. The word is thus often translated simply as a "story," moreover, one not seen as standing in a position diametrically opposed to reason.[26]

The myth/story Protagoras relates tells of humans originally coming together to form cities in order to better preserve themselves. But

> they treated each other with injustice, not possessing the art of running a city, so they scattered and began to be destroyed once again. So Zeus, fearing that our race would be wholly wiped out, sent Hermes bringing conscience and justice to mankind, to be the principles of organization of cities and the bonds of friendship. Now Hermes asked Zeus about the manner in which he was to give conscience and justice to men: "Shall I distribute these in the same way as the arts? These are distributed thus: one doctor is sufficient for many laymen, and so with the other experts. Shall I give justice and conscience to men in that way too, or distribute them to all?"
>
> "To all," said Zeus, "and let all share in them; for cities could not come into being, if only a few shared in them as in the other arts."[27]

---

25. Plato, *Protagoras*, ed. with an introduction by Gregory Vlastos, trans. Benjamin Jowett, extensively revised by Martion Owtwald (Indianapolis and New York: Bobbs Merrill, 1956), 320c, 18.

26. See, e.g., C. C. W. Taylor's translation in *Protagoras*, trans. and notes by C. C. W. Taylor (Oxford: Clarendon Press, 1996), 320e, 16.

27. Ibid., 322b–d, 18–19.

Some commentators are struck by the curiosity that Protagoras's originary scene provides us with a story involving recourse to divine aid, given that he was agnostic. This would seem to reinforce the suspicion that Protagoras is simply trafficking in deception here. And, yet, if one keeps in mind the self-consciously fictional quality of myth, this fact is perhaps not so surprising. We might accordingly see Protagoras's story as one that crystalizes and vividly represents the essential commitments of Athenian democracy in an imaginative way, thus helping to further embed what were, at the time, relatively recent democratic commitments into the broader, more settled context of Greek culture. For some of Protagoras's listeners, perhaps the references entangling the gods with democracy might have increased their sense of the fundamental validity of the Athenian commitment to that political form by persuading citizens that this democratic ground was divinely endorsed. Given the recent and extraordinary character of the democratic order in fifth-century BCE Athens (when Protagoras lived), it is hardly surprising that some might have remained a bit uncomfortable with fully acknowledging the purely human artifice behind that order. Better to have a story containing a little help from the gods for creating the ground on which your political life stands. Otherwise, as an Athenian you have to boldly face the fact that you are almost simultaneously creating that ground and standing on it. Humans have traditionally not been very comfortable with fully acknowledging such a status. The passage of time may help in moderating the sense of precariousness induced by confronting the depth of human artifice, but even with time, the additional sense of security offered by an external guarantor is a powerful support that has been hard to relinquish. Perhaps the Athenians Protagoras was addressing were not so different from the undergraduates above who affirm "God-given rights."

Protagoras may have been trying simultaneously to nudge his listeners to become more comfortable living without any theistic security. As one Plato scholar puts it, the myth/story "brings together two realms, cosmos and community," and yet, "order in these realms is to be understood not as transcendent, but as built up through interaction, . . . the world of experience." In short, the story "is itself part of the process it interprets, part of the dynamic (democratic) process."[28] If so, then in Protagoras's story there is no deity whose generative will literally stands transcendent, as in Locke's.

The scenes carried in such myths/stories help us interpret the significance of events around us and motivate us to be our best selves in politics. They are functioning well if they imaginatively represent what we have come to take ourselves to be in the most basic ontological-ethical sense and thereby help provide us with initial orientation and motivation in ethical-political space. While Protagoras's resort to the gods' intervention might have seemed to Plato to be no different from his own recourse to the myth of the metals, there is a crucial difference. The former's departure from strict truth can be understood and accommodated recursively, over time, by *all* those who hear the story.[29] Any deception in the scene can accordingly be judged, on balance, to be relatively harmless in a democratic sense, functioning only as an imaginative vivifier of the shared cultural-political background for the story. In short, this mythic scene seems intended not to cast doubt on democracy but rather to be central to the emerging democratic self-understanding in Athens.

Our goal in the next chapter is to articulate an originary scene in a weak ontological sense that is somewhat comparable to Protagoras's. More specifically, we sketch a core constellation of meaning animated by a conception of the place of autonomy and equality in modern democratic life as those values have emerged and developed historically.[30] But before we turn to this constructive project, it is first necessary to further elucidate what is implied by the general idea of an exemplary scene, as well as its entanglement with a mythic dimension.

---

28. Cynthia Farrar, *The Origins of Democratic Thinking: The Invention of Politics in Classical Athens* (Cambridge: Cambridge University Press, 1988), 12, 47.

29. Of course, "all" here means all Greek men who were accorded the right to citizenship in Greek democracies.

30. We are aware that the Greeks did not have the same sense of the place of individual autonomy in democracy as we moderns do.

## II. EXEMPLARY SCENES

### A. Their Character

Why use the term "exemplary" to describe the sort of scenes we have in mind? And why distinguish between what we have called "specific" exemplary scenes and "originary" exemplary scenes? Regarding the first question, the term "exemplary" is useful because it carries two sorts of connotations. One is particularizing, as in the notion of a particular "example," the other is generalizing or more expansive in its potential significance, in the sense of a "model" or "pattern" for further insight and action (see the *Oxford English Dictionary*). The latter characteristic means that something exemplary thus illuminates more broadly than a particular example; in short, it orients perceptions of significance and inspires action across a greater range of settings.

Our second question asks why distinguish between an *originary* exemplary scene and the more familiar type of *specific* exemplary scene? "Specific" refers in the present context to historical or aesthetically created scenes that are generative of significance beyond their immediate context but usually in relation to a relatively limited set of values.[31] For example, one can see a prominent historical event like the Constitutional Convention of 1787 or an ancient Greek play like *Antigone* as having this kind of exemplary significance for political life. But such scenes nevertheless typically illuminate only relatively restricted dimensions. Thus, we see the need to think as well in terms of more abstract scenes that both fully embody the most important democratic values, as well as portray their interconnection. Such scenes are "originary" not in some traditional, strong foundational sense of ultimate origins, but rather in the sense that they provide a fuller representation of the sources that animate us as democratic citizens. These

---

31. Obviously, specific historical exemplary scenes are not literally imagined like either specific aesthetic scenes or originary exemplary scenes. But a prominent, specific historical event like, say, the Tennis Court Oath, will likely be heavily worked over in an aesthetic sense.

values do not stand transcendentally independent of us; rather, they constitute the deepest layer of our interpretive frames in the sense of what we have recourse to finally when pushed by events and counterclaims to explain and justify why we take some normative stand in political contestation. So, although our idea of an originary exemplary scene has an abstract, generalized character, it nevertheless retains a final rootedness in particularity in the sense that it is an interpretive rendering rooted in what is historically specific, namely, the tradition of modern democracy in the West.[32] Thus, the generalizing, originary character of this sort of exemplary scene is always conditioned in a way that distinguishes it from the kind and degree of abstraction found in strong foundations.[33]

And yet such a scene is nevertheless more abstract than specific, exemplary aesthetic or historical scenes. It provides, in effect, a proto-narrative stripped of most of the details one expects in specific exemplary scenes that give them their immediate, vivid traction in our consciousness. An originary scene is "proto" in the sense of its occupying the furthest point in the stages of our moral-political reflections. Of course, as a weak ontological figuration, this finality does not imply that the character of the scene is immaculately uncriticizable, rather only that to criticize or get beyond, at this level, involves taking on the task of refiguring the deepest understanding of how we imagine ourselves and our collective life embedded in democratic traditions. In short, the authority of such a scene is one it accrues historically, and one that must be re-authorized toward the future. In this sense, the scene is never fully in the past, as with many traditional origin stories; rather it is a continually operative, aspirational sketch of

---

32. Later, we will show another way in which particularity plays a central role in this scene, namely, because of the way it vividly emphasizes the continual appearance of what is different or "other" to generalized expectations.

33. It should be distinguished as well as from the abstraction involved in the sort of scenes we think of as "thought experiments" that tie into some determinate theory, as was the case with Rawls's initial understanding of his "original position," or that embedded in rational choice scenarios that are supposed to model what would be *the* determinate rational decision in a given set of circumstances.

how to orient ourselves to the events of political life. In short, the scene is "proto-" in the sense of being merely a bare sketch of a story whose specifics must be further narrated by contemporary actors.

Thinking in terms of an exemplary scene populated with abstract figures, as is the case with our originary one, has a clear disadvantage compared to thinking with the aid of more specific, concrete scenes, whether from art, literature, or history. With the former we obviously lose much of the latter's narrative richness, embodied in particular details and vivid characters that are often powerful vehicles for carrying the force of an illustration. Nevertheless, the abstract or generalized quality of an originary scene has a distinct advantage in the way it allows us to more consciously order and highlight ontological features, values, and affects embodied in the portrait that can, in turn, serve to roughly integrate our reactions to a broader range of ethical-political interactions.[34] Having recourse to an originary scene thus allows us to have a more coherent and consistent democratic orientation in the face of widely differing events in our political world. Specific exemplary scenes, with their narrow range of reference, can sometimes project a correspondingly limited understanding of what a fully democratic orientation to the world should look like. For example, the specific exemplary scenes that portray one or the other of what we have called the two faces of democracy, can, on their own, be drawn in disturbingly undemocratic directions (a danger we illustrate further in the next chapter).

As a means of better grasping the distinction between specific and originary scenes, it might be helpful to return momentarily to Honig's work. She can be interpreted as taking a position that is different from, but not necessarily opposed to, the one we are presenting. As she says, our attachments to positions in political theory can never be cleanly divorced from the force of "fables or fantasy."[35]

---

34. This abstract character also keeps the identity of the actors undetermined. Specific scenes and traditional originary scenes are often biased by specific racial and gender issues.

35. Honig, *Political Theory and the Displacement of Politics* (Ithaca, NY: Cornell University Press, 1993), 210.

But, unlike Connolly and us, Honig does not appeal to anything like an originary, generalizing scene. She prefers rather to deploy multiple specific scenes from novels, the Hebrew Bible, classical Greece, and film. Her engagements with them typically involve agonistic portrayals of the harms of gender and racial inequality, as well as the admirability of acts of resistance to them.[36] Despite the often compelling quality of these scenes, for a reader following the trajectory of her thought, it is hardly unreasonable to wonder whether there is some more generative, generalizing ontological-ethical figuration embodying a sense of equality and autonomy that is persistently, if tacitly, structuring her selection of one such illustrative scene rather than another. Honig, however, does not pursue reflections in this direction. And yet there also does not seem to be any principled opposition on her part to the idea of a more generalized scene. Notably, she appears to affirm the value of Connolly's originary scene of identity/difference for her own thinking.[37] Perhaps it constitutes for her a distinctive sort of "fable," namely a generalized one that aims to encourage further critical reflection along certain significant lines.[38] One can thus see the two kinds of scenes, specific and originary, not as direct competitors but as mutually supplementary. That is how we see the relationship between, on the one hand, the specific historical scenes, highlighted in the Introduction and, on the other hand, the more generalized understanding of their significance provided by our originary scene.

36. See, e.g., *Antigone Interrupted* (Cambridge: Cambridge University Press, 2013), and "12 Angry Men: Care for the Agon and the Varieties of Masculine Experience," *Theory & Event* 22, no. 3 (July 2019): 701–716.

37. Honig, "What Is Agonism," *Contemporary Political Theory*, 666.

38. Honig, *Political Theory and the Displacement of Politics,* 210. She also sees an idealized view of Athenian democracy functioning for Arendt as a generalized "fable" for a renewal of contemporary politics. In effect, then, it has something like the status of our idea of an originary exemplary scene.

## B. The Myth Problem

When one has recourse to specific scenes that are at least partially fictional and appeal to our imagination, we can appreciate them without worrying too much that they might displace what one hopes is the underlying, reason-based framing of democratic politics. However, when one speaks, as we are, of an originary, generalizing scene that is somewhat imaginary and intended to be action orienting, as well as presumed to stand at the center of our understanding of democracy, then things may start to look—as we indicated above—a bit more unsettling, even manipulative. Reason and imagination seem to get entangled in unclear ways. Is our action oriented by reason or by affect and enthusiasm that are corroding reason and are potentially entwined with some inconspicuous strategy of power? If the latter, we have entered the uncertain territory of political myth.

As indicated a moment ago, we want to hold the myth issue in the foreground and show how our originary scene can be understood as embodying the qualities of a democratic mythic. But rather than plunging directly into a conceptual unpacking of this question, we want to approach it obliquely, but hopefully in a fashion that opens the topic effectively. As a means of starting to think broadly about myths in this context, it is useful to begin with specific exemplary scenes related to the two faces of democracy and try to show first that they involve a mythic dimension. That should make it easier to see how such a dimension is more entangled with familiar figures of thought than we might initially imagine.

Although references to, say, the Boston Tea Party or the "Minutemen" at Lexington and Concord, might not seem to immediately involve anything mythic, a moment's reflection begins to problematize that presumption. Admittedly, they do not include fantastic figures like gods in classical myths, but that should not be an immediately disqualifying feature. In fact, we would argue that a typical characteristic of the modern democratic mythic is that its narratives often feature ordinary people doing extraordinary things—in short, the ordinary becomes linked to the heroic or fantastic.

After one makes this single shift, our two historical scenes seem to share most of the other features scholars associate with myths and how they help us see the significance of events confronting us at a later time. In terms of sensemaking, myths differ from scientific or religious explanations by exerting their force through "concrete reference and temporal perspective."[39] Conceptually, they generate sense through "a narrative that coagulates and reproduces significance." And this significance is not transmitted in an affectively neutral way; rather, such "narratives put a drama on stage." And, finally, in myths this sort of dramatic generation of significance has a practical force: it offers "orientation and stimulation for action."[40]

The Tea Party and Minutemen narratives possess these characteristics, having continually inspired Americans' imagination from the eighteenth century until the present, toward what people see as public-spirited actions in defense of their political community.[41] Prominent examples include signing up for the military after the attacks of 9/11 or on Pearl Harbor in 1941. But more controversial examples come into view as well, such as joining "militias" in the first two decades of the twenty-first century with the aim of foiling "tyranny" by the leftist "deep state," against which Donald Trump defined his presidency. Most Americans would probably find the former motivations to be democratically admirable, while fewer would find the latter qualifying for such a description. This dispute over different directions of interpretation

39. Henry Tudor, *Political Myth* (London: Pall Mall Press, 1972), 126.

40. Chiara Bottici, *A Philosophy of Political Myth* (Cambridge: Cambridge University Press, 2007), 123–132, 196, 243.

41. One might object that there is nothing imaginary about specific historical episodes like the Boston Tea Party. It is a piece of history. But clearly that scene has a significance beyond its pure historical reality as one episode leading up to the American Revolution. The vivid positive symbolic appeal it has accrued for the American imagination today contrasts somewhat with the more ambivalent significance it had at the time it occurred. Almost no one remembers that many otherwise anti-British Bostonians were not happy about this event and the crowd that carried it out. See Benjamin L. Carp, *Defiance of the Patriots: The Boston Tea Party and the Making of America* (New Haven and London: Yale University Press, 2010), 166–167, 191, 218–222.

points toward a crucial, but complex question: What exactly draws a given mythic figuration toward democratic, rather than an antidemocratic, significance? In what follows we delineate a set of features that characterize a distinctly democratic mythic. But, importantly, these features are quite often not embodied fully in a given, specific narrative or aesthetic scene. Accordingly, one of our key claims is that these specific scenes and their detailed features need finally to be animated by, and mutually entwined with, an underlying originary scene that portrays more fully the connection of these features with a core set of democratic values that constitute our most basic moral sources.

## C. The Democratic Mythic and Its Critical Work

At this point, Protagoras's story is once again instructive. It is doubly relevant: not only because it constitutes what is perhaps the earliest Western example of a democratic mythic, but also because it is simultaneously an originary scene. That makes it somewhat different from stories of specific historical events, like the actual dumping of tea into the water of Boston harbor in 1773. Clearly, in antiquity, myths about origins were quite common, usually featuring gods (as does Protagoras's or Plato's) or other fantastic creatures. A familiar example of that sort of originary story is the founding of Rome by fictional brothers Romulus and Remus, who were raised by a wolf. For the present discussion, an obvious question thus arises: What might a plausible originary political mythic look like, given that appeals to fantastic characters, or a creator God or gods, do not have as much resonance as in the past? The answer in short is that all we can appeal to are the deepest interpretive resources that we democratic actors have, historically, authorized. These can provide us with a proto-story that we narrate to ourselves, vivifying our sense of autonomy and equality; this is what functions, in effect, as a democratic mythic. But what exactly do we mean by introducing this unusual term "democratic *mythic*" rather than the more familiar sounding one "democratic myth"?

When one thinks about myths in the classic sense, what tends to come to mind is a fixed story with a cast of larger-than-life actors.[42] An emphasis on such characteristics may indeed be useful in distinguishing the status of a myth and its significance from a scientific explanation, but this contrast can also create the impression that myths are always self-contained, fixed entities with what is, in effect, a frozen meaning. That quality may be evident in some myths, but it is most often associated with attempts by intellectuals, groups, and regimes to police traditional myths, especially ones about national origins, in ways that support certain values and collective interpretations.[43] Absent such efforts to achieve an authoritative congealing of meaning, myths are often quite pliable, in the sense that their transmission involves pluralization and mutation that occur in the process of the continual reappropriation of meaning as new actors try to draw significance from them for their present circumstances. In effect, myths are frequently less like frozen entities than something always in motion.[44] We find this characterization especially true when one thinks about myths today, especially when they are cut off from the authority of beyond-human figures. As a way of bringing this dynamic character into the heart of our reflections, we have spoken of a democratic "mythic" not of democratic "myths." Thus, to speak of stories, scenes, images, and so forth as possessing "mythic" qualities is to envision them as not necessarily

---

42. What we refer to here as "classic" are myths that exist in a literary mode or are attached to significant historical events, not the more amorphous tales of modern life that circulate at a semi-conscious level and tend to remain remarkably resilient in the face of palpable contrary evidence. The latter include, for example, the familiar tales of welfare recipients who drive their Cadillacs to the social services office to pick up their checks. Keum refers to the former as "philosophical" and the latter as "deep" myths; Keum, *Plato and the Mythic Tradition*, 5–7, 212–223, 237–238.

43. See the interesting discussion of President Akayev's efforts to deploy an epic poem to foster a mythic origin story for the new nation state of Kyrgyzstan after it emerged as an independent entity in 1991, in Rogers M. Smith, *Stories of Peoplehood: The Politics and Morals of Political Membership* (Cambridge: Cambridge University Press, 2003), 1–5. Although Smith exhibits some sympathy for such efforts, it is hard in retrospect not to see the rather heavy hand of authoritarianism increasingly guiding the whole effort.

44. Bottici, *A Philosophy of Political Myth*, 126–129. In this view, she is following Hans Blumenberg, *Work on Myth* (Boston: MIT Press, 1985).

carrying either the full sense of a discrete "myth" in the classical mold or as possessing the primarily negative associations attached typically to the adjective "mythical," a term that often implies something deceptively fictive, at least when one is speaking about political matters.

Regarding the dynamic character of myth, consider again Protagoras's originary narrative. The setting of Plato's dialogue is Athens, where such a story about democratic origins would have had some degree of immediate fit with the political order. But the narrative is not exclusively about Athens, as the story of Romulus and Remus is about Rome. Rather, Protagoras's story has a potentially generalizing reach, referring only to "men" and "cities." Thus, it has the capacity to travel as it is retold elsewhere and potentially open up democratic questions in broader contexts, at the very least in other Greek city-states that did not have democratic constitutions. The relating of this originary story could thus do critical work.[45]

So, if myths help "coagulate" significance, this is not a process that is inherently scripted to fit the needs of any given political regime. Of course, that sort of constriction often occurs. But when a narrative gets coopted in this way, there is a good basis for saying that it is being transformed into something that is better described as an ideological or propagandistic distortion of the mythic; in effect, what happens is that the mythic dimension becomes reified. Against this background, we suggest that mythic significance in democratic life is especially attuned to pluralization and

---

45. Another example of the mobility and critical potential of originary myths can be seen in Rousseau's work. In the *Discourse on the Origin of Inequality*, he took the familiar scene/story of the state of nature that had, by the 1750s, sunk into consciousness as part of the modern Western political imaginary and turned it into a deeply critical indictment of some of its normal components. His mythic portrayal of a natural condition flipped the standard script: the emergence of political life out of the state of nature becomes a tale not of the progress and superiority of Western modernity but of regress and oppression. The way Rousseau does this is captured beautifully in the frontispiece of the essay, where the central subject is not a European "everyman," but a "primitive" everyman who had been taken as a child from his native homeland to be educated in Europe. The scene shows him as an adult standing before a group of Europeans. He is telling them that he has decided to give up all things modern, preferring instead to return "to his equals." He is saying "no" to a "superior" modern life. Rousseau, *The First and Second Discourses*, ed. Roger Masters, trans. Roger Masters and Judith Masters (New York: St. Martin's Press, 1964), 76. See the discussion in Bottici, *A Philosophy of Political Myth*, 143–145.

reappropriation, as well as the uncertainty and precarity tied to a cultivation of such a sensibility; accordingly, it is always in tension with efforts at systematic reification.

In order to illuminate more precisely the substantive character of a democratic mythic, we again want to back away momentarily from the focus on originary scenes and attend to another specific exemplary scene, one portrayed in a recent work of art. This allows us to present a particularly vivid representation of the character and force of a democratic mythic. The work of art to which we turn is richly illustrative; in fact, so much so that it is also somewhat extraordinary in the sense of how fully it captures the range of features of that mythic. After having laid out these features, we will turn in the next chapter to explaining how they are embodied in our originary scene.

As we saw already in the case of Protagoras, a cardinal characteristic of a democratic mythic is its moving of everyday people into heroic roles, ones that may have been formerly occupied by revered, authoritative, even semi-divine characters. The critical edge this can have is clearly displayed in the context of the recent controversy over the statues of Confederate leaders in the city of Richmond, Virginia. Of course, many southern cities have recently faced this kind of issue. But the case of Richmond is distinctive. As the capital of the Confederacy, it has always had a special symbolic significance. Moreover, in this case, it was not just a matter of the presence of an individual statue, but an entire avenue—Monument Avenue—dedicated to and lined with such statues, creating what was perhaps the most powerful visual portrayal of the myth of the "lost cause": the belief that the Civil War was a noble defense of states' rights and not really about the oppressiveness of slavery. Monument Avenue is the widest, most beautiful, tree-lined street in the city. On it were five huge statues of Confederate generals and other leaders of the Confederacy spaced over a stretch of ten unusually long blocks. Erected in the Jim Crow era, these were central symbols sustaining the myths of the Confederacy. The statues were literally monumental: imposing in size, seemingly immovable, even slightly fantastic. The one of General Robert E. Lee towered a full sixty feet above the street. Collectively, the statues had a palpable, unmistakable significance: the supposed truth and rectitude of the southern cause in the Civil War was bronzed and made solid, unalterable in time. The scene portrayed in this outdoor drama, was about as far from a democratic mythic as one can get. It was meant to present frozen significance, embodied in almost beyond-human figures.

Beginning in 2013 in the U.S., growing signs of protest began to appear with the Black Lives Matter movement in the wake of national outrage over the acquittal of George Zimmerman for the murder of Trayvon Martin. These protests swelled to the broadest in U.S. history in the summer of 2020 after the murder of George Floyd by a police officer.[46] At that point, sufficient public pressure was exerted in Richmond to have the Confederate monuments dismantled and removed by the end of 2021.[47] While simple removal is one way to combat an antidemocratic mythic force, another—symbolically richer—is represented by replacing the statue with a new one: a piece that operates creatively on a democratic mythic register.[48] Kehinde Wiley recently sculpted a mounted figure in bronze

---

46. See Lara Putnam, Erica Chenoweth, and Jeremy Pressman, "The Floyd Protests Are the Broadest in U.S. History—And Are Spreading to White, Small-Town America," *Washington Post*, June 6, 2020, https://www.washingtonpost.com/politics/2020/06/06/floyd-protests-are-broadest-us-history-are-spreading-white-small-town-america/.

47. Earlier efforts to promote an aesthetic-political thaw of the frozen panorama of Monument Avenue had a less than felicitous outcome. Amidst great controversy on both sides, a relatively small statue of Arthur Ashe was installed at one end of the street. Ashe, a top professional tennis player and hometown, humanitarian hero in the last decades of the twentieth century, had grown up in Richmond and faced discrimination, being denied the right as a kid to play on what were public, but white-only, courts. The insertion of a new, comparatively diminutive statue of him in the context of Monument Avenue seemed to many promoting civil rights to carry a whiff of mockery. In that regard, the statue existed in a strange limbo, comparable to the symbolic legacy of Martin Luther King Jr. in the state, when Virginia decided in 1984 to honor his memory by including him in a state holiday officially named "Lee, Jackson, King Day," thus allowing King to trail behind Robert E. Lee and Thomas "Stonewall" Jackson. In 2000, King finally got a separate holiday.

48. Our analysis below of Wiley's statue in relation to the myths of the Confederacy would seem to constitute the sort of mythic work Keum hopes for when she suggests that the deployment of new "philosophical myths" (which we take to include the aesthetic and historical scenes we are analyzing) might help undermine the deleterious effects of undemocratic myths, both "literary" and "deep myths"; Keum, *Plato and the Mythic Tradition in Political Thought*, 5–7, 212–238. The statues on Monument Avenue propagated an antidemocratic, aesthetic scene drawing out particular interpretations of associated historical scenes. And the effect was to provide

**Figure 5.1.** Major General J. E. B Stuart, by Frederick Moynihan, Richmond, Virginia, erected 1907; removed in 2020.
*Source:* Wikipedia.

entitled *Rumors of War* that does mythic work on the original scene of Monument Avenue, especially the statue of J. E. B. Stuart, the most famous Confederate cavalry general (Figure 5.1). Stuart was portrayed astride a bucking horse, evoking a sense of imminent battle. With his body turned slightly backward, his drawn sword and commanding gaze seem to urge his troops into the fight.

Wiley's statue is a comparably monumental size, and the audacious rider is also astride a similarly posed steed—only Wiley's subject is a contemporary young black man with dreadlocks, jeans, and tennis shoes (Figure 5.2). This figure brings a frozen myth to transmogrified life, transforming the "fantastic" subject into a contemporary individual who is a generalized, anonymous "everyman": an ordinary black man, one

powerful sustenance to numerous deep myths about the inferiority of African Americans and the baselessness of their claims about unaddressed historical injustices.

**Figure 5.2.** *Rumors of War* by Kehinde Wiley, Virginia Museum of Fine Arts, Richmond, 2019. Purchased with funds provided by Virginia Sargeant Reynolds in memory of her husband, Richard S. Reynolds, Jr., by exchange, Arthur and Margaret Glasgow Endowment, Pamela K. and William A. Royall, Jr., Angel and Tom Papa, Katherine and Steven Markel, and additional private donors.
*Source:* Stephen K. White photograph.

of those locked into subordination and invisibility in the settled, official southern myth of the Confederacy. Here an aristocratic, military figure of authority has morphed into a larger-than-life but still ordinary person of democratic bearing.

But Wiley's work (that now stands on a street intersecting Monument Avenue, relatively near the location of the original Confederate statue) not only brings the figure of the hero down to democratic earth, it operates as well on another, related level of generalization that helps delineate a second quality of a democratic mythic. And that involves the democratization not just of the actor but also the interpreter who must evaluate and justify what is to be done. That feature was already on display, as we have seen, in Protagoras's narrative. In *Rumors of War*, we are all invited/incited—by the man's looking backward to all those who might be reacting to the continuing racial violence in America—to these tasks of citizenship. Thus, there is mobility and plurality not only in the substitution of figures but also in who is conceived as capable of interpretating what is at stake. There is no clear superior-subordinate relation here; no one is being ordered by the arm and gaze of authority. There are only other citizens (us, the viewers) beckoned by the young man's body language into sharing a mutual responsibility as equals to think and act for ourselves—in short, to take up our role in the drama of democratic autonomy.

Finally, there is a third crucial characteristic of a democratic mythic. Wiley's young man, entangled in the foregoing questions, subtly evokes a sense of precarity in a twofold way. The first is highlighted by this figure's being not just a common man but also a black man, who pointedly carries the precarity of a class of people historically oppressed in an ostensibly democratic country. Wiley's individual is clearly stepping up to fight against this racial injustice, but he does not carry a sword or other weapon. His muscularity and audacity are thus also layered with an embodied vulnerability.[49] Precarity in this sense involves both individual bodily vulnerability as well as the "socially induced" precarity" of some actors, the latter being a kind of vulnerability that legitimately haunts the always recurrent tendency toward democratic self-satisfaction on the part of those who enjoy more secure economic and political positions in society.[50]

A second sense of precarity involves the vulnerability of judgment rather than embodied vulnerability. It is related to the character of

---

49. See Kriston Capps, "Kehinde Wiley's Anti-Confederate Memorial," *The New Yorker*, December 24, 2019, https://www.newyorker.com/culture/culture-desk/kehinde-wileys-anti-confederate-memorial.

50. Judith Butler, *Notes Toward a Performative Theory of Assembly* (Cambridge, MA: Harvard University Press, 2015), 11, 21–22.

political judgment, more specifically to its fallibility. This young man calls us to democratic judgment, but he does not evoke a militarized sense of self-certainty that effaces the burdens of interpretation and decision. The tasks that *Rumors of War* urges us to embrace are entangled with difficult questions: Is this a war or something else? Who stands where? What should we do? Importantly, the precarity evoked here is not that of a figure immobilized by indecision. But the young man also does not represent a militarized image of democratic self-certainty. In the next chapter, we will contrast this evoking of a moment of precarity and reflection with the militarized certainty and bravado so proudly embodied in contemporary right-wing populism's political imagination.

As we noted earlier, Wiley's statue is extraordinary for how fully it portrays the democratic mythic. Most historical or aesthetic representations give us more partial portrayals.[51] Importantly, we sense this partiality precisely because we perceive these representations against the background of an originary scene that embodies the fuller array of intuitions we have about the moral core of democracy. This sensing of partiality becomes one impetus for the interpretive "work" of a democratic mythic.[52] This will become clearer in the Chapter 6.

---

51. Another example of recent aesthetic work that, like Wiley's, carries a remarkably full embodiment of a democratic mythic can be seen in the creations of the South African artist Sethembile Msezane. In the setting of confrontations with huge monuments in that country memorializing the apartheid past, she has created aesthetic experiences where she embodies a contrast with the sublime force of these larger-than-life statues. She does this by performances at the monuments that put the small, vulnerable living body of a common person, dressed in a way symbolic of opposition, in contrast to the gigantic metallic leaders of a racist South Africa. But this evocation of precarity and hope is balanced with the scene or prospect of those figures being toppled. In the most famous case, the performance was in front of a statue of Cecil Rhodes about to taken down. The entwining of precarity and the counter-sublimity of the falling monument (a counter to the one-dimensional way authoritarian power seeks to clothe itself in a pure masculinist sublimity) beautifully captures key characteristics of a democratic mythic. See Msezane's TED Talk, August 2017, https://www.ted.com/talks/sethembile_msezane_living_sculptures_that_stand_for_history_s_truths/transcript.

52. We have used the notion of "work on myth" several times in this chapter. In this we are following Hans Blumenberg's approach in *Work on Myth*. Although this idea might seem to imply manipulation of myth in an ideological sense, the work Blumenberg refers to is associated generally with the development of myth. "Work" here refers broadly to our efforts to symbolically manage, over time, the existential "*Angst*" embedded in human consciousness of finitude, 3–10.

## III. CONCLUSION

We have now laid out the basic qualities that a representation of the weak ontological core of democracy would have to embody today. The old metaphor of foundations, with its image of something that independently precedes and secures a dwelling for its occupants, is no longer convincing to many. Nevertheless, in situations of ongoing political contestation, we are periodically forced to have recourse to our most basic commitments, our moral sources of what we take ourselves to be as people in a democratic community. In this world, any notion of a "foundation" must imagine itself as just as dependent upon the building and its occupants as they are on it.

What is the best way to conceive this reimagined relationship? We have proposed the idea of thinking in terms of having recourse to exemplary scenes that capture, conceptually and affectively, the sense of our moral sources. In the case of democratic life, these are primarily equality and autonomy. Two sorts of exemplary scenes need to be distinguished. *Specific* scenes involve historical or aesthetic settings rich in detailed figures, images, or narratives that represent some aspect of these sources in a vivid fashion, as do the different scenes we have identified with the two faces of democracy. But these specific exemplary scenes need to be related to an *originary* one that constitutes a template of both of our underlying sources and their mutually constitutive relationship. Such a scene is originary, not in an ultimate metaphysical sense, but only in the sense that it is the final representation, where our efforts to imagine ourselves as democratic citizens run out of any further grounds of justification.

If there are advantages to shifting away from the language of strong ontological foundations to that of exemplary scenes, there would seem to be as well a significant disadvantage. To speak of scenes and their attraction is to enter the realm of imagination, and that raises fears of reason's role in our political reflections being dangerously demoted. Images of the worst sorts of undemocratic states and their reliance on the perpetration of myths immediately come to mind. We have tried to respond to this problem by sketching the specific characteristics of a democratic mythic.

Wiley's *Rumors of War* is beautifully illustrative here. It provides us with an aesthetic exemplary scene that embodies these traits in an unusually rich fashion. Three are crucial. A democratic mythic will portray a *generalized capacity to contest authority and to act politically*, often appearing as the substitution of the everyman or everywoman for some superior or privileged figure. Related to that, it will portray the *generalized capacity to interpret political life*. And, finally, it will evoke moments of *precarity, opening into a sense of the need for mutual support and collective cooperation of the vulnerable, as well as a willingness to admit the persistence of uncertainty* in our judgments of political life. This is the idea that democratic power and confidence are always provisional in relation to time, audience, and our tendency to forget our finitude; they must remain continually open to reevaluation.

We brought these traits forward in the context of their remarkable display in Wiley's specific exemplary scene, but there will be many scenes, both aesthetic and historical, that embody something less than all three. In fact, that is more typically the case. And that is perfectly okay, just as it is acceptable for people in a given situation to be inspired by scenes of only one or the other of the two faces of democracy. But one can also see here the template role that needs to be played by an originary scene: it embodies, even if abstractly, all three of these aspects of a democratic mythic. Thus, it can always work as a resource for gently vivifying for us this fuller meaning of a democratic ethos.

In sum, we have laid out the broad criteria that would have to be satisfied to have a weak ontological "foundation" for democratic politics. It would take the form of an originary exemplary scene that adequately portrays the moral sources most relevant to politics and highlights the traits we have identified with a democratic mythic. We turn now to the task of sketching such a scene.

# 6
# An Exemplary Scene of the Moral Equality of Voice

Chapter 5's goal was to clarify the role an originary exemplary scene can play and specify some of the criteria a critical, democratic one would have to model. We now turn to the task of elaborating the character of the particular scene we believe can admirably embody those criteria, as well as provide a sense of the interconnectedness of those two faces of democracy that have such intuitive force for us. To give coherence to those intuitions, the scene must weave together, at the level of social ontology and imagination, a portrayal of the agonism present in political relations, on the one hand, and an idea of how individual moral status and mutual communicative obligation are reciprocally constituted, on the other hand. This two-foldedness is displayed in the way our scene manifests the values of autonomy and equality embodied in the concept of the moral equality of voice. Section I begins the task of elaborating the originary scene of our communicative model. Section II attends to how the scene brings to life the moral equality of voice in a way that constitutively intertwines both what deliberativists as well as agonists wish to emphasize. Further, we show how this scene models the characteristics of a democratic mythic that were delineated in the previous chapter. Much of the critical interpretive "work" of this mythic occurs in the interaction of this implicit scene with more specific historical and aesthetic scenes. Finally, in Section III, some possible lines of criticism of our perspective are considered.

## I. DRAWING ON AND DEPARTING FROM HABERMAS

Rather than constructing an originary exemplary scene *ab initio*, we will be drawing upon one that is already somewhat familiar in the world of contemporary social and political thought, even if it was not originally offered as a scene in the sense we have in mind. We both borrow from, and substantially revise, a figure of thought that first appeared several decades ago in Habermas's portrayal of "communicative action."

### A. The Scene of "Communicative Action"

Of course, such a starting point is likely to be maximally suspicious to those in the agonist camp. They charge Habermas with framing the discourse of justice so as to thoroughly preclude access to the discourse of agonism. The idea of an originary exemplary scene drawn from Habermas immediately calls up the image of the frequently derided "ideal speech situation" (ISS) that portrays actors as situated in a perfectly fair setting and who exchange arguments until consensus is reached. One might here call attention again to the scene referenced in Chapter 5 from the *Oxford Handbook of Deliberative Democracy*. It could be taken as a sort of watered-down version of this idealization. The difficulty with this figuration of the core ideal is, of course, that it foregrounds only one of the two faces of democracy, that associated with reasonable discussion and debate. We are called to a scene where agents gather soberly to carry on the reasonable negotiation of significant issues. The problem is not so much that this is a patently bad exemplary scene; rather, it is simply one-sided, orienting us only to the first face of democracy that emphasizes discussion and reasonableness. When this face is given such unqualified prominence, it encourages, once again, the emergence of familiar lines of critique charging that the deliberative approach underplays contestation, power, resistance, and conflict. Proponents of the *Handbook* version of the ideal may counter that such phenomena can in fact be comprehended, secondarily at least, within the deliberative perspective. But, as we have shown in the preceding chapters, even some sympathetic critics have not found this broad strategy to be successful. Concerns have been voiced that the continual expansion of the ideal of deliberation to cover all sorts of *non-deliberative* actions, such as, for example, expressive protest, has resulted in an implicit strategy of "concept stretching" that makes almost any kind of political speech and action somehow "deliberative." And the more radical, agonist critics have persistently accused deliberativists of proceeding in a way that underrecognizes domination and injustice.

In short, the idea of turning to even a watered-down version of the Habermasian ideal for inspiration here hardly seems like a promising avenue for imagining an exemplary scene that can vivify agonism as emphatically as it would deliberation. But what if there are in fact resources in Habermas's work that can be interpreted in a less one-sided fashion?

There are indeed grounds for being suspicious of such a suggestion, but there are also good reasons not to let that suspicion be the final word. Below, we argue that we should indeed reject some of the central claims associated with Habermas's deliberative ideal. But we also argue that there nevertheless remains in the core of his general account of communicative action several elements crucial to the portrayal of a more capacious and persuasive originary scene. In what follows we draw out how this core can be understood in a way that continually casts doubt on structures of inequality and domination, thus making it far more sensitive to difference and resistance than typically thought.

The qualities we wish to emphasize become more easily visible as a result of Habermas's recent relinquishing of his strong foundationalist claim, according to which, as he famously announced, "the *telos* of language is understanding," meaning that language, *in its essence*, orients us toward agreement.[1] Our intuitive understanding of the criteria of a fair agreement is no longer an immovable ontological anchor for him; rather, it is now simply the fruit of deep, but always uncertain and precarious,

---

1. Habermas, *The Theory of Communicative Action*, vol. 1: *Reason and the Rationalization of Society*, trans. Thomas McCarthy (Boston: Beacon Press, 1984), 286–288.

"moral-practical learning processes" associated with modernity.[2] With no telos behind this movement, nothing is guaranteed and the progressive, self-congratulatory attitude formerly implied appears now as unjustified and dangerous.[3] With this change, the notion that Habermas's framework has some foundational orientation that draws all social interaction toward consensus loses its relevance. His perspective can no longer be cast as an all-ordering consensus machine that grinds different views into commensurable material, methodically processing us toward a just, common "yes." Similarly, it is no longer tied to an essentialist view of language, according to which its "action-coordinating" function is central, whereas its more aesthetic "world-disclosing" disruptive function is secondary.[4]

Accordingly, when we speak of a "communicative" model of democracy, it does not have to seem so one-sided from the start. Habermas's ideal is now rooted only in a depth hermeneutic in the sense of our most

---

2. Habermas, *Auch Eine Geschichte der Philosophie,* Band 2: *Vernünftige Freiheit: Spurren des Diskurses über Glauben und Wissen* (Frankfurt: Suhrkamp, 2019), 806. The original strong ontological claim appears, e.g., in Habermas, *The Theory of Communicative Action,* 1:286–288.

3. The objection that Habermas has not adequately acknowledged this changed status of claims about a learning process has been voiced even by sympathetic critics. His argument in *Auch Eine Geschichte der Philosophie* about this process emerges from a story focused on the Western voices. Seyla Benhabib argues that he has thus left himself open to the charge that his learning process may be too close to Hegel's in the *Phenomenology.* "Unless the concept of a learning process is further clarified," it may still imply the kind of exclusivist dangers that exist in Hegel; in effect, it would constitute a privileged, exclusive narrative of Western modernity, rather than one that is always opening itself increasingly to being a "narrative of global modernity"; see Benhabib, "Habermas's New *Phenomenology of Spirit:* Two Centuries after Hegel," *Constellations* 28 no. 1 (2021): 37–40. See also Steven Gormley's critique in *Deliberative Theory and Deconstruction, A Democratic Venture* (Edinburgh: Edinburgh University Press, 2022), 249–253. Given the interpretative direction we have taken in this book toward a revised Habermasian framework, there would be no grounds on which one could plausibly assert the trajectory of a learning process, without seeing that as a contestable narrative open to non-Western voices, as well as any other voices that may have been disempowered or neglected in the initial story. This simply reflects the continuing application of the idea of moral equality of voice to the normative content of that narrative.

4. Habermas, *The Philosophical Discourse of Modernity: Twelve Lectures,* trans. Frederick Lawrence (Cambridge, MA: MIT Press, 1987), 178, 199–210. This earlier privileging of the "action-coordinating" function of language (oriented toward agreement) over the "world-disclosing" function (which may interrupt that coordination) now loses its justification. See fn. 18. The latter function of language is obviously more closely aligned with social practices that unmask and disrupt settled power structures; in short, something agonists would affirm.

basic weak-ontological framework. In other words, the communicative ideal represents our most basic, historically informed intuitions about the best way to array core values that have accompanied the rise of democracy. More specifically, Habermas's ideal is based on the idea that a legitimate politics should be tied to public speech claims about what is in the common interest.

But many would nevertheless continue to find this chastened frame suspicious. Two problems stand out. First, the Habermasian picture still imagines political life as only about clashes between actors who are all essentially the same, except for the fact that they embrace different interests. Managing conflicting interests through deliberation thus becomes the key task. This makes issues of identity/difference either invisible or matters convertible into interest clashes.[5] But, if Connolly is right, as we think he is, then this is a deeply flawed portrait of mortal creatures who are existentially faced with an agonism of identity/difference that continually animates political life. We will come back to this issue in a moment and try to show how it might be better accommodated within our radicalized portrait of communicative action.

The second problem with the Habermasian frame is that, even after the foundational claim is dropped, the ISS still seems to be firmly at the center of things. Here we want to make a departure from Habermas that is crucial to our perspective, and yet it is one that is implicit in some of his work. Its significance becomes decidedly more prominent, however, once we have given up the earlier, strong-ontological foundation. Our claim is that the ISS is *not* the central concept in Habermas. It is indeed important, but it is not the dominant character in the drama of communication Habermas offers. Rather, the originary scene of his account of "communicative action" has the following shape.[6]

---

5. On the way in which Habermas's theory fails to account for power in the sphere of identity formation and dynamics, see Amy Allen, *The Politics of Our Selves: Power, Autonomy, and Gender in Contemporary Critical Theory* (New York: Columbia University Press, 2008), 110–122.

6. Habermas's general account of "communicative action" is laid out in *The Theory of Communicative Action*, vol. 1. Our interpretation below of this aspect of communicative action was first laid out in Stephen K. White, *A Democratic Bearing: Admirable Citizens, Uneven Injustice and Critical Theory* (Cambridge: Cambridge University Press, 2017), 16–17.

He asks us to imagine a setting of ongoing, linguistically mediated interaction that is proceeding cooperatively with the actors sharing an at least implicit sense of the rightness of how that interaction is unfolding. This is the default background picture of unproblematic communicative action. But then there is a rupture, with one actor interrupting the flow by saying "no" to some aspect of the normative expectations built into the scene, on which its unproblematic unfolding had constantly depended. That actor challenges the normative framing of things and demands a justification of some aspect of that order; in effect, they demand some response from others that could justify continuing to interact cooperatively. This scene highlights two interconnected moments: a frictional, "anarchic" moment of challenge and a reference to some basis for repairing cooperation that could be agreed to by both the "no-sayer" as well as those who embrace the challenged normative frame.[7]

The character of this scene is not pulled entirely out of thin air; rather, it reflects criteria of what sociologists refer to as the condition of the possibility of social life: a context of interaction within which humans can symbolically reproduce themselves and their relationships over time. This is a way of capturing the sense that ongoing human social life cannot be imagined as reproducing itself simply on the basis of force and strategic incentives alone; rather it must involve some degree of cooperative interaction tied to normative bonds. But those bonds must also be represented in such a way that humans do not appear as mere automatons who simply follow norms.

The scene has, accordingly, three crucial aspects. First, there is the sustaining, unproblematic symbolic reproduction in which actors, at least implicitly, accept the validity of the regnant norms guiding existing patterns of interaction. It is this bondedness that underlies unproblematic cooperation. But, second, there is also a figuration of the capacity to

---

7. Habermas, *Between Facts and Norms: Contributions to a Discourse Theory of Law and Democracy* (Cambridge, MA: MIT Press, 1996), xl and 307; and Habermas, "Commentary on Cristina Lafont, *Democracy Without Shortcuts*," *Journal of Deliberative Democracy* 16, no. 2 (2020): 14, https://doi.org/10.16997/jdd.397.

contest norms. It is especially this latter aspect that Habermas wants to emphasize in the scene of ongoing interaction, namely, the *interruption* of it; in short, our capacity and motivation to *say no* to this flow of normative interconnectedness, to stand up in speech and contest norms that are directing our lives.[8] Finally, this scene is animated by an aspirational ethical core that reflects our hope and expectation of how we might repair the interruption.[9] Together, these three aspects display the complex idea we call the moral equality of voice: a shared intuition that each individual possesses the standing to challenge the regnant norms that govern their lives and to expect justification from those for whom the norms are unproblematic. So, the scene develops from ongoing, unproblematic interaction to a given actor's "turning" on a normative context that is now experienced as oppressive in some way and demanding justification. The force of autonomy and equality here means that the other actors involved, explicitly or implicitly, are challenged to answer with persuasive arguments that could stand up in a deliberative context. Their obligation to respond is rooted in the fact that they are implicated in the claim to rightness that underlies this ongoing, shared context of communicative interaction.[10]

This is the heart of our radicalized, communicative model of democracy. It is a scene of linguistic interaction encompassing moments of challenge, rupture, and some sense of the shape of potential repair. The concepts and values embedded in this scene focus our attention and constitute a proto-setting in which multiple questions—of a distinct character—arise for participants who have taken a stance of no-saying. Prominent here are questions related to the suspicions that precede or accompany that

---

8. See Stephen K. White and Evan Robert Farr, "No-Saying in Habermas," *Political Theory* 40, no. 1 (Feb. 2012): 32–57; and White, *A Democratic Bearing*, 152–157.

9. The phenomenon of "no-saying" is posited by Habermas as rooted in the nature of language and understood as an emergent characteristic of Western modernity, thus making available a natural normative foundation for legitimate politics today. It seems to us that, along with the foundationalism, one can abandon the "Western" part and simply associate the persistent rise of "no-saying" with modernity generally.

10. This is our reading of Habermas's idea of a "speech-act immanent obligation," once one has dropped the strong foundationalist claim; Habermas, *Communication and the Evolution of Society* (Boston: Beacon Press, 1979), 63–64. See White, *A Democratic Bearing*, 61–62.

challenge to a given norm—most prominently: Does this norm simply embody domination of some sort and thus fail to have the generalized validity it claims for itself? The Habermasian account of communicative action and deliberation has often been thought of as failing to perceive many of the ways that power structures social life.[11] Although we would argue that it offers a good understanding of some forms of power, the key question is not so much whether it offers a specific, sufficient account of power, but whether it broadly casts a light of suspicion and thus persistently invites hypotheses regarding possibly illegitimate relations of power. If so, then there is no reason to see it as somehow deflecting attention from inconspicuous structures and forms of power; rather, it welcomes all hypotheses about possible ways in which normative contexts might embed domination and inequality, whether they be Foucauldian, feminist, Bourdieuean, and so forth.[12]

Another, related line of questions emerges here regarding the possible reparative-constructive direction from that challenge toward a more defensible normative context. Here is where serious misunderstanding of the ISS continues to distract. It was never meant as the sketch of an ideal form of social life, a blueprint that either could be brought to life now or in the future. Rather, it is better understood as a cluster of intuitions about what persuasion in speech should look like if it were to reflect the moral equality of voice (remaining, of course, always alert to how power may inconspicuously occlude such initial intuitions). In our judgment, it would make good sense to simply drop the term ISS in favor of something like "intuitions about fair communication" in relation to normative contestation. When rephrased in this fashion and understood in the context of the exemplary scene of communicative action, it becomes clear that the most immediate role of these positive intuitions is how they animate inferences

---

11. For example, Ian Shapiro argues that Habermas concentrates on the ideal speech situation and ignores power; *The State of Democratic Theory* (Princeton: Princeton University Press, 2003), 33–34. It is difficult to see how anyone could read the last one hundred pages of vol. 2 of *The Theory of Communicative Action: Lifeworld and System* (Boston: Beacon Press, 1987) and conclude that power is not an issue of great significance for Habermas.

12. White develops this point further in *A Democratic Bearing*, 138–145 and Ch. 7.

as to the possible *failures* of existing social and political structures to live up to democratic expectations. The intuitions continually function as the basis for counter-institutional critique and activity.[13] Insofar as these intuitions also point in a positive direction, that guidance is always chastened by the idea that any projection of what fairness implies is ultimately dependent, Habermas argues, on its justification to "all-affected" by a given norm. The equal status of each speaker implies that, in relation to a norm that either applies to given speakers directly or affects them indirectly, justification is owed to them in terms of how that norm is fair or not. This qualification gives the idealization of the communicative model an inextricable moment of uncertainty, as the reach of a given claim of justification remains perpetually open to new, potentially resistant voices.[14]

## B. Identity/Difference in the Scene

This radicalized communicative component of our exemplary scene, embodying the moral equality of each voice, embraces greater contestation and disruption than more familiar accounts of deliberation. But, as we noted earlier, it still operates in a world where conflicts unfold only at the level of interests and their possible accommodation, either through consensus or "fair compromises."[15] More agonism is now in play, but it is clearly not as essentially constitutive of this scene as agonists would legitimately expect. In sum, at this point our deliberative scene does not

---

13. A radicalized deliberative ideal establishes this scene of challenge at the center of its entire approach. Even though we think Habermas would today affirm this, his talk in the past of language's "telos" has led many to conclude that all social interaction is subtly drawn toward the end point of the ideal speech situation, and thus precedence seems to be given not to the starting scene of challenge but the concluding one of consensus. Within our radicalized reading, there is no clear end, rather, only the vivid initial scene and some persistent intuitions about possible, normatively admirable paths forward.

14. Habermas, *Between Facts and Norms*, 107–111.

15. Although Habermas has always used the concept of "fair compromises," its significance becomes far greater in our radicalized communicative model. See the discussion of this in White, *A Democratic Bearing*, pp. 158–159.

embody a sufficiently rich understanding of the dynamics of human identity to provide the basis for comprehending agonism and power in their full senses.

We need an exemplary scene that can vivify comparably significant roles for both the dynamic of identity/difference and the radicalized deliberative ideal. As we have suggested, each is insufficient on its own, and yet neither is constitutively closed to being interwoven and exerting a mutually chastening influence. For agonism to be tempered, actors must extend to one another a sense of agonistic respect, but that can only be adequately motivated when one already affirms the sense of autonomy and equality provided by the idea of moral equality of voice. And for the deliberative ideal to be adequately radicalized, it needs to accommodate the insights that agonists (especially Connolly) have generated about identity/difference.[16] Our realization of this mutual insufficiency can draw us toward imagining a more complex, but still coherent, exemplary scene that illuminates a possible interdependence of agonism and the radicalized deliberative ideal.

It is important at this point to highlight the sharp contrast between what we see as the defensibility of this composite arrangement and a lack in this regard on the part of the one Mouffe proffers. As demonstrated earlier, she begins with a Schmittean ontology that essentially defines politics as a field of immanent conflict between friends and enemies, but then she tries to insert into that fully self-sufficient world democratic norms that remain patently outranked by the prescriptions authorized by its central conceptual and affective dynamics.

The two onto-ethical scripts we seek to bring into engagement can, on the contrary, be compatibly entwined. An actor in our exemplary scene is

---

16. And once one accepts the difficulties for political interaction that arise with the identity/difference dynamic, what Arletta Norval calls the existential significance of "rhetoricality" becomes a crucial matter. We mean this in the sense that breaking through the barriers created and maintained by "othering" will often require more than rational arguments. In this context, Norval develops a perceptive account of Wittgenstein on "aspect change," in short, ways of causing substantial shifts in perception through recourse to all sorts of means, pragmatic and imaginative; Norval, *Aversive Democracy, Inheritance and Originality in the Democratic Tradition* (Cambridge: Cambridge University Press, 2009), 105–140.

aware of the intractability of political life in relation to consensual hopes, an awareness rooted at least partially in an acceptance of the fundamental dynamic of identity/difference in a world of becoming.[17] Agreements will now be expected to be more elusive, temporary, and subject to suspicion about agendas possibly tied to systematically negative perceptions of others that go beyond overt clashes of interest.[18] But, in their ongoing exchange of speech act claims, agents struggling with the identity/difference dynamic are also imagined as experiencing the subtle pull of intuitions about the moral equality of voice. In any given setting, there may be many sources that pull against this one, but actors in the modern world know that this sense of fairness cannot simply be ignored and conclusively sidelined, even if it can often be temporarily avoided or silenced by deception and oppression.[19] How exactly do these intuitions tune one's perception of, and motivation to inhabit, this space of tensional congruence? It

17. Our acceptance of an ontology of becoming is inflected differently than Connolly's in that we make an explicit, if partial, differentiation between the becoming of nonhuman nature and the becoming of humans, the latter occurring partially in the symbolic dimension, including speech claims.

18. Because, in this exemplary scene, there is a greater appreciation of the many ways a given social context may deeply, and often inconspicuously, undermine the prospects of achieving a fair outcome of argumentation, any commitment to equality of voice must now be ready to go beyond the narrow "action-coordinating" orientation to language, embodied in the orthodox deliberative ideal, and frequently have recourse to a "world-disclosing" one; see Stephen K. White, *Political Theory and Postmodernism* (Cambridge: Cambridge University Press, 1991), 19–28. Actors in this scene no longer understand language as having an essentially action-coordinating function; rather, it has a world-disclosing one as well that is of equal importance. The deployment of aesthetic-expressive language, such as rhetoric or narrative, as well as non-linguistic forms of expression, such as silence or artistic performance, can sometimes help begin an evolution of someone's initial hostility or incomprehension in relation to racial, ethnic, religious, or economic "others" toward a greater understanding of, and respect for, their difference.

19. How might a tempered agonist like Honig react to this conception of equality embedded in our exemplary scene? She speaks of not wanting the two impulses of agonism and justice to be posited simply in mute opposition; rather, we must "negotiate" between them. She gestures accordingly toward a politics of "self-overcoming" in which the necessary "closures represented by law, . . . state, community" are continually open to a contestation regarding the "remainders" that resist those closures. We would argue that the intuitions that our exemplary scene embodies help us imagine actors who would be motivated to engage in just such negotiation. See Honig, *Political Theory and the Displacement of Politics* (Ithaca, NY: Cornell University Press, 1993), 13–14, 200–211.

involves the specific way equality of voice is figured in our scene, and we turn now to a fuller elaboration of that.

## II. VIVIFYING EQUALITY OF VOICE AND THE DEMOCRATIC MYTHIC

Crucial to the elucidation of our originary scene is a fuller accounting of the connotations carried by our notion of the moral equality of voice, and how it functions within that scene. Additionally, we need to provide a more adequate explanation of the philosophical status and significance of the scene, especially the way it functions as an animator of a democratic mythic.

The notion of moral equality of voice prioritizes distinctive interpretations of autonomy and equality. Drawing from the familiar connotation of "voice" in political contexts, the concept emphasizes the embodied demand of each for autonomy, manifesting in the appearance of contestation—"resistant voice"—as an actor "turns" on the extant normative context and says "no," demanding justification. Second, drawing from the deliberative tradition, the equal status of all "no-sayers" is given its shape through the force of a preexisting intersubjective background that both carries the social weight of extant normativity and yet remains continually liable to appeals for re-justification through the potential agreement of all speakers who are subject to that norm. The conceptualization of autonomy highlights resistance in political life, and the conceptualization of equality highlights each speakers' shared status as a resister, as well as how that status is attached to an intersubjective context—conceived as the constitutively presupposed background of linguistic interaction that embodies the continual expectation of fair justification for both norms and the resistant claims that confront them.[20]

---

20. Rainer Forst offers a somewhat parallel shift in the Habermasian deliberative tradition of positing the "right to justification" in the face of normative orders as the central concept. But he conceives this as rooted in a Kantian, strong ontology; see *The Right to Justification* (New York: Columbia University Press, 2012). Our overlaps and differences are laid out in

This compound ideal of the moral equality of voice is an abstract universal that we imagine to be embodied in voices. It is situated in *the seam between the felt experience of injustice and resistance to it, on the one hand, and the desire to articulate a more admirable context of justice that could be authorized by our sense of fairness, on the other hand.* Within this exemplary scene, agonism and an otherwise underdetermined sense of associated respect become *intimately and explicitly* aligned with that core sense of fairness. Hence, the scene provides that clear explication of equality and autonomy that was absent in the otherwise admirable examples of tempered agonism considered in Chapter 4.

The world imagined in our originary scene is one in which the resilience of conflict can thus be affirmed, but in such a way that newly emergent voices are always already constrained by an intersubjective context of justification. As noted above, this context embodies not just the closed fields of existing, power-structured normativity but also an implicit, continually open one, available, at least virtually, to all those affected by contested norms. This idealizing force, animated by the expectation of equal voice, allows a moment of questioning to always subtly accompany settled political arrangements. In this context, one can better grasp the significance of Habermas's remark that the collective, "communicative power" imagined in such a scene "is exercised in the manner of a siege" of established institutions.[21] Thus, this portrayal of equality and autonomy possesses a porosity in the sense of unpredictable upwellings of resistant voice that can challenge the appropriateness of any actor's or group's efforts to encompass—or ignore—that voice within some interpretive frame, whether that reflects an account of what a just order demands or agonistic respect implies.

The proto-narrative instantiated in this scene traces a circuit of action, thought, and affect on the part of imagined subjects. In referring to a "circuit," we mean that this narrative does not have a necessary starting and

---

White, "Does Critical Theory Need Strong Foundations?," *Philosophy and Social Criticism* 41 no. 3 (2015): 207–211.

21. Habermas, *Between Facts and Norms*, 486.

ending point, rather the story can be engaged at different points—at the moment of resistance or at the moment of deliberation—depending on the given experience that initiates the actor's reflections.[22] The scene's role is to help actors comprehend themselves and the events they encounter in a certain light, namely, as bearing democratic significance in a fashion that encourages certain sorts of interpretations and actions. This influence occurs on both the conceptual and motivational level, although the motivational force of such a second-order, proto-scene will typically, by itself, not match that of a richer, more specific exemplary scene, at least in the short term. But the proto-scene nevertheless helps us draw out more carefully, over time, how adequately or poorly a specific one reflects democratic qualities.[23]

---

22. As we saw in Chapter 5, there may be good reasons to follow the lead of tempered agonists who assign an initial priority to resistant voice protesting harm. And it seems Habermas does just this (following Adorno) in favoring the primacy of a version of morality that refers "negatively to the damaged life instead of pointing affirmatively to the good life"; Habermas, *Moral Consciousness and Communicative Action*, trans. C. Lenhardt and S. Weber Nicholson with an introduction by T. McCarthy (Cambridge, MA: MIT Press, 1990), 205. For this Adornoian side of Habermas, see Odin Lysaker, "Bodily Felt Integrity: The Anarchic Core of Communication in Jürgen Habermas's Democratic Thought," *Distinktion: Journal of Social Theory* 22, no. 3 (2021): 277–298, DOI: 10.1080/1600910X.2021.2014629.

23. The need for thinking in terms of a democratic mythic that carries this second-order sense of an originary scene of the sort we suggest can be seen in Jason Frank's otherwise excellent work on the aesthetics of democratic imagination. Like us, he wishes to show the importance of myths or "sustaining fictions" for democracy. He surveys a variety of historical examples of eruptive popular gatherings and says we should understand these as manifestations of a "democratic sublime." This interpretive turn to "aesthetic peoplehood" allows us to recover "democracy's dormant or 'sleeping' radicalism." In short, building on multiple, specific exemplary scenes, he fashions what is presented as the central category of democratic imagination. He resists the traditional objection of some that such identification of the spirit of democracy with mass appearances in the streets leads to authoritarian or totalitarian directions. Frank is right to resist this blanket condemnation, but he fails to adequately acknowledge that mass appearances do not always embody democratic values. The populist insurrection of Trump supporters on January 6, 2021, is a prominent case in point. Thus, the popular assemblies that Frank wants to valorize are better understood as phenomena that are underdetermined in terms of their democratic character. It thus might be better to use the more ambivalent term "populist sublime" rather than "democratic sublime" for the phenomena he thematizes in order to emphasize that the democratic character of a specific mass assembly is validated over time through a reflective process in which a given, individual exemplary scene of protest is evaluated by considering it in the fuller light of the democratic mythic we have sketched in tandem with an originary exemplary scene. Seen in this way, eruptive, popular assemblies can retain "their

For purposes of explication, we will cut into our originary scene at the point of an actors' experiencing the generalizing, binding force of norms in contexts of ongoing social life in which we all find ourselves. It is in relation to this constraining force that a further moment arises, namely, that of a particular actor's taking a stand we have called no-saying: essentially turning against the force of some part of the normative context as it bears upon them. This is a crucial moment of freedom or autonomy that links in our imagination everything from Antigone's defiance of Creon, to Martin Luther's "Here I stand, I can do no other," to the Boston Tea Party, to Hegel's master-slave dialectic, to Rosa Parks's refusal to move from her seat on the segregated bus, to the mass demonstrations in Tiananmen Square in 1989, to the appearance of the young black rider in *Rumors of War*. This heroization of common people standing up in protest against the force of dominant normative structures (and their enforcers) resonates deeply in multiple strains of modern political consciousness, and it portrays the first two aspects of a democratic mythic: the sense of every person having the status to both challenge the prevailing interpretations of that norm and to join in resistant action.

But, taken alone, these two characteristics can sometimes be figured in dramatically different ways, not all of them democratic. In short, the presence of these moments in specific scenes does not fully portray all the dimensions of a democratic mythic we identified in the preceding chapter. It is that partialness that tends to incite the critical work of bringing to bear additional interpretive figuration provided by a richer portrayal of a democratic mythic.[24]

---

centrality for the democratic political imagination" without also accepting a claim that they are automatically democratic in character. See Frank, *The Democratic Sublime: On Aesthetics and Popular Assembly* (New York: Oxford University Press, 2021), xii, 2–11, 20, 66, 72, 93–94.

24. Here we return to the issue from Chapter 5 regarding "work on myth" that can take place when a given aesthetic or historical scene only partially represents the core features of a democratic mythic. Our picture of this kind of work on a democratic mythic might seem somewhat removed from Blumenberg's characterization of such work as representing our symbolic efforts to manage existential *Angst*. But he sees Hobbes's political theory as precisely trying to address this fear, only the latter thinks (incorrectly for Blumenberg) this is a problem that can be definitively solved by reason alone. We suggest that all political theory is at least partially an attempt to manage the existential problem of fear of disorder. Thus, work on a *democratic*

The sort of potential problem that may arise here can be seen in the way that common people who step onto the stage of history in protest sometimes interpret themselves as fully sovereign enactors whose significance is apotheosized and reified. In such versions these actors envision themselves as immaculately prior to any structure of social normativity beyond their will. Consider a case of how such reification could unfold. Some on the populist right in the U.S. have attempted to render mythic the insurrection mounted at the Capitol in Washington, DC on January 6, 2021. Republican Congresswoman Marjorie Taylor Greene has argued that the insurrection was exactly in line with the Declaration of Independence.[25] At first glance, the insurrection might indeed seem to manifest characteristics that could embody a democratic mythic. Here one might highlight the insertion of common people into the chambers of the elite in the Capitol during that event. This was crystallized in the much-publicized photo of the man who broke into the office of the speaker of the House of Representatives, Nancy Pelosi, sat in her chair, and put his feet up on her desk.[26] But such acts of substitution alone do not adequately capture the full spirit of a democratic mythic. For that to be persuasively embodied, it is necessary to portray not just an insertion of the resistant, common people's voice into the social world but also a ventilating, chastening moment in which an element of precarity and humility make their presence felt. This third trait of a democratic mythic is philosophically modeled in our scene in the way the character of resistant voice is constitutively tied to two further qualities of how that resistant voice manifests itself. First,

---

mythic in the sense we have elucidated addresses exactly this problem in a distinctive fashion, namely, one that requires all people to participate in deciding how to both define and meet it. See "Translator's Introduction" to Hans Blumenberg, *Work on Myth* (Cambridge, MA: MIT Press, 1985), xiv–xv.

25. Aaron Blake, "Marjorie Taylor Greene Says Jan. 6 Riot Was in Line with the Declaration of Independence," *Washington Post*, October 26, 2021, https://www.washingtonpost.com/politics/2021/10/26/marjorie-taylor-greene-says-jan-6-riot-was-line-with-declaration-independence/.

26. For this image, see Bill Chappell, "Man Who Posed for Photos Sitting at a Desk in Pelosi's Office Has Been Arrested," NPR, January 8, 2021, https://www.npr.org/sections/insurrection-at-the-capitol/2021/01/08/954940681/man-who-posed-for-photos-sitting-at-desk-in-pelosis-office-has-been-arrested/.

people's resistance is embedded in acts and speech that appeal to the judgment of all others potentially affected by their interpretations and actions; and they may, in turn, contest their views, something which deserves at least initial respect. Second, people are also imagined as chastened by an awareness of how their resistance may be animated and distorted by their susceptibility to transforming difference into otherness.

In the case of the insurrectionists, these aspects of a democratic mythic are starkly absent. They styled themselves less as the embodiment of the democratic people and more as militarized fighters, with many clad in body armor or other tactical gear, and with a set strategy, unquestioningly defending their leader's frozen assertions about his being the real president, a claim that simply ignored the larger context of democratic opinion and the facts about the actual election outcome. Congresswomen Greene's claim that the Declaration of Independence justifies the insurrection of January 6, fails to remember that most of that text was devoted to a careful elucidation of the *reasons* for such a declaration. The authors saw that as demanded by "a decent respect to the opinions of mankind." The stance of Greene and her allies also actively disdains any manifestation of self-scrutiny as to whether their interpretations of political situations are crucially dependent on a continual symbolic production of "others" who are held responsible for social ills. These deficits mean that any attempt to dress the January 6th insurrection in the clothing of a democratic mythic will likely end up as a scene that more closely mirrors the militarized certainty carried by fascist crowds that have assaulted democratic polities in the past. For them, any sense of precarity or openness to counter-interpretations is simply viewed with contempt as a deplorable sign of weakness.

This kind of stylization and reification of the moment of agonistic resistance arrests the play of reflection and imagination evoked by a democratic mythic. Such tendencies toward cognitive and affective rigidification are unsettled when that image of resistance is animated by the originary scene we propose. There, agonistic resistance is interpreted through the lens of the moral equality of voice, and that draws the unfolding of the narrative not just to the moment of the resistant no-saying but also to two further moments. First, that claim of wrong or injustice is raised in broader contexts of other voices, equal in status to interpret and judge claims. Second, there is a carefulness not to allow the propensity to transform our difference into otherness to join with the seductions of self-righteousness. The first moment involves the sense of an expanded audience, in which the force of the claim embodied in a particular no-saying is implicitly tied to a broader test of fairness to others, something that extends its challenge beyond the specific claim outward toward any extant normative background or interpretation-resistant, collective fantasy. The second moment involves an openness to more fully listening to and engaging with those who represent differences that fundamentally challenge our interpretive frameworks. Insofar as we open ourselves to these moments of reflection and questioning of motivation, we allow the intuitive attractions of *individual or specific group* autonomy to be seen as always tied intrinsically to *pluralistic democratic* autonomy.

Internalizing these moments moves us beyond *my*—or *my group's*—resistance in a universalizing direction. But this is not reducible to a mandate of universalization pursued as a step in the process of determinate theory construction, as it is in a thinker like Rawls. The generalization portrayed in this movement carries less of a claim to certainty; rather, it opens the issues thematized by no-saying to criteria of fairness and agonistic respect among larger, but never fully determinate, audiences. This pressure to expand the range of concern is best understood not as an abstract mandate but as a work order open to continual reconfiguration.

The foregoing orientation to either openness or reification surrounding questions of identity/difference and "all affected" is frequently apparent in struggles over who is seen as having full membership in the "people" of a given nation. Constraints here, at least in reasonably democratic countries, are typically ones that operate tacitly, below the level of formal legal restrictions. A striking example of how the tendency to reification and "othering" can be loosened by an aesthetic object's deployment of a democratic mythic is apparent in the way Jacques Louis David's classic painting of the Tennis Court Oath (Figure 6.1) was recently reimagined by a 2012 French campaign poster titled "NOUS SOMMES (AUSSI) LA NATION"

**Figure 6.1.** Jacques Louis David, *The Tennis Court Oath*, 1790–94.
*Source:* Wikipedia.

(Figure 6.2).²⁷ The original work helped render mythic that moment in which the resistance of a variety of voices in eighteenth-century France became explicitly the generalized voice of the people, constituting itself in the act of collectively stepping onto the stage of history as democratically autonomous. In the campaign poster version, the scene of the oath and the actors' gestures in the original are repeated, but now the actors represented are present-day French Muslims. This democratic reworking of the national myth of the people was not appreciated by the French authorities; they quickly had the poster removed from Paris Metro stations.²⁸

---

27. We would like to thank Andrew Gates, whose dissertation drew Stephen's attention to this poster; "Reclaiming Rights: Subaltern Praxis and Counterhegemonic Strategy in French and Canadian Social Movement Politics," University of Virginia, 2020.

28. Antoine Blua, "Anti-Islamaphobia Posters Banned from Paris Metro," *Radio Free Europe, Radio Liberty,* November 15, 2012, https://www.rferl.org/a/islam-tolerance-posters-banned-paris-metro-france/24772022.html. A poignant agonistic edge to the opposition's appeal is subtly inserted into the portrayal of the space where the oath takes place. In the poster version, as opposed to David's painting, there is a slight modification of the background. Both take place in a large, relatively dark room. In the original, the room houses a tennis court with windows high above providing light. A strong breeze is blowing the curtains, presumably the wind of

**Figure 6.2.** "WE ARE **ALSO** THE NATION." Election campaign poster by the Collectif Contre l'Islamophobie en France (CCIF), 2012.
*Source:* Héléne Irving and Marwan Muhammad, "It's Not Just a 'Muslim' Thing," *Voices*, Open Society Foundation, December 6, 2012.

This controversy helps shed light on how the French majority's traditional sense of what immaculately displays a democratic mythic can be seen as falling short today, insofar as it fails to embody any sense of uncertainty and humility that are grounded in our originary scene's portrayal of the problem of identity/difference and all-affected. When David's splendid eighteenth-century scene is merely mechanically reproduced in twenty-first-century minds, the democratic, revolutionary "people" of France becomes rigidified, constituted essentially and eternally by a fixed

democratic change. In the poster, there is no wind; in fact, the windows have bars on them, thus evoking how the new historical actors feel imprisoned by what they experience as having been frozen out of the category of "the people," as it has been interpreted through the normalized, majoritarian French invocations of the country's revolutionary past.

set of ethnic and gender characteristics.[29] The way in which a fuller evocation of the democratic mythic can unsettle that sort of reification of the nation is captured powerfully in the election poster. New historical actors have been inserted into the scene of the people voicing resistance.[30] And it is worth highlighting that the "people" here are not violently trashing the seat of a democratic legislature; rather they are being imaginatively expanded through an aesthetic scene of protest that is appealing to the reflective judgment of a wider audience.

Creative reworking of a democratic mythic through portrayals rooted in the intuitions of our originary scene can occur without the sort of striking aesthetic strategies of substitution that we see in the campaign poster or in Wiley's statue. One can generate insight more prosaically simply by initiating trains of reflection on ordinary action situations or

---

29. Historically, this sort of reification of the social-political body has certainly taken even more extreme forms and become fused with mythic scenes like the "Dolchstoss" (stab in the back), according to which the German war effort in World War I supposedly was undermined by internal enemies, especially Jews, and supposedly caused Germany's defeat. Such narratives are also characterized by their being frozen in the sense of becoming immune from critical interpretation. One of the most disturbing trends in U.S. political life during the Trump era has been the degree to which the political right has been willing to invest in this sort of antidemocratic myth making, most notably the lie that the 2020 election was "stolen."

30. This example shows how the relationship between a democratic mythic and national myths can work to leaven the degree to which the latter are sometimes heavily tied to distortions of reality that cloak injustice. The full range of issues surrounding democracy and national myths is a complex one that cannot be fully treated here. A useful analysis of the complexities is Arash Abizadeh, "Historical Truth, National Myths and Liberal Democracy: On the Coherence of Liberal Nationalism," *The Journal of Political Philosophy* 12, no. 3 (2004): 291–313. The general approach we take is that when national myths are entangled with truth claims denying significant injustices, a healthy democratic mythic works, over time, to move those myths away from that entanglement. In some cases, this process may largely dissolve those myths, as we are seeing, for example, with the myth of the Lost Cause of the Confederacy. In other cases, the process may operate to maintain the symbolic power of certain mythic formations while also drawing people away from interpretations that passed over gross injustices. For example, for decades after World War II, the story of that struggle was related to the American people as a completely unblemished one. But increasingly in recent years, the horrendous story of Japanese-American internment has been brought into the foreground. We see this in the widely acclaimed multipart, 2007, TV series on America's experience in World War II by Ken Burns and Lynn Novick. It presented the conflict as a story of American greatness while unblinkingly covering the internment. The overall point is that myths of national unity can and should be leavened by a democratic mythic, so that they do not function as instruments that obscure injustice.

specific exemplary scenes through direct recourse to the conceptual, aesthetic, and affective insights animated by the originary scene. Consider again, how specific scenes like the Boston Tea Party and the Minutemen have been drawn upon to motivate and justify political resistance in recent years. As we noted above, they have been deployed both in ways that are democratic, as well as in ways that are of questionable democratic character, especially in the cases of right-wing populist groups, such as the recent one that called itself simply the "Tea Party," as well as the so-called militia movement in the U.S. that styles itself as a grassroots gathering and arming of revolutionary patriots.[31] These groups draw precisely—and only—on the interpretation they prefer from their favored scenes, ignoring actual history and repressing any evidence that supports alternative interpretations. The scenes are reified to fit tightly with certain ideological criteria, thereby restricting the way our reflection and imagination might reconstrue our recollection of these events.

For someone not already fully invested in such frozen scene-scapes, recourse to the originary scene we have sketched might help foster some suspicion regarding the hermeneutical lockdown this reification involves. For example, one might look more carefully at the particulars of the actual historical episode that came to be called the Boston Tea Party. The participants were asserting the broadly shared feeling of colonists that the British government was tyrannically denying them the rights of a free people. The contemporary Tea Party and militia movement have appropriated this gesture by baldly announcing that the American government is just an updated version of that tyranny. Any questioning of the aptness of that description, as well as their claim to be the authentic embodiment of the people, is simply brushed aside.

This deployment of the historical event in Boston as the animator and justifier of a claim to speak in the name of the people opens up a range of questions that contemporary populists avidly avoid. Those who dumped the tea in 1773 were disguised as Native American Mohawks.

---

31. See, e.g., David Niewert, *Alt-America: The Rise of the Radical Right in the Age of Trump* (London and New York: Verso Books, 2017).

Who, then, was really speaking and acting for the people in this scene? One intention behind that disguise was to show that the participants were no longer English but true Americans who were ferociously attached to their freedom.[32] But the rebels thereby entangled themselves in a rather conflicted self-image, unintentionally raising the question: Who, indeed, were the true American people, the white colonists or the Mohawks, or both? The participants claimed to represent the general category of the people while categorically restricting it to include only white male inhabitants. The groups who now drape themselves in this mythic figuration are unintentionally exposing the old contradictions and yet failing to confront the fact that these cannot plausibly be ignored today. To persist in valorizing such selectively frozen scene-scapes, to abide no uncertainty or ambivalence about historical scenes of patriotic purity, is to move increasingly, even if unintentionally, onto the terrain of undemocratic mythics.

## III. OBJECTIONS

Although we have emphasized that our exemplary scene of communicative democracy is not to be construed as leading to a determinate theory of justice, it still has a core of moral values. This core is accorded a status that is fixed and fundamental in a certain sense, even if this constraint allows wide latitude as to the range of what is justifiable regarding the shape of collective actions, institutions, or policies. In short, our originary scene, like any other possible one, enacts certain restrictions of the imagination and judgment and thus establishes its own closures, a fact that will be flagged by at least some agonists. They have encouraged us to be suspicious of abstract universals, since they can function in ways that misperceive and denigrate difference. This caution is well taken. But at the same time, as we showed in Chapter 4, agonists themselves either quietly

---

32. For the full range of "mixed meanings" carried by the disguise, see Benjamin L. Carp, *Defiance of the Patriots: The Boston Tea Party and the Making of America* (New Haven: Yale University Press, 2010), 141–160.

affirm, but fail to fully explicate, the value of certain universals, namely equality and autonomy (Connolly and Honig); or fulsomely affirm them but provide no coherent account of how that affirmation aligns with their prior, primary commitment to a world defined essentially in terms of friends and enemies (Mouffe).

We affirm explicitly a particular interpretation of autonomy and equality by constituting their sense in the context of an originary scene. Tempered agonists, as we argued earlier, do pursue the admirable goal of keeping "the agon open" or fair, but they achieve this through a deus ex machina gesture that tacitly installs the value of an equal openness to resistance from all voices.[33] The aim of our scene is to provide a moral and mythic infrastructure that can illuminate more fully the significance of that value.

How should we weigh the dangers associated with the role of this core universal of moral equality of voice as it appears in our proposed scene? Here we would note again that affirming this value and embedding it in an exemplary scene does not give rise to a determinate theory of justice but rather helps minimize the potential closures that agonists have typically associated with such universals. Of course, some will continue to worry that any ethical universal will unacceptably occlude difference. No one has made this point more vividly than Theodor Adorno.[34] For him, all thinking with universal concepts homogenizes the diversity of life and thus has a kind of illicit, reductive character. It thus participates in a "dialectic of enlightenment," whereby what appears to be rational and progressive morphs into a vehicle of unreason and regression, transforming dreams of ever-increasing control of the world into nightmares.[35] Adorno's response to this threat is to promote more purely aesthetic ways of encountering difference in the world.[36] He hopes to find modes of tending to nature, the

---

33. Honig, *Political Theory and the Displacement of Politics*, 33–34.

34. Theodor Adorno, *Negative Dialectics*, trans. E. B. Ashton (New York: Continuum, 1973).

35. Max Horkheimer and Theodor Adorno, *Dialectic of Enlightenment: Philosophical Fragments*, ed. Gunzelin Schmid Noerr and trans. Edmund Jephcott (Stanford, CA: Stanford University Press, 2002).

36. Adorno, *Negative Dialectics*.

world, and the human other in ways that do not subsume them wholesale in the category of potentially controllable stuff.

Our conception of communicative democracy embodies significant gestures in this direction, even if they would not satisfy Adorno.[37] These include the "all-affected" requirement, according to which our sense of community rightness must persistently remain open to potential disruption by initially excluded voices. The effect of that rule is deepened and radically extended by our embrace of the need to continually challenge the tendency to transform difference into otherness; in short, the need for the agonistic respect that we incorporated from the tempered agonism of Connolly. And, finally, by accepting the democratic mythic as inextricably entangled with our reasoned defenses of democratic life we vivify the precarity of all our moral-political constructs and our unending obligation as democratic citizens to actively, but critically, support them.

Adorno's suggestions about more purely aesthetic ways of encountering difference should always be allowed to resonate as a leavening influence on our perception and reflection. But our wager is that the dangers of our exemplary scene and the universal moral equality of voice it models are relatively minimal, given how it encompasses various gestures toward its own unsettling. When that is weighed against alternatives that draw pretty much exclusively on aesthetically oriented modes of engaging difference, with only allusive references to a moral core, it seems to us that the costs of our option are not, on balance, excessive.

If one possible danger carried by our approach emerges around the problem of abstract universals in general, a second one attaches to the character of the specific universal we are singling out for affirmation: the shared human status as language creatures. Traditionally, language has functioned both as a marker of our right of dominion over nonhuman nature and as a cardinal characteristic that is presumed in the construction

---

37. We don't claim that these gestures "solve" the problem Horkheimer and Adorno highlighted in the *Dialectic of Enlightenment*; to conclude that would be to presume that one had not really comprehended the problem in its fullness.

of our political ideals. Over the last few decades, there has been a powerful turn away from highlighting this capacity on the grounds that it blinds us to harms and injustices, including to nonhuman nature, that we need to take more seriously. These are significant concerns, but sometimes they can be expressed in ways that fail to appreciate the possible resilience of more nuanced appeals to language. We would argue that our approach constitutes such an appeal. Consider two ways we might respond to challenges potentially evoked by our prioritization of language.

First, there is the problem of dominating nonhuman nature. Against that, we would argue that by relinquishing any strong-ontological foundation that marks us as superior beings in the world from the start, we have perhaps made it easier to imagine a future of progressively learning how to affirm our language capacity differently than in the past. In this vein, we do better not to worry exclusively about the distance between humans and nonhuman species in relation to their capacity for language; clearly, we are finding that the distance is less than we thought in the past. But the reality, here and now, is that humans are the only creatures who can collectively interpret the world and redirect its possible course, both human and nonhuman, and thus we have a default responsibility for the path we take into the future—whether we try to avoid this burden or not. This way of seeing things gives us a certain specialness, but it is a political specialness, in which any sense of privileged status is shadowed by the weight of the obligation inextricably attached to it.[38] For younger generations facing the challenge of climate change, imagining this shift of perspective requires far less of a leap of imagination than it did for earlier generations. Moreover, there is no reason we cannot imagine a democratic proto-narrative such as ours being interwoven with another proto-narrative that

---

38. Here we overlap to a degree with George Kateb on how to think about putting an emphasis on language in our thinking about human dignity, so that one both centers and decenters us in the world; *Human Dignity* (Cambridge, MA: Harvard University Press, 2011), 132–171. See also the excellent treatment of the theme of language in this context in Joshua Dienstag, "Dignity, Difference and the Representation of Nature," *Political Theory* 49 no. 4 (Aug. 2021): 613–636.

stages all inhabitants of the earth as facing a common threat of environmental crisis.[39]

Second, one can argue that there are human characteristics other than language capacity that should be accorded a central status. As we saw in Chapter 5, Butler provides an apt example of this when she puts our bodily and psychic vulnerability, and the need to respond to them, at the core of her originary scene.[40] As we just indicated, there is nothing wrong with affirming additional exemplary scenes that may highlight one or another crucial human quality or moral source and their possible orienting roles. But if we are right, such originary scenes cannot simply displace the one we have sketched, at least if we affirm democratic processes as being at the center of public life. This preeminence of our scene is rooted finally in the notion that the crucial values that other scenes might prioritize must present themselves *as candidates* for animating democratic publics. What this means is simply that those values need to be publicly interpreted and justified. In the case of vulnerability, this means that democratic consideration, fleshed out through deliberation and contestation, has to determine exactly what we mean by vulnerability and how it should align with other basic values if it is to take a more prominent position in the structuring of public policy. In short, something like a commitment to the moral equality of voice must always provide part of the underlying structure of justification for democratic political commitments and policies related to other important values, such as vulnerability.

---

39. On the idea of such a planetary proto-narrative, see Rogers M. Smith, *Stories of Peoplehood: The Politics and Morals of Political Membership* (Cambridge: Cambridge University Press, 2003), 168–169.

40. Vulnerability, as shown earlier, is not neglected in our scene, but it does not have the singular prominence that Butler gives it.

**7**

# Conclusion

### The Communicative Model of Democracy

Democracy today faces both theoretical and practical problems. Theoretically, there has been a lack of clarity on how to understand the interconnectedness of what we call the two faces of democracy: one emphasizing reason, civility and discussion, and the other emphasizing conflict, protest, and resistance. Each seems to be intuitively part of what is essential to democratic life, yet there is less certainty about exactly how they are bound together. This impasse is displayed in the conflict between the two leading theoretical approaches to democracy, the deliberative and agonistic. Our volume has offered a framework that illuminates why the two do not need to understand themselves, as is often the case, to be aligned in unrelenting opposition. Still, while we seek to get beyond sheer opposition, we maintain that our effort should not be understood as analogous with a peace negotiation between enemies, where the negotiator pragmatically strives to identify common ground. Rather we have developed a communicative model of democracy that decenters both contending perspectives and yet claims to embody their most admirable insights.

The elaboration of this model also helps address a pressing practical problem facing democrats today. The recent emergence of right-wing populism in various countries presents a striking challenge. Many within the populist camp affirm variants of racism and ethno-nationalism that depart markedly from democratic ideals. Others drawn to this movement may not explicitly accept these views or clearly understand how deeply they cut against such ideals. Defenders of democracy who seek to develop coalitions that can both contest and effectively engage this variegated group need to proceed in a way that does not fulfill the populists' own image of their enemies as either leftist pure agonists or chattering deliberative idealists who will melt under the pressure of political confrontation. Our account of the moral core of democracy can help provide a better grounding for how democrats should think and act in this context.

Here it is useful to review the claims we have made about how our approach offers a more persuasive orientation to the present challenges than either deliberative or agonistic ones offer on their own.

## I. DECENTERING DELIBERATION

In Chapter 2, we presented the deliberative model of democracy both as it emerged in the last decade of the twentieth century and as it evolved since. As we have shown, defenders of the deliberative model have offered a variety of responses to concerns over what is seen as the deliberative ideal's elusive and exclusive nature. For example, the deliberative systems approach expanded the model by showing how even non-deliberative and even anti-deliberative acts could contribute to the deliberative quality of a political system. Others, however, in assessing the current state of deliberative democratic theory, have argued that these adaptations have so expanded and distorted the deliberative ideal as to render it useless. In other words, as we showed in Chapters 2 and 3, efforts to decenter deliberative democracy are well under way in democratic theory. If with their systems approach to deliberative democracy, Mansbridge et al. removed the practice of deliberation from pride of place, then a recent emphasis on "problem-based" approaches to democratic theory has completed the demotion.

In current debates among deliberativists, however, those who emphasize the limits of deliberation (e.g., Warren) extend those further such that they imply the exhaustion of the deliberative model as a whole. To the extent that the normative commitments of the deliberative model point to a practice that is not, in fact, ideal, then what is the value of those normative commitments in the first place?

In Chapter 3, we made the case for maintaining key normative commitments of the deliberative model while decentering the practice of deliberation *within* that model. We did this by reinterpreting the normative value of the deliberative model, showing that its normative commitments do not, in fact, support a single-minded pursuit of the practice of deliberation. Instead, the key contribution of the deliberative model is that it provides an account of how to understand the concept of democracy itself within contexts of deep difference and disagreement. By adopting a consciously decentered approach to the practice of deliberation within the model, we can consider all the practices that bear on the democratic quality of a collective decision, including voting and resisting, without discarding or weakening the valuable standards that derive from the normative core of the model.

How might deliberativists respond to our call to decenter the primacy originally placed on the practice of deliberation? For those who study deliberation from an empirical perspective, the contributions we've made here may seem so abstract as not to apply to their research. How should someone studying deliberative mini-publics in practice, for example, think about what we've said about the need for both faces of democracy? It could be that these scholars simply reframe their work on deliberation, noting that it is just one practice among several that are relevant for democracy. We think, however, that such a simple response would be a mistake. Recognizing the common normative core of the two faces of democracy provides important insights for democratic practice. And so, we maintain that our investigation into the importance of both faces of democracy could help reshape even the empirical study of deliberation. For example, in order to take seriously the tension and congruence of these two faces, we might have to reconsider certain assumptions regarding how best to design deliberative forums. Our work, as Young's before us, might even point to the value of designing deliberative procedures so that they allow for disruptions and allow people to speak out of turn, for example.[1] As one of us (Molly) has shown, however, simply allowing disruptive speech in deliberation will not ensure the relevant people will listen.[2] Ultimately, further work and creative thinking may be required if empirical work relating to discrete deliberative forums is to account adequately for both faces of democracy.

What about those normative theorists, including Owen and Smith and Warren, for example, who have called for dropping the "deliberative" emphasis in democratic theory? How might they respond to our calls to decenter deliberation while retaining key normative commitments of the deliberative model, including a commitment to the moral equality of voice? We imagine that they might be somewhat sympathetic to our aims here. A major part of what we take to be animating Warren's "problem-based approach" is a desire to move democratic theory beyond the unproductive turf wars that result from unnecessarily rigid "model-based" thinking. In highlighting the tensional congruence between these various ways of imagining democracy, we show that, while it's not as simple as moving past the deliberative-agonistic divide, there are more productive "cross-model" conversations to be had, including the one we have had in this volume.

## II. DECENTERING AGONISM

Turning now to our effort to decenter agonism, Chapter 4 showed that an agonism grounded in Schmitt's ontology of politics has a fatal propensity to draw its adherents toward a stance that corrodes democratic norms. This "imperializing" form of agonism was contrasted with "tempered" ones, offered by Connolly and Honig, which offer admirable modes of conceiving spirited political contestation that envision themselves to be

---

1. Iris Marion Young, *Inclusion and Democracy* (Oxford: Oxford University Press, 2000), 57.

2. Mary F. Scudder, *Beyond Empathy and Inclusion: The Challenge of Listening in Democratic Deliberation* (New York: Oxford University Press, 2020), 34.

in fundamental accord with core democratic values. But, as we showed, although these thinkers invoke at different points the orienting force of autonomy and equality in relation to agonism, they have not sufficiently elaborated the character and status of these values. Our articulation of an originary exemplary scene embodying the idea of moral equality of voice is meant to address that shortcoming and, in doing so, illuminate how agonism needs to open itself to some of the deliberativists' insights.

How will agonists respond to our effort to decenter some of their fundamental claims? It seems likely that there be will greater skepticism expressed here than from deliberativists faced with a comparable push to reconceptualize. Our efforts to see a certain interconnectedness between the two perspectives will be taken by some agonists to be nothing more than a wholesale attempt to disempower the force of their insights. In one sense, this suspicion is perfectly welcome and not at odds with our perspective. In today's setting, with its challenges of right-wing populism as well as social and racial injustice, a given political actor may have good reasons to start with, and persist in, prioritizing resistant political interaction. There is nothing in the orienting force of our originary exemplary scene that necessarily opposes such a stance. But, over time and across wide-ranging situations, pure agonistic reactions will frequently appear inadequate in the face of the full spectrum of challenges faced. The quick stylizing of opponents as enemies does not eliminate the difficulties of, for example, managing one's own internal group organization and coalition building with groups that have similar or overlapping objectives. Nor does it eliminate the potential need to rethink one's initial judgment of at least some of one's adversaries. In relation to these challenges, one has to have recourse to arguments about which stances are more democratic than others, and this will have to draw on some basic sources of insight. At that point, our originary scene would claim to provide the best source of a democratic orientation, even if it is only a rough one.

In relation to lingering agonist suspicions regarding our perspective, it is important to emphasize that what might appear to be a somewhat reconciliatory framing of political interaction can nevertheless also constitute an emerging justification for an eventual stance of vehement confrontation and resistance. Such a shift can be justified when one is facing actors who manifest an increasingly clear antidemocratic character. Crucial here is the character of the ethos with which one approaches a decision to increase one's level of contestation. What we mean is that there is more than one way to confront those who confidently infuse a friend-enemy orientation into every political setting. One is by simply adopting an agonism that confidently matches the sovereign clarity and ironclad certainty of the populist right, only now we reverse the direction of the "enemy" status. But the articulation of a tempered agonism embodied within the communicative model of democracy points to a different strategy, one that cultivates a refusal to affirm patterns of reaction that may lead, even if unintentionally, to a premature participation in the corrosion of democratic norms. The key issue involves clarifying the sorts of reflections that should condition one's moving toward an increasingly agonistic stance.[3]

Our approach does not depend on a full, determinate theory of a just democratic order, against the background of which we might clearly delineate who constitutes an antidemocratic threat. Rather we tie our thinking to an originary exemplary scene that provides what is only an imprecise orientation to our political actions and institutions. This orientation embodies an agonistic dimension, but its activation does not spring, as imperializing agonists believe, from a sovereign decision delineating the world into friends and enemies. Instead, our recourse to the cognitive and aesthetic-affective sources provided by the exemplary scene draws us into a set of reflections that condition agonistic stances toward political opponents. As we have shown, these reflections will include, first, concerns about the inevitable susceptibility of our thinking to identity/difference dynamics that can distort our perceptions of the identities of

---

3. Some work on the issue of responding to hate speech nicely illustrates the complexity of contending democratically with those who oppose you, requiring separation of types of speakers/hearers and modes of responding, with some situations calling for more discursive responses and others for more agonistic ones. See Corrado Fumagalli, "Counterspeech and Ordinary Citizens: How? When?," *Political Theory* 49, no. 6 (Dec. 2021): 1021–1047. It is just such flexibility and complexity that would find justification from the moral core of our communicative model.

others we engage in political life and, second, concerns about multiple ways we may fall short in including the input (actual or virtual) of all-affected by contested normative arrangements. When these concerns are embraced seriously, the force of a third one embodied in a democratic ethos also becomes clear: we cannot, once and for all, eliminate precarity and ambivalence from our stances and thus the need for a subtle, abiding political humility. But it is crucial to highlight that this aspect of a democratic bearing, with its persistent respect for equality of voice, does not amount to a pusillanimous indecisiveness or a willingness to back away from political contest. Rather it simply means that judgments in politics should develop an increasingly antagonistic character only in reaction to one's opponents' *progressively defining themselves* as enemies of democracy by speech and action that fail to honor the full sense of the moral equality of voice. In effect, they read themselves out of the script of a possible democratic "we."

The orientation we affirm thus requires a certain ethical-political self-discipline, exercised over time, in how one reacts to political engagement with opponents. The populist right is also attracted to self-discipline, but its phenomenology is quite different. For them, discipline only comes into play after one has identified one's enemies. This existential identification is a decision that provides great cognitive and emotional solace, opening into a soothing sense of self-righteousness and non-precarity around which adherents can mobilize an army of metaphors of military discipline.

In the Introduction, we referenced two sorts of classic moments of democratic politics, the two faces. Our evocation of these moments was a way of appealing to the common intuitions of a democratic "we." But the appeal to this "we" always remains an aspirational one that hopes to better weave—or reweave—together a loose community of those who share at least some elements of an originary exemplary scene. When, however, some political actors give repeated and thus increasingly clear evidence of rejecting the animating influence of that scene, they thereby progressively justify our adoption of increasingly vehement modes of opposition to them. In short, our perspective does not deny the significance of agonism but infuses it with the necessity of also continually engaging in certain modes of ethical-political cultivation rooted in the core commitments of democracy itself.[4]

But if we should always be ready to walk back from increased agonistic contestation, we also need to admit that the democratic significance of agonism is not always adequately appreciated when that perspective is taken to be merely a minor adjunct to an otherwise deliberative orientation. A tempered agonism, when comprehended as a core component of an originary scene, helps vivify awareness of the underlying twofold character of the democratic imagination that must always animate public life, something that can be forgotten when too much faith is invested in narrow interpretations of either deliberation or agonism.

Hannah Arendt's work is useful for highlighting this point. She suggests that our ontologies of politics will always participate in a subtle orientation either toward death or toward life. The latter emerges for her only when a view of politics emphasizes the "natality" of speech and action, by which she means only when one both affirms the precarity and promise of speech in public contexts suffused with plural perspectives and tries to generate by persuasion the phenomenon of democratic power.[5] When political theory forgets this, it expresses a subtle political death wish: a desire for the quietude of a political life beyond pluralism and contentiousness.

We think our efforts to envision a perspective that allows both faces of democracy to express themselves moves in the general direction Arendt affirms. What we mean here is that when either face, the deliberative or agonistic, is affirmed in a one-sided fashion that implies a failure to fully

---

4. Connolly has articulated his political ontology with this issue of imagining the world as continually throwing up difference and urging an attitude of generosity as a way in which we honor that character of the world with a mimetic attitude. Although the sort of cultivation being emphasized here is one of restraint that resists sliding quickly into a stance of full-bore agonism, a democratic citizen should also be open to the possibility of more directly generous engagements with others. As Connolly has emphasized under the heading of "presumptive generosity," this kind of orientation would reflect a fuller acknowledgment of our mortality and acceptance of being as becoming. A sense of how this might be part of a broader democratic ethos is explored in Stephen K. White, *A Democratic Bearing: Admirable Citizens, Uneven Justice, and Critical Theory* (Cambridge: Cambridge University Press, 2017), 68–76.

5. Hannah Arendt, *The Human Condition*, with an introduction by Margaret Canovan (Chicago and London: University of Chicago Press, 1998), esp. 243–247.

acknowledge the challenges of political life: a tacit turning away from the difficulty of working in the context of a continual plurality of contending voices. By itself, the deliberative face carries the danger of persistently, if implicitly, expecting too much reduction of that contention, ardently hoping to clear up the persistent cacophony of different voices, thereby betraying an implicit wish for a peace that really comes only with a withdrawal from public life. The agonistic face, when it manifests in what we have called the imperial variant, carries a similar danger, even though, at first glance, it seems rather to extol the continual tumult of political contestation. That extolling of liveliness, however, is haunted by a different wish because the self behind this face ultimately seeks an elimination of "enemies" and thus implicitly a blissful immersion in a placid community of "friends." Its secret desire is thus finally the perpetual peace of the graveyard.

The implicit wish for this peace beyond politics thus haunts both faces when they are embraced in a one-sided way. But when we imagine them both animated by our reading of an originary scene of democratic life, that recurrent human wish is continually open to interruption and leavening. This reciprocal vivifying of the two faces is what we must affirm if our democratic life is to effectively engage the multiple challenges of the future.

# BIBLIOGRAPHY

Abizadeh, Arash. "Does Collective Identity Presuppose an Other? On the Alleged Incoherence of Global Solidarity." *American Political Science Review* 99, no. 1 (Feb. 2005): 45–60.

Abizadeh, Arash. "Historical Truth, National Myths and Liberal Democracy: On the Coherence of Liberal Nationalism." *The Journal of Political Philosophy* 12, no. 3 (2004): 291–313.

Adorno, Theodor. *Negative Dialectics*. Translated by E. B. Ashton. New York: Continuum, 1973.

Allen, Amy. *The Politics of Our Selves: Power, Autonomy, and Gender in Contemporary Critical Theory*. New York: Columbia University Press, 2008.

Arendt, Hannah. *The Human Condition*. Chicago: University of Chicago Press, 2013.

Bächtiger, André, and Dominik Hangartner. "When Deliberative Theory Meets Empirical Political Science: Theoretical and Methodological Challenges in Political Deliberation." *Political Studies* 58, no. 4 (2010): 609–629.

Bächtiger, André, and John Parkinson. *Mapping and Measuring Deliberation: Towards a New Deliberative Quality*. Oxford: Oxford University Press, 2019.

Benhabib, Seyla, ed. *Democracy and Difference: Contesting the Boundaries of the Political*. Princeton: Princeton University Press, 1996.

Benhabib, Seyla. "Habermas's New *Phenomenology of Spirit*: Two centuries after Hegel." *Constellations* 28, no. 1 (2021): 33–44.

Benhabib, Seyla. "Toward a Deliberative Model of Democratic Legitimacy." In *Democracy and Difference: Contesting the Boundaries of the Political*, edited by Seyla Benhabib, 67–94. Princeton, NJ: Princeton University Press, 1996.

Blake, Aaron. "Marjorie Taylor Greene Says Jan. 6 Riot Was in Line with the Declaration of Independence." *Washington Post*, October 26, 2021. https://www.washingtonpost.com/politics/2021/10/26/marjorie-taylor-greene-says-jan-6-riot-was-line-with-declaration-independence/.

Blua, Antoine. "Anti-Islamaphobia Posters Banned from Paris Metro." *Radio Free Europe, Radio Liberty*, November 15, 2012. https://www.rferl.org/a/islam-tolerance-posters-banned-paris-metro-france/24772022.html.

Blumenberg, Hans. *Work on Myth*. Cambridge, MA: MIT Press, 1985.
Bottici, Chiara. *A Philosophy of Political Myth*. Cambridge: Cambridge University Press, 2007.
Burns, Alexander, and Jonathan Martin. "Trump Onslaught Against Biden Falls Short of a Breakthrough." *New York Times*, November 7, 2020. https://www.nytimes.com/2020/09/12/us/politics/biden-trump-poll-wisconsin-minnesota.html.
Butler, Judith. *Antigone's Claim: Kinship Between Life and Death*. New York: Columbia University Press, 2000.
Butler, Judith. *The Force of Nonviolence: An Ethico-Political Bind*. London and New York: Verso, 2020.
Butler, Judith. *Notes Toward a Performative Theory of Assembly*. Cambridge, MA: Harvard University Press, 2015.
Capps, Kriston. "Kehinde Wiley's Anti-Confederate Memorial." *The New Yorker*, December 24, 2019. https://www.newyorker.com/culture/culture-desk/kehinde-wileys-anti-confederate-memorial.
Carp, Benjamin L. *Defiance of the Patriots: The Boston Tea Party and the Making of America*. New Haven: Yale University Press, 2010.
Chambers, Simone. "Deliberative Democratic Theory." *Annual Review of Political Science* 6, no. 1 (2003): 307–326.
Chambers, Simone. *Reasonable Democracy: Jürgen Habermas and the Politics of Discourse*. Ithaca, NY: Cornell University Press, 1996.
Chambers, Simone. "Rhetoric and the Public Sphere: Has Deliberative Democracy Abandoned Mass Democracy?" *Political Theory* 37, no. 3 (2009): 323–350.
Chappell, Bill. "Man Who Posed for Photos Sitting at a Desk in Pelosi's Office Has Been Arrested." NPR, January 8, 2021. https://www.npr.org/sections/insurrection-at-the-capitol/2021/01/08/954940681/man-who-posed-for-photos-sitting-at-desk-in-pelosis-office-has-been-arrested/.
Cohen, Joshua. "Deliberation and Democratic Legitimacy." In *The Good Polity: Normative Analysis of the State*, edited by Alan Hamlin and Philip Petit, 17–34. Oxford: Basil Blackwell, 1989.
Connolly, William. *Aspirational Fascism: The Struggle for Multifaceted Democracy Under Trumpism*. Minneapolis: University of Minnesota Press, 2017.
Connolly, William. *The Augustinian Imperative: A Reflection on the Politics of Morality*. Newbury Park, London, and New Delhi: SAGE, 1993.
Connolly, William. *The Ethos of Pluralization*. Minneapolis: University of Minnesota Press, 1995.
Connolly, William. *Identity\Difference: Democratic Negotiations of Political Paradox*. 2nd rev. ed. Ithaca, NY and London: Cornell University Press, 1991; University of Minnesota Press, 2001.
Connolly, William. *A World of Becoming*. Durham and London: Duke University Press, 2011.
Coppedge, Michael, John Gerring, David Altman, Michael Bernhard, Steven Fish, Allen Hicken, and Matthew Kroenig, et al. "Conceptualizing and Measuring Democracy: A New Approach." *Perspectives on Politics* 9, no. 2 (2011): 247–267.

Derrida, Jacques. *The Politics of Friendship*. Translated by G. Collins. London and New York: Verso, 1997.

Dienstag, Joshua. "Dignity, Difference and the Representation of Nature." *Political Theory* 49, no. 4 (2021): 613–636.

Dryzek, John S. *Foundations and Frontiers of Deliberative Governance*. Oxford: Oxford University Press, 2010.

Ercan, Selen A., and Andre Bächtiger. "Deliberative Democracy: Taking Stock and Looking Ahead." *Democratic Theory* 6, no. 1 (2019): 97–110.

Farrar, Cynthia. *The Origins of Democratic Thinking: The Invention of Politics in Classical Athens*. Cambridge: Cambridge University Press, 1988.

Fishkin, James, Alice Siu, Larry Diamond, and Norman Bradburn. "Is Deliberation an Antidote to Extreme Partisan Polarization? Reflections on 'America in One Room.'" *American Political Science Review* 115, no. 4 (2021): 1464–1481.

Forst, Rainer. *The Right to Justification: Elements of a Constructivist Theory of Justice*. New York: Columbia University Press, 2012.

Frank, Jason. *The Democratic Sublime: On Aesthetics and Popular Assembly*. New York: Oxford University Press, 2021.

Fumagalli, Corrado. "Counterspeech and Ordinary Citizens: How? When?" *Political Theory* 49, no. 6 (2021): 1021–1047.

Fung, Archon. "Deliberation Before the Revolution: Toward an Ethics of Deliberative Democracy in an Unjust World." *Political Theory* 33, no. 3 (2005): 397–419.

Gates, Andrew. "Reclaiming Rights: Subaltern Praxis and Counterhegemonic Strategy in French and Canadian Social Movement Politics." PhD diss., University of Virginia, 2020.

Geuss, Raymond. *Philosophy and Real Politics*. Princeton: Princeton University Press, 2008.

Ginsburg, Benjamin L. "My Party Is Destroying Itself on the Altar of Trump." *Washington Post*, November 1, 2020, https://www.washingtonpost.com/opinions/2020/11/01/ben-ginsberg-voter-suppression-republicans/.

Glover, Robert. "Games Without Frontiers? Democratic Engagement, Agonistic Pluralism and the Question of Exclusion." *Philosophy and Social Criticism* 38, no. 1 (2012): 81–104.

Goodin, Robert. "If Deliberation Is Everything, Maybe It's Nothing." In *The Oxford Handbook of Deliberative Democracy*, edited by Andre Bächtiger, John S. Dryzek, Jane Mansbridge, and Mark Warren, 883–889. Oxford: Oxford University Press, 2018.

Goodin, Robert. *Reflective Democracy*. Oxford: Oxford University Press, 2003.

Goodin, Robert. "Sequencing Deliberative Moments," *Acta Politica* 40, no. 2 (2005): 182–196.

Gormley, Steven. *Deliberative Theory and Deconstruction: A Democratic Venture*. Edinburgh: Edinburgh University Press, 2022.

Gutmann, Amy, and Dennis Thompson. *Why Deliberative Democracy?* Princeton: Princeton University Press, 2004.

Habermas, Jürgen. *Auch Eine Geschichte der Philosophie. Band 2: Vernünftige Freiheit: Spurren des Diskurses über Glauben und Wissen*. Frankfurt: Suhrkamp, 2019.

Habermas, Jürgen. *Between Facts and Norms: Contributions to a Discourse Theory of Law and Democracy*. Cambridge, MA: MIT Press, 1996.

Habermas, Jürgen. "Commentary on Cristina Lafont, *Democracy Without Shortcuts*." *Journal of Deliberative Democracy* 16, no. 2 (2020): 5–10.

Habermas, Jürgen. *Communication and the Evolution of Society*. Boston: Beacon Press, 1979.

Habermas, Jürgen. *Legitimation Crisis*. Boston: Beacon Press, 1975.

Habermas, Jürgen. *Moral Consciousness and Communicative Action*. Translated by C. Lenhardt and S. Weber Nicholson with an introduction by T. McCarthy. Cambridge, MA: MIT Press, 1990.

Habermas, Jürgen. *The Philosophical Discourse of Modernity: Twelve Lectures*. Translated by Frederick Lawrence. Cambridge, MA: MIT Press, 1987.

Habermas, Jürgen. "Reconciliation Through the Public Use of Reason: Remarks on John Rawls's Political Liberalism." *Habermas and Rawls: Disputing the Political* 92, no. 3 (1995): 109–131.

Habermas, Jürgen. *The Theory of Communicative Action*. Vol. 1. *Reason and the Rationalization of Society*. Translated by Thomas McCarthy. Boston: Beacon Press, 1984.

Habermas, Jürgen. "Three Normative Models of Democracy." *Constellations* 1, no. 1 (1994): 1–10.

Honig, Bonnie. "12 Angry Men: Care for the Agon and the Varieties of Masculine Experience." *Theory & Event* 22, no. 3 (July 2019): 701–716.

Honig, Bonnie. *Antigone Interrupted*. Cambridge: Cambridge University Press, 2013.

Honig, Bonnie. *Democracy and the Foreigner*. Princeton: Princeton University Press, 2001.

Honig, Bonnie. *Political Theory and the Displacement of Politics*. Ithaca, NY: Cornell University Press, 1993.

Honig, Bonnie. "What Is Agonism?." *Contemporary Political Theory* 8, no. 4 (2019): 661.

Horkheimer, Max and Theodor Adorno. *Dialectic of Enlightenment: Philosophical Fragments*. Edited by Gunzelin Schmid Noerr and translated by Edmund Jephcott. Stanford, CA: Stanford University Press, 2002.

Ingo, Farin, and Jeff Malpas, eds. *Reading Heidegger's Black Notebooks 1931–1941*. Cambridge, MA and London: MIT Press, 2016.

Jackson, Jeff. "Dividing Deliberative and Participatory Democracy Through John Dewey." *Democratic Theory* 2, no. 1 (2015): 63–84.

Kateb, George. *Human Dignity*. Cambridge, MA: Harvard University Press, 2011.

Keum, Tae-Yeoun. *Plato and the Mythic Tradition in Political Thought*. Cambridge, MA: Harvard University Press, 2020.

Krause, Sharon R. *Civil Passions: Moral Sentiment and Democratic Deliberation*. Princeton: Princeton University Press, 2008.

Lafont, Cristina. "Democracy Without Shortcuts." *Constellations* 26, no. 3 (2019): 355–360.

Lavi, Shai. "Should We De-Mythologize Politics?" Presented at the Force of Myth: Authority, Illusion, and Critique in Modern Imaginaries Conference, Van Leer Jerusalem Institute, June 2021.

Leonard, Miriam. "Theater and the Dispersal of the Agon." *Contemporary Political Theory* 18, no. 4 (2019): 658–659.

Levinson, Sanford. "The Brooding Presence of Carl Schmitt in Contemporary Jurisprudence: Reflections on William Scheuerman's *The End of Law: Carl Schmitt in the 21st Century*." *Philosophy and Social Criticism* 47, no. 2 (2021): 178–182.

Locke, John. *Two Treatises of Government. Second Treatise.* Cambridge: Cambridge University Press, 1960.

Lysaker, Odin. "Bodily Felt Integrity: The Anarchic Core of Communication in Jürgen Habermas's Democratic Thought." *Distinktion: Journal of Social Theory* 22, no. 3 (2021): 277–298. https://doi.org/10.1080/1600910X.2021.2014629.

Mansbridge, Jane. "Everyday Talk in the Deliberative System." In *Deliberative Politics: Essays on Democracy and Disagreement*, edited by Stephen Macedo, 211–240. Oxford: Oxford University Press, 1999.

Mansbridge, Jane J., James Bohman, Simone Chambers, Thomas Christiano, Archon Fung, John R. Parkinson, Dennis F. Thompson, and Mark Warren. "A Systemic Approach to Deliberative Democracy." In *Deliberative Systems: Deliberative Democracy at the Large Scale. Theories of Institutional Design*, edited by John Parkinson and Jane Mansbridge, 1–26. Cambridge: Cambridge University Press, 2012.

Markovits, Elizabeth. *The Politics of Sincerity: Plato, Frank Speech, and Democratic Judgment*. University Park: University of Pennsylvania Press, 2008.

Maxwell, Lida, Cristina Beltrán, Shatema Threadcraft, Stephen K. White, Miriam Leonard, and Bonnie Honig. "The 'Agonistic Turn': Political Theory and the Displacement of Politics in New Contexts." *Contemporary Political Theory* 18, no. 4 (2019): 640–672.

McCormick, John. *Machiavellian Democracy*. Cambridge: Cambridge University Press, 2011.

McCormick, John. "Teaching in Vain: Carl Schmitt, Thomas Hobbes, and the Theory of the Sovereign State." In *The Oxford Handbook of Carl Schmitt*, edited by Jens Meierhenrich and Oliver Simons, 269–290. Oxford: Oxford University Press, 2016.

McKean, Benjamin. "Toward an Inclusive Populism? On the Role of Race and Difference in Laclau's Politics." *Political Theory* 44, no. 6 (2016): 797–820.

Mehring, Reinhard. *Carl Schmitt: A Biography*. Translated by Daniel Steuer. Cambridge, UK and Malden, MA: Polity Press, 2014.

Meierhenrich, Jens, and Oliver Simons. "'A Fanatic of Order in an Epoch of Confusing Turmoil': The Political, Legal, and Cultural Thought of Carl Schmitt." *The Oxford Handbook of Carl Schmitt*, edited by Jens Meierhenrich and Oliver Simons, 3–70. Oxford: Oxford University Press, 2016.

Meierhenrich, Jens, and Oliver Simons, eds. *The Oxford Handbook of Carl Schmitt*. Oxford: Oxford University Press, 2019.

Morgan, John. "Chantal Mouffe: Only Populism Can Save the Left." *Times Higher Education*, April 4, 2019, https://www.timeshighereducation.com/features/chantal-mouffe-only-populism-can-save-left.

Morrell, Michael E. *Empathy and Democracy: Feeling, Thinking, and Deliberation*. University Park: Pennsylvania State University Press, 2010.

Mouffe, Chantal. *Agonistics: Thinking the World Politically*. London and New York: Verso, 2013.
Mouffe, Chantal. "Carl Schmitt and the Paradox of Liberal Democracy." In *The Challenge of Carl Schmitt*, edited by Chantal Mouffe, 38–53. London: Verso Books, 1999.
Mouffe, Chantal. *The Democratic Paradox*. New York: Verso, 2000.
Mouffe, Chantal. *For a Left Populism*. London: Verso, 2018.
Mouffe, Chantal. "Introduction: Schmitt's Challenge." In *The Challenge of Carl Schmitt*, edited by Chantal Mouffe, 1–6. London: Verso Books, 1999.
Mouffe, Chantal. *On the Political*. London: Routledge, 2005.
Mouffe, Chantal. *The Return of the Political*. London and New York: Verso, 1993.
Msezane, Sethembile. "Living Sculptures That Stand for History's Truths." TED Talk. August 2017. https://www.ted.com/talks/sethembile_msezane_living_sculptures_that_stand_for_history_s_truths/transcript.
Müller-Doohm, Stefan. *Habermas: A Biography*. Translated by Daniel Steuer. Cambridge: Polity Press, 2016.
Mutz, Diana C. "Is Deliberative Democracy a Falsifiable Theory?" *Annual Review of Political Science* 11, no. 1 (2008): 521–538.
Neblo, Michael. "Thinking through Democracy: Between the Theory and Practice of Deliberative Politics." *Acta Politica* 40, no. 2 (2005): 169–181.
Neblo, Michael A., Kevin M. Esterling, Ryan P. Kennedy, David M. J. Lazer, and Anand E. Sokhey. "Who Wants to Deliberate—And Why?" *American Political Science Review* 104, no. 3 (2010): 566–583.
Neblo, Michael A., Kevin M. Esterling, and David Lazer. *Politics with the People: Building a Directly Representative Democracy*. Cambridge: Cambridge University Press, 2018.
New York Times/Siena College Poll. "Biden Leads Trump 50-41%." October 15–20, 2020. https://scri.siena.edu/2020/10/20/the-new-york-times-siena-college-national-poll-biden-leads-trump-50-41/.
Nietzsche, Friedrich Wilhelm. "Homer Contest." In *On the Genealogy of Morality*, edited by Keith Ansell Pearson, 187–194. New York: Cambridge University Press, 1994.
Nietzsche, Friedrich Wilhelm. *Human, All Too Human: A Book for Free Spirits*. Translated by R. J. Hollingdale with an introduction by Eric Heller. Cambridge: Cambridge University Press, 1986.
Nietzsche, Friedrich Wilhelm. *Thus Spoke Zarathustra: A Book for All and None*. Edited by Adrian del Caro and Robert B. Pippin and translated by Adrian del Caro. Cambridge: Cambridge University Press, 2006.
Niewert, David. *Alt-America: The Rise of the Radical Right in the Age of Trump*. London and New York: Verso Books, 2017.
Norval, Aletta J. *Aversive Democracy: Inheritance and Originality in the Democratic Tradition*. Cambridge: Cambridge University Press, 2009.
O'Flynn, Ian. *Deliberative Democracy*. Cambridge: Polity Press, 2021.
O'Neill, Daniel, and Michael Bernhard. "Perspectival Political Theory." *Perspectives on Politics* 17, no. 4 (2019): 953–956.
Ott, Hugo. *Martin Heidegger: A Political Life*. Translated by Allan Blunden. New York: Basic Books, 1993.
Owen, David. *Nietzsche, Politics and Modernity*. New York and London: SAGE, 1995.

Owen, David, and Graham Smith. "Deliberation, Democracy, and the Systemic Turn." *Journal of Political Philosophy* 23, no. 2 (2015): 213–234.

Pareene, Alex. "Give War a Chance: In Search of the Democratic Party's Fighting Spirit." *The New Republic,* June 20, 2019. https://newrepublic.com/article/154113/democratic-party-fighting-spirit-give-war-chance.

Parkinson, John. *Deliberating in the Real World: Problems of Legitimacy in Deliberative Democracy.* Oxford: Oxford University Press, 2006.

Parkinson, John. "Models, Metaphors, and Their Consequences: The Curious Case of Deliberative Systems." ECPR Joint Sessions. Pisa, 2016.

Paxton, Marie. *Agonistic Democracy: Rethinking Political Institutions in Pluralist Times.* London and New York: Routledge, 2020.

Plato, *Protagoras*. Edited with an introduction by Gregory Vlastos, translated by Benjamin Jowett, extensively revised by Martin Ostwald. Indianapolis and New York: Bobbs Merrill, 1956.

Plato, *Protagoras*. Translated and notes by C. C. W. Taylor. Oxford: Clarendon Press, 1996.

Plato, *The Republic*. Translated with an introduction and interpretive essay by Allan Bloom. New York: Basic Books, 1968.

Putnam, Lara, Erica Chenoweth, and Jeremy Pressman. "The Floyd Protests Are the Broadest in U.S. History—And Are Spreading to White, Small-Town America." *Washington Post,* June 6, 2020.

Rawls, John. "The Idea of Public Reason Revisited." *University of Chicago Law Review* 3 (1997): 765–807.

Rawls, John. *A Theory of Justice.* Cambridge, MA: Harvard University Press, 1971.

Rousseau, Jean-Jacques. *The First and Second Discourses.* Edited by Roger Masters and translated by Roger Masters and Judith Masters. New York: St. Martin's Press, 1964.

Rousseau, Jean-Jacques. *The Social Contract and Other Later Political Writings.* Edited and translated by Victor Gourevitch. Cambridge: Cambridge University Press, 1997.

Sanders, Lynn. "Against Deliberation." *Political Theory* 25, no. 3 (1997): 347–376.

Satkunanandan, Shalini. "Beyond Belief: Passing by Others in Nietzsche's *Zarathustra*." Paper delivered to Political Theory Colloquium, University of Virginia, November 2019.

Scheuerman, William. "Getting Past Schmitt? Realism and the Autonomy of Politics." In *Politics Recovered: Realist Thought in Theory and Practice*, edited by Matt Sleat, 270–295. New York: Columbia University Press, 2018.

Schmitt, Carl. *The Concept of the Political.* Translated with an introduction by George Schwab, with a new foreword by Tracy Strong. Chicago and London: University of Chicago Press, 1996.

Schmitt, Carl. *The Nomos of the Earth in International Law of the Jus Publicum Europeum.* Translated by G. L. Ulmen. Candor, NY: Telos Press, 2003.

Scudder, Mary F. *Beyond Empathy and Inclusion: The Challenge of Listening in Democratic Deliberation.* Oxford: Oxford University Press, 2020.

Scudder, Mary F. "Deliberative Democracy, More Than Deliberation." *Political Studies,* Online First (August 2021): 1–18. https://doi.org/10.1177/00323217211032624.

Scudder, Mary F. "The Ideal of Uptake in Democratic Deliberation." *Political Studies* 68, no. 2 (2019): 504–522.

Searle, John. *Speech Acts: An Essay in the Philosophy of Language*. Cambridge: Cambridge University Press, 1969.
Shapiro, Ian. *The State of Democratic Theory*. Princeton: Princeton University Press, 2003.
Shklar, Judith N. *The Faces of Injustice*. New Haven and London: Yale University Press, 1990.
Smith, Rogers M. *Stories of Peoplehood: The Politics and Morals of Political Membership*. Cambridge: Cambridge University Press, 2003.
Specter, Matthew G. "What's 'Left' in Schmitt? From Aversion to Appropriation in Contemporary Political Theory." In *The Oxford Handbook of Carl Schmit*, edited by Jens Meierhenrich and Oliver Simons, 426–456. Oxford: Oxford University Press, 2016. ., André Bächtiger, Markus Spörndli, and Jürg Steiner. "Measuring Political Deliberation: A Discourse Quality Index." *Comparative European Politics* 1, no. 1 (2003): 21–48.
Tanasoca, Ana. *Deliberation Naturalized: Improving Real Existing Deliberative Democracy*. Oxford: Oxford University Press, 2020.
Taylor, Charles. *Modern Social Imaginaries*. Durham and London: Duke University Press, 2004.
Taylor, Charles. *Sources of the Self: The Making of Modern Identity*. Cambridge, MA: Harvard University Press, 1989.
Tudor, Henry. *Political Myth*. London: Pall Mall Press, 1972.
Tully, James. *Public Philosophy in a New Key*. Vol. 1: *Democracy and Civic Freedom*. Cambridge: Cambridge University Press, 2008.
Vitale, Denise. "Between Deliberative and Participatory Democracy: A Contribution on Habermas." *Philosophy & Social Criticism* 32, no. 6 (2006): 739–766.
Wang, Rui, James S. Fishkin, and Robert C. Luskin. "Does Deliberation Increase Public-Spiritedness?" *Social Science Quarterly* 101, no. 6 (2020): 2163–2182.
Warren, Mark E. "A Problem-Based Approach to Democratic Theory." *American Political Science Review* 111, no. 1 (2017): 39–53.
White, Stephen K. *A Democratic Bearing: Admirable Citizens, Uneven Justice, and Critical Theory*. Cambridge: Cambridge University Press, 2017.
White, Stephen K. "Does Critical Theory Need Strong Foundations?" *Philosophy and Social Criticism* 41, no. 3 (2015): 207–211.
White, Stephen K. *Political Theory and Postmodernism*. Cambridge: Cambridge University Press, 1991.
White, Stephen K. *The Recent Work of Jürgen Habermas: Reason, Justice, and Modernity*. Cambridge: Cambridge University Press, 1988.
White, Stephen K. *Sustaining Affirmation: The Strengths of Weak Ontology in Political Theory*. Princeton: Princeton University Press, 2001.
White, Stephen K., and Evan Robert Farr. "'No-Saying' in Habermas." *Political Theory* 40, no. 1 (2012): 32–57.
Williams, Bernard. *In the Beginning Was the Deed: Realism and Moralism in Political Argument*. Princeton: Princeton University Press, 2005.
Williams, Melissa S. "The Uneasy Alliance of Group Representation and Deliberative Democracy." In *Citizenship in Diverse Societies*, edited by Will Kymlicka and Wayne Norman, 124–154. Oxford: Oxford University Press, 2000.

Wingenbach, Ed. *Institutionalizing Agonistic Democracy: Post-Foundationalism and Political Liberalism*. London: Routledge, 2011.

Wolin, Richard. "Carl Schmitt: The Conservative Revolutionary Habitus and the Aesthetics of Horror." *Political Theory* 20, no. 3 (Aug. 1992): 436–444.

Young, Iris Marion. "Communication and the Other: Beyond Deliberative Democracy." In *Democracy and Difference: Contesting the Boundaries of the Political*, edited by Seyla Benhabib, 120–135. Princeton: Princeton University Press, 1996.

Young, Iris Marion. "De-Centering Deliberative Democracy." In *Democratizing Deliberation: A Political Theory Anthology*, edited by Derek W. M. Barker, Noelle McAfee, and David W. McIvor, 113–128. Dayton, OH: Kettering Foundation Press, 2012.

Young, Iris Marion. *Inclusion and Democracy*. Oxford: Oxford University Press, 2000.

Young, Iris Marion. "Justice and Communicative Democracy." In *Radical Philosophy: Tradition, Counter-Tradition, Politics*, edited by Roger S. Gottlieb, 123–143. Philadelphia: Temple University Press, 1993.

# INDEX

*For the benefit of digital users, indexed terms that span two pages (e.g., 52–53) may, on occasion, appear on only one of those pages.*

Figures are indicated by an italic *f* following the page/paragraph number.

Abizadeh, Arah, 90–91n.42
Adorno, Theodor, 167–68
aggregative model of democracy, 23–24, 25–26, 29, 35
agonism
    and conflict and contestation, 8–10, 81–82, 177–78
    and creativity, 95–97
    criticisms of, 15, 104
    and debate with deliberativists, 32, 45, 71–72
    decentering, 107–8, 174–75
    definition of, 4
    and democratic values, 73–74, 82
    and fairness, 93
    and foundations, 109
    and the goal of this book, 12, 174–75
    and Habermas, 145–46
    and identity/difference, 90–92, 97–100, 117–18, 148, 153–55, 161–62
    imperializing, 72–73, 80–83, 176–77
    and injustice, 111–13
    and Nazism, 14–15
    as normalized, 71, 72
    and pluralism, 82–83, 91–92
    political reflections on, 7–8, 10–12, 11n.13, 14–15
    and preferential ordering, 103–4
    and realism, 5–6
    and recurring impulses, 99–100
    and respect, 97, 98–99, 100, 105n.65, 110n.4, 153, 168
    the rules of, 85–86
    tempered, 72–73, 82, 85–86, 85n.30, 89, 91, 95n.51, 96, 100–3, 109, 153, 156, 157n.22, 167, 168, 174–76, 178
    and the two faces of democracy, 20, 43–44, 152–53, 171
    *See also* autonomy; equality; friends and enemies; injustice; justice (theories of); "no-saying"; resistance
*Agonistic Democracy* (Paxton), 11n.13
Akayev, Askar, 134n.43
American Political Science Association, 6
*Antigone* (Sophocles), 119
anti-Semitism, 76–77, 78–79, 81–82, 164n.29, *See also* injustice; racism
apartheid, 141n.51
Arendt, Hannah, 178
Ashe, Arthur, 137n.47

*Auch Eine Geschichte der Philosophie* (Habermas), 147n.3
autonomy
    and agonism, 14–15, 72–73, 89, 103, 104, 105–6, 107–8, 109, 156
    and consensus, 56–57
    and the deliberative model, 13, 46, 56, 60, 107–8, 149–50
    democratic, 139–40
    and individual sovereignty, 102, 159–61, 175–76
    and inequality, 60
    and moral equality of voice, 153, 155–56
    and an originary scene, 15–16
    and resistance, 101–2, 103, 105–6, 155, 156, 158, 159–61
    and the two faces of democracy, 109
    *See also* equality; moral equality of voice; "no-saying"
*Aversive Democracy* (Norval), 11n.13

Bächtiger, André, 51–52, 55, 56n.37, 62
Benhabib, Seyla, 23–24, 147n.3
*Beyond Empathy and Inclusion* (Scudder), 38, 174
Biden, Joe, 17n.19
Black Lives Matter, 137–38
Blumenberg, Hans, 141n.52, 158–59n.24
Butler, Judith, 118–19, 170

Cavell, Stanley, 11n.13
Chambers, Simone, 21–22, 21n.5, 25, 28–33, 34, 63
the Civil War, 116–17, 136–38
Cohen, Joshua, 21–23, 21n.5, 23n.8, 24–25, 27–28, 29, 30–31, 36
Collectif Contre l'Islamophobie en France (CCIF), 161–64, 163*f*
collective will, 23–24, 27–28, 31–32, 36–37, 54–55, 57–59, 60, 173
communicative model of democracy
    background on the, 10–12, 17–18, 171–72
    in defense of the, 175–79
    and fair compromise, 152n.15
    foundations for a, 108

and language, 168–70
and the moral equality of voice, 15–16, 144, 149–60, 166–68
    possible criticisms of the, 166–67, 168, 175–76
    in relation to agonism, 72
    in relation to the deliberative model, 9–10, 13–14, 31, 52–53, 64, 68, 69
    *See also* agonism; deliberative democracy
"The Concept of the Political" (Schmitt), 74, 77–79
concept stretching, 42–43, 45–46, 47–48, 50, 52–53, 62–63, 145–46
the Confederacy, 116–17, 136–38, 164n.30
Connolly, William, 72–73, 89–92, 94–95, 97–99, 100–2, 103–4, 105–6, 110n.4, 117–18, 129–30, 148, 174–75, 178n.4
consensus, 29–30, 36–37, 56–57, 71–72, 146–47, 152–53
conspiracy theories, 102–3
constitutive rules, 114–17
criteria weakening, 48

David, Jacques Louis, 161–64, 162*f*
"Deliberation and Democratic Legitimacy" (Cohen), 22–23
deliberative democracy
    the advantages of, 24
    calls to move away from the, 48–49, 50, 52, 53, 55, 61–62, 69–70, 174
    and the communicative process, 26, 28–29, 30, 31, 33–34, 37–38, 40, 41–42, 43–44, 46, 53, 57–59, 65, 68, 147–48
    and compromise, 21–22
    criticisms of, 5, 9–10, 11n.13, 12–13, 14, 20–21, 35–37, 38–39, 41–43, 45–46, 48, 53, 55, 145–46
    and decentering deliberation, 62–63, 64–67, 68, 69–70, 107–8, 172, 173–74
    defending, 61–62
    the dominance of, 19–20, 35
    the epistemic function of, 41
    foundations of, 108–9
    global challenges to, 45

Index

and the goal of this book, 12
and ideal theory, 5–6, 20–21, 22–23, 29, 33, 35, 36–39, 43, 49, 53, 62–63, 64, 146, 152n.13, 153, 172–73
limitations of the, 55, 59–60, 61, 172–73
the maturation of, 46–47
and non-deliberative practices, 42–43, 46–48, 49, 53, 62–63, 65, 66, 67, 68–69, 145–46, 172
the normative core of, 13, 20–21, 41–44, 46, 49–50, 52–53, 56–57, 58, 59–60, 62–63, 64–67, 69–70, 72–73, 173, 174
the practices of, 46, 52, 62–63, 64n.59, 65–67
and reason and debate, 8–10, 13–14, 20
and scale, 36, 40
and the two faces of democracy, 20, 32, 34–35, 39, 41–43, 152–53, 171
*See also* communicative model of democracy; concept stretching; consensus; criteria weakening; disagreement; empiricism; Habermas, Jürgen; informal deliberation; injection approach; legitimacy; listening; persuasion; pluralism; problem-based approach to democratic theory; realism; systems approach
*Deliberative Theory and Deconstruction* (Gormley), 11n.13
deliberative timbre, 51–52, 55, 62
deliberative wrongs, 66–67
*A Democratic Bearing* (White), 15n.18
democratic mythic, 111, 122–26, 131–41, 142–43, 144, 155, 157–58n.23, 158–62, 163–66. *See also* myth; political imaginary
democratic norms
commitments to, 8
and conflict, 33, 73, 80–81, 153
the corrosion of, 2–4, 6–7, 83–85, 174–75
determining, 28
and political institutions, 83–84
and Trump, 82, 83–84
and the two faces of democracy, 2, 9, 10–12, 14–15, 73–74
Democratic Party, 3–4
democratic procedure, 21–26, 27–32, 33, 35, 173–74
democratic theory. *See* aggregative model of democracy; agonism; communicative model of democracy; deliberative democracy
Derrida, Jacques, 80n.24
Dewey, John, 28–29
difference, 110n.4, 154n.18
difference democrats, 34, 35
direct democracy, 27–28
disagreement, 21–22, 31–32, 33–35, 57–58. *See also* pluralism
*Discourse on the Origin of Inequality* (Rousseau), 135n.45
Dryzek, John, 24–25, 30–31

election denying, 2–3, 6–7n.10, 83–84, 116n.14, 164n.29, *See also* voting
elites. *See* formal deliberation
empiricism, 19–20, 36, 37, 56, 173–74
equality
and agonism, 72–73, 89, 92–93, 95–102, 103, 105–6, 109
and communicative democracy, 13, 15–16
and the deliberative model, 107–8, 149–50
and legitimacy, 27–28
and participation, 29
and the two faces of democracy, 14–15, 109
*See also* autonomy; inequality; moral equality of voice
exclusion, 30–31, 34, 36–38, 40, 45–46. *See also* inclusion
exemplary scenes
of Butler, 118–19
and communicative action, 9–10, 145–47, 148–56, 166–70
and Connolly, 91–92, 97–99
definition of, 127

exemplary scenes (*cont.*)
  and democratic mythic, 111, 122–26,
    131–41, 142–43, 144, 155, 157–58n.23,
    158–62, 163–66
  and fair argument, 154n.18, 155–56
  and friends and enemies, 74
  and imagination, 110–11, 113–17, 118–19,
    121–22, 125, 131, 132–33, 142–43, 157–
    58n.23, 163–64
  and Locke, 119–22
  and moral sources, 15–16, 105–6, 107–8,
    109–14, 116–17, 119–20, 142, 170
  and myth, 110–11, 123–26, 129–30, 131–
    32, 133–35
  originary, 15–16, 15n.18, 108, 110–11,
    113–16, 117–32, 133, 135, 141, 142, 143,
    144–46, 148–60, 164–67, 174–75,
    177–78, 179
  and the *Protagoras*, 123–26, 133, 135
  as proto-narratives, 15, 110, 119–20, 128–
    29, 133, 150–51, 156–57, 169–70
  and recurring impulses, 99–100
  and the relation of an originary
    scene to a specific or particular
    scene, 114–16, 119, 127–31, 136–41,
    142, 164–65
  in relation to reason, 131, 142–43
  and the state of nature, 113, 114–15, 118–
    21, 135n.45
  *versus* strong foundations, 110–11
  and the two faces of democracy,
    120n.20, 129, 131, 143, 144, 145–46,
    153–55, 178
  *See also* constitutive rules; foundations
    (moral core of democracy); moral
    equality of voice; political imaginary;
    regulative rules

fascism, 2–3, 74–75, 77–79, 116n.14, 122–
  23, 123n.24, 160. *See also* Nazism
Floyd, George, 3–4, 17–18, 116–17, 137–38
formal deliberation, 10, 27, 28, 36, 39, 54.
  *See also* informal deliberation
Forst, Rainer, 155–56n.20
Foucault, 71

foundations (moral core of democracy),
  15–16, 107–9, 110, 112–13, 141–42, 146–
  47. *See also* exemplary scenes; strong
  ontology; weak ontology
Frank, Jason, 157–58n.23
friends and enemies, 3–4, 6–7, 34, 74,
  77–84, 85–86, 90–91, 102–4, 153,
  166–67. *See also* Mouffe, Chantal;
  Schmitt, Carl

Ginsberg, Benjamin, 116n.14
"Give War a Chance" (Pareene), 3–4
Gormley, Steven, 11n.13
Greene, Marjorie Taylor, 159–60

Habermas, Jürgen
  and collective agenda and will
    formation, 58–59
  and collective decision-making, 58–59
  criticisms of, 4–5, 73–74, 105, 145–46,
    147n.3, 148
  and the democratic process, 28–29, 32–
    33, 56, 57, 58, 146
  and the emergence of deliberative
    theory, 12, 20, 21–22
  and empowered inclusion, 58–59
  and exemplary scenes, 145, 146, 148–50
  and fair compromise, 33–34, 152–53
  and foundations, 146–48
  and the ideal, 146–47
  as influence, 9–10, 23n.8, 28, 29, 31–32
  and justice, 104
  and language, 146–47, 150nn.9–10,
    152n.13
  and morality, 157n.22
  and Nazism, 75n.10
  and political unfreedom, 57
  and Rousseau, 58–59
  and strong ontology, 146–47, 148
  and the two-track model, 27, 28–29, 39
  and Young, 30–31
  *See also* deliberative democracy
Hegel, 147n.3
Heidegger, Martin, 76–77, 77n.14, 81–82
Hobbes, Thomas, 119–20

"Homer's Contest" (Nietzsche), 4n.4, 92–93
Honig, Bonnie, 72–73, 89, 92–95, 97, 99–102, 103–4, 105–6, 129–30, 174–75

ideal speech situation (ISS), 145–46, 148, 151–52
*Identity/Difference* (Connolly), 90–92, 97–100, 117–18, 129–30, 148
imagination, 15–16. *See also* exemplary scenes
inclusion, 30, 31, 33–34, 38, 41, 45–46, 52, 54–55, 57–59. *See also* exclusion
inequality, 36–37, 38, 42, 60–61, 91–92, 97, 123n.24, 129–30. *See also* equality
informal deliberation, 27–29, 27n.26, 39, 67. *See also* formal deliberation
injection approach, 50–51, 52–53, 60–61
injustice, 5, 7–8, 10–12, 16–18, 91–92, 97–98, 105, 111–12, 164n.30, 175. *See also* anti-semitism; justice (theories of); racism
*Institutionalizing Agonistic Democracy* (Wingenbach), 11n.13
interest-based theory of democracy. *See* aggregative model of democracy
intersubjectivity, 9–10, 57–58, 68, 93–94n.49, 96n.53, 101–2, 155, 156

Jackson, Jeff, 42
justice (theories of), 4–5, 10–12, 91–92, 97–98, 99–100, 103–4, 105–6, 167–68. *See also* injustice; Rawls, John

Kateb, George, 169n.38
Keum, Tae-Yeoun, 134n.42
King Jr., Martin Luther, 137n.47

Laclau, Ernesto, 4
language, 168–70, 178
Lavi, Shai, 111n.5
law and order, 16–18, 17n.19
legitimacy
 and autonomy, 56–57
 and democratic procedure, 20–26, 29–30, 31–32, 33, 35, 57–58

 and disagreement, 32, 33
 and informal discourse, 28–29
 and participation, 22–23, 24–25
 and theory, 1–2, 4–5, 36
 threats to, 29–30
 *See also* deliberative democracy
*Legitimation Crisis* (Habermas), 22–23, 23n.8
Levinson, Sanford, 77n.15
listening, 38, 107–8
Locke, John, 58–59, 114–15, 119–22

Machiavelli, 93n.48, 119–20
Mansbridge, Jane, 40–41, 42–43, 50, 172
Markovits, Elizabeth, 123n.24
militias, 2–3, 132–33, 164–65
Monument Avenue, 136–41
moral equality of voice
 and agonism, 11n.13, 153–55, 160–61
 and autonomy, 153
 for a better political world, 100
 and challenging norms, 149–52, 158, 159–60
 and the communicative model of democracy, 15–16, 144, 149–53, 155–60, 166–69, 174–75
 and the deliberative model, 13, 46, 60, 62–63, 66–67, 152–53
 and exemplary scenes, 144, 149–51, 153–60, 168
 explanation of the, 176–77
 and the learning process, 147n.3
 potential dangers of the, 167–70
 and the two faces of democracy, 105–6, 144, 153–55
 *See also* autonomy; equality; "no-saying"
Mouffe, Chantal, 4, 11n.13, 14–15, 70, 73–75, 78, 80–87, 89, 90–91n.42, 102, 105, 153. *See also* friends and enemies
Msezane, Sethembile, 141n.51
myth, 116n.14
 and art, 136–41
 and dangers in politics, 15, 122–23, 135–36, 142–43, 159–60, 164nn.29–30
 and democracy, 123–24, 131

myth (*cont.*)
  and imagination, 15, 110–11, 131, 132–33
  and Plato, 123–26
  as pliable, 134–35
  work on, 137–41, 141n.52, 144, 158–59n.24, *See also* democratic mythic

natural law, 119–22
Nazism, 14–15, 74–79, 77n.14, *See also* fascism
*New Republic*, 3–4
Nietzsche, 4n.4, 72–73, 91, 92–97
*Nietzsche, Politics and Modernity* (Owen), 89n.40
Nixon, Richard, 16–17
nonviolence, 118, 119n.19
Norval, Arletta, 11n.13, 85n.30, 86n.33, 153n.16
"no-saying," 32–33, 111–13, 114–15, 149–50, 158, 160–61. *See also* autonomy; moral equality of voice

Obama, Barack, 2–3
O'Flynn, Ian, 38–39
ontology. *See* strong ontology; weak ontology
original position, 15–16
ostracism, 92–95
Owen, David, 42–43, 47–48, 49–52, 58, 65, 66–67, 89n.40, 93–94n.49, 174
*Oxford Handbook of Carl Schmitt*, 76n.12
*Oxford Handbook of Deliberative Democracy*, 61n.53, 108, 145–46

Pareene, Alex, 3–4
Parkinson, John, 50–52, 55, 62
particular exemplary scenes, 15–16
partisanship, 37, 42–43, 46–47, 49, 65, 71–72, 82
Paxton, Marie, 11n.13
*Perspectives on Politics*, 6
persuasion, 25–26, 29–32, 33, 34, 36, 50
Plato, 123–26, 133, 135
pluralism, 21–22, 32, 35, 36, 53, 56–58, 65, 69–70, 82–83, 91–92. *See also* disagreement

political imaginary, 115–17, 119, 121–23. *See also* democratic mythic; exemplary scenes; social imaginary
*Political Theory and the Displacement of Politics* (Honig), 92
Popper, Karl, 123n.24
populism, 2–3, 86–87, 140–41, 157–58n.23, 159–60, 164–66, 171–72, 175–76, 177
problem-based approach to democratic theory, 48–50, 54–55, 58–60, 62, 172, 174
procedure. *See* democratic procedure
*Protagoras* (Plato), 123–26, 133, 135
protest
  and autonomy, 101–2
  background on, 1
  and the deliberative model, 65, 67–68
  and othering, 34, 161–62
  and the removal of statues, 137–38, 138*f*, 141n.51
  and the systems approach, 40, 41, 46–47
  and tension with law and order, 16–18
  and the two faces of democracy, 7–8
  violent, 1–2
  *See also* resistance
public opinion, 28–29

racism, 78–79, 86–87, 122–23, 129–30, 137–40, 171–72, 175. *See also* anti-semitism; injustice
Rawls, John, 4–5, 11n.13, 15–16, 21n.5, 73–74, 104, 105, 128n.33, 161. *See also* justice (theories of)
realism, 5–6, 25, 28
*Reasonable Democracy* (Chambers), 31–32
regulative rules, 114–17
representation, 55
republican model of democracy, 56–57
resistance
  background on, 1, 10–12
  and civility, 16–17
  and communicative action, 146
  and the communicative model, 151–52, 155
  and injustice, 111–13

and the political right, 2–3, 6–7, 17–18, 132–33, 164–66, 171–72
violent, 3–4, 17n.19
See also agonism; protest
rhetoricality, 153n.16
Rousseau, Jean-Jacques, 56–57, 58–59, 135n.45
rule of law, 2–3, 73, 80–81, 82
*Rumors of War* (Wiley), 137–41, 139f, 142–43

Satkunanandan, Shalini, 95, 96
Schmitt, Carl, 14–15, 72–73, 74–87, 90–91, 102, 105, 153, 174–75. See also friends and enemies
Scudder, Mary F., 38, 174
*Second Treatise* (Locke), 119–20
Shapiro, Ian, 151n.11
Shklar, Judith, 5
silent majority, 16–17
Smith, Graham, 42–43, 47–48, 49–52, 58, 65, 66–67, 174
social imaginary, 113–15, 117, 118–19, 123n.23, See also exemplary scenes; political imaginary
social media, 102–3
Sophocles, 119
*Sources of the Self* (Taylor), 109n.3
state of nature, 15–16
strong ontology, 15–16, 87–89, 102, 103–4, 105, 113, 142–43, 146–47, 148, 155–56n.20, See also foundations (moral core of democracy); weak ontology
Stuart, J.E.B., 137–38, 138f
summative quality, 51. See also injection approach
systems approach, 20–21, 35, 39–44, 46–49, 52, 66–67, 69

Taylor, Charles, 88, 109n.3, 110n.4, 113–15

*The Faces of Injustice* (Shklar), 5
*The Force of Nonviolence* (Butler), 119n.19
*The Nomos of Earth* (Schmitt), 79–80
*Theory of Communicative Action* (Habermas), 23n.8
*The Phenomenology of Spirit* (Hegel), 147n.3
*The Republic* (Plato), 123–24
*The Tennis Court Oath* (David), 161–64, 162f
"Three Normative Models of Democracy" (Habermas), 56
*Thus Spoke Zarathustra* (Nietzsche), 94–96
translation, 94n.50, 95
Trump, Donald, 2–3, 17–18, 82, 83–84, 101, 116n.14, 132–33, 157–58n.23, 164n.29
Tully, James, 72–73n.2

violence, 79–80, 100
voting, 23–26, 29, 54, 60–61, 82, 115–16. See also election denying

Warren, Mark, 48–50, 54–55, 58–62, 61n.53, 64–65, 174
weak ontology, 15, 87–89, 109, 110n.4, 126, 128–29, 142, 143, 147–48. See also foundations (moral core of democracy); strong ontology
"We Are Also The Nation," 161–64, 163f
White, Stephen K., 15n.18
white nationalism, 2–3
Wiley, Kehinde, 137–40, 139f, 142–43
Wingenbach, Ed, 11n.13
Wittgenstein, Ludwig, 11n.13, 85–86, 86n.33, 116n.15, 153n.16
Wolin, Richard, 78n.18

Young, Iris Marion, 9–10, 21–22, 26, 29–31, 33–34, 36–38, 64, 66, 68, 173–74